BAPTISTS IN EARLY NORTH AMERICA SERIES

Volume X

General Editor
William H. Brackney†

An Abridgment of the Church History of New-England from 1602 to 1804, By Isaac Backus, A.M.

BAPTISTS IN EARLY NORTH AMERICA SERIES

General Editor

William H. Brackney

Volume I
SWANSEA, MASSACHUSETTS
Ed. William H. Brackney with Charles K. Hartman

Volume II
FIRST BAPTIST, PROVIDENCE
Ed. J. Stanley Lemons

Volume III
NEWPORT, RHODE ISLAND, SEVENTH DAY BAPTISTS
Ed. Janet Thorngate

Volume IV
FIRST BAPTIST CHURCH, BOSTON, MASSACHUSETTS
Ed. Thomas McKibbens

Volume V
WELSH NECK, SOUTH CAROLINA
Ed. John Barrington

Volume VI
MEHERRIN, VIRGINIA
Ed. Fred Anderson

Volume VII
FIRST BAPTIST CHURCH, PHILADELPHIA, PENNSYLVANIA
Ed. Deborah Bingham Van Broekhoven

Volume VIII
MIDDLETOWN BAPTIST CHURCH, NEW JERSEY
Ed. John D. Inscore Essick

Volume IX
ABBOTT'S CREEK, NORTH CAROLINA, BAPTIST CHURCH
Ed. J. Kristian Pratt

BAPTISTS IN EARLY NORTH AMERICA SERIES

Volume X

General Editor
William H. Brackney†

An Abridgment of the Church History of New-England from 1602 to 1804, By Isaac Backus, A.M.

Edited by James P. Byrd

MERCER UNIVERSITY PRESS
Macon, Georgia
2023

MUP/ H1033

© 2023 by Mercer University Press
Published by Mercer University Press
1501 Mercer University Drive
Macon, Georgia 31207
All rights reserved

27 26 25 24 23   5 4 3 2 1

Books published by Mercer University Press are printed on acid-free paper that meets the requirements of the American National Standard for Information Sciences—Permanence of Paper for Printed Library Materials.

Printed and bound United States of America.

This book is set in Times New Roman; Palatino Display

Cover/jacket design by Burt&Burt.

ISBN978-0-88146-883-0
Cataloging-in-Publication Data is available from the Library of Congress

CONTENTS

Series Introduction   xi

Preface and Acknowledgments   viii

Part I. Historical Introduction to Isaac Backus's
*An Abridgment of the Church History of New-England
from 1602 to 1804*   ix

Part II. Text of Isaac Backus's
*An Abridgment of the Church History of New-England
from 1602 to 1804*   1

Bibliography   207

Indexes   213

Series Introduction
to Volume X

The historical work of Isaac Backus, while confined to New England (he also included a brief, concise account of Baptists in the southern parts of America), is of paramount importance to the origins and development of Baptists in the United States. Even more, his writings articulate the Baptist principle of the separation of church and state. A long line of Backus biographers has sought to recover his life: William B. Sprague (1856), Alvah Hovey (1859), William Cathcart (1881), Edwin S. Gaustad (1958), Clarence C. Goen (1962), Thomas B. Maston (1962), William G. McLoughlin (1967; 1971), and Stanley Grenz (1983). Professor McLoughlin reproduced and annotated Backus' diary (Brown University Press, 1979), providing a major resource for American religious historians. His method of presentation and critical apparatus has been a model for this Series.

Across two decades, Backus published a three volume *History of New England, with Particular Reference to the Denomination of Christians Called Baptists* (1777–1796), followed by a single volume, *An Abridgment of the Church History of New-England from 1602 to 1804* (1804). We chose the 1804 work for this Series because it reflects his revised thoughts and his final historical interpretation. It has also been out of print for many years.

We are delighted that a distinguished American religious historian has prepared this volume. Dr. James P. Byrd is currently Professor of American Religious History, Cal Turner Chancellor's Chair of Wesleyan Studies, and Associate Dean for Graduate Education at Vanderbilt University. His education includes a B.A. from Gardner-Webb, an M.Div. from Duke University Divinity School, and a Ph.D. from Vanderbilt University, where his dissertation, "Roger Williams's Radical Biblicism: Scripture Versus Christendom in Puritan New England" was prepared under John R. Fitzmier.

A specialist in the work of Roger Williams, Dr. Byrd has produced four noteworthy books covering major events and personalities in American religious history: *The Challenges of Roger Williams: Religious Liberty, Violent Persecution, and the Bible* (2002); *Jonathan Edwards for Armchair Theologians* (2008); *Sacred Scripture, Sacred War: The Bible and the American Revolution* (2013); and *A Holy Baptism of Fire and Blood: The Bible and the American Civil War* (2021), plus a forthcoming book on the assassination of Abraham Lincoln. He has authored articles in numerous professional journals and many book reviews, including, "The New World of North America and

Historical Introduction

Canada and the Globalization of Critical Biblical Scholarship" in *The Hebrew Bible / Old Testament: The History of Its Interpretation, Vol. III: the Nineteenth and Twentieth Centuries*); "Baptist Tradition and Heritage" in *Encyclopedia of Religion in America,* and several articles in *The Cambridge Dictionary of Christianity*, building his reputation as a widely respected contemporary authority on American religious culture.

Dr. Byrd found Backus's history to be inspired and heroic, a kind of denominational epic. From his own earlier research, Byrd underscores the importance of fidelity to the Scriptures in Backus's account of the Baptists. He reminds us of the impact of Backus upon revivalism, and vice versa, in the eighteenth century. Also a specialist in Wesleyan thought, the editor usefully contrasted Backus with the Methodists. Ever sensitive to contemporary issues, the editor is aware of a sensitivity to race and culture in both Backus and his main hero, Roger Williams.

We are greatly indebted to the editor of this volume for providing a fresh, new window on Isaac Backus. He has carefully checked and rechecked the text against the original. His notations, bibliography, and indexes bring the Backus historiography up to date and ably fulfill the objectives of the Series.

William H. Brackney†, M.A., Ph.D.
General Editor
Baptists in Early North America Series

Preface and Acknowledgments

I am grateful to William H. Brackney for the invitation to contribute to this important series, and especially for the opportunity to explore the historical work of Isaac Backus. I have long been fascinated by Backus, a champion of religious liberty—as he understood it—and defender of Baptists against those who threatened, debated, and lampooned them. He was also a leading historian of colonial American Baptists. Even as he was pastoring a church, traveling hundreds of miles to preach, and writing treatises on various subjects, Backus was collecting and collating evidence for publication in his histories. He wrote and revised, always looking for insights into what made the Baptists important. The end products were his narratives of Baptists, but not only Baptists. They were only understandable, he believed, when placed in their colonial New England context. Backus's historical vocation has received less attention than it deserves, and I have appreciated the opportunity to shed additional light on Backus the historian.

This project was greatly improved by the expertise of Alex Ayris, who worked with me as a research assistant while he was a PhD student at Vanderbilt. Ayris helped to proof and transcribe Backus's history in a document electronically scanned from the original text, which is in the possession of William Brackney, and measures 12.5 mm x 21.5 mm, 72 p, leatherbound. I am also thankful to Mercer University Press for publishing this series, and especially to Dr. Marc Jolley for guiding this project through to completion. In addition, as always, I am thankful for my family, especially my wife, Karen Byrd, and our daughters, Caroline and Olivia.

EDITOR'S NOTE:
In the introduction that follows, page numbers referred to in Backus's text refer to the original page numbers which are clearly indicated on each page.

Part I.

Historical Introduction to Isaac Backus's

An Abridgment of the Church History of New-England

Isaac Backus (1724–1806) helped to shape the historical events he recorded. Born and baptized in 1724, he lived the first years of his life as a member of a prominent family in Norwich, Connecticut. Isaac's father, Samuel, had done well as a farmer and leader in the community, and Isaac's grandfather, Joseph Backus, had been a justice of the peace, a position that included considerable authority. Isaac, then, was born into a home of farming and privilege. He saw slavery from an early age, as the family household included one enslaved African American and a Native American servant. Backus, his parents, his five sisters, and five brothers worshiped in a Congregationalist church, which enjoyed the privileges of tax support as a church established by the state. Later, Backus became one of the most zealous protesters of church establishments. After his conversion during the outbreak of revivals later called the Great Awakening, Backus navigated the spiritual labyrinth from Congregationalist (and religious insider) to outsider Baptist living on the fringes of New England's religious society.[1]

A trailblazer on the cutting edge of Baptist growth, Backus was a pastor and activist who supported Baptist churches and associations. He was a tireless writer who published often, defending Baptists and advocating for their concerns, especially for religious liberty as he understood it. Backus was, as

---

[1] For a brief overview of Backus's family background, see William G. McLoughlin, *Isaac Backus and the American Pietistic Tradition*, The Library of American Biography; (Boston, MA: Little, Brown, and Co., 1967), 1–5. McLoughlin's work has led the way in historical assessments of Backus and his thought. His publications related to Backus include: *Soul Liberty: The Baptists' Struggle in New England, 1630–1833* (Hanover, MA: University Press of New England and Brown University Press, 1991); William McLoughlin, *The Diary of Isaac Backus* (Providence, RI: Brown University Press, 1979); William McLoughlin, *New England Dissent, 1630–1833; The Baptists and the Separation of Church and State* (Cambridge, MA, Harvard University Press, 1971); Isaac Backus and William McLoughlin, *Isaac Backus on Church, State, and Calvinism: Pamphlets, 1754–1789*, The John Harvard Library (Cambridge, MA: Belknap Press of Harvard University Press, 1968).

Mark Noll wrote, "the key figure in the rise of the Baptist denomination in New England." During his lifetime, and partially due to his efforts, Baptists grew in the region—"from only 25 congregations in 1740 to nearly 24,000 members in 312 churches and 13 regional associations by 1804."[2] This transformation needed to be recorded and remembered, Backus believed, and in his view history was crucial to ministry. The title of Backus's history revealed what he thought mattered most:

> An Abridgment of the Church History of New-England, From 1602 to 1804. Containing a View of Their Principles and Practice, Declensions and Revivals, Oppression and Liberty. With a Concise Account of the Baptists in the Southern Parts of America, and a Chronological Table of the Whole.[3]

From just a perusal of the title page, we see that Backus wanted readers to know that this was a "*Church History of New-England*" with a particular slant, focusing on "*principles and practice,*" and giving extensive treatment to Baptists. This was a book about ebbs and flows—"*Declensions and Revivals,*" because Baptists owed their growth mainly to the revivals that surged through the colonies in the eighteenth century, disrupting the traditional, respectable, and tax-supported churches of New England. Understandably, then, Backus embraced revivalism, and much of this history gives us a firsthand view of revivals and the disputes that erupted in their wake.

Through all the controversies they faced, including clashes over revivals and church establishments, Baptists struggled with "*Oppression and Liberty.*" But the "oppression" that occupied Backus's mind was mainly the mistreatment of white Baptists at the hands of magistrates and ministers who defended their established churches. The far more appalling oppressions of slavery and the slave trade apparently did not concern Backus much for most of his life. In 1788, while advocating the ratification of the Constitution in Massachusetts, Backus excused the Constitution's failure to abolish slavery. "No man abhors that wicked practice more than I do, and would gladly make use of all lawful means towards the abolishing of slavery in all parts of the land," Backus said. But he was in no hurry. It was enough for him that the Constitution left open the option of prohibiting the slave trade in future years. He did not object that the Constitution said nothing about abolishing slavery, instead leaving that decision to the states. As Backus wrote, "slavery grows more and

---

[2] Mark A. Noll, *America's God: From Jonathan Edwards to Abraham Lincoln* (New York: Oxford University Press, 2002), 149.

[3] Isaac Backus, *An Abridgment of the Church History of New-England, From 1602 to 1804* (Boston, MA: Manning & Loring, 1804). Henceforth abbreviated as Backus, *Abridgment of the Church History*.

Historical Introduction

more odious through the world; and as an honorable gentleman said [here] some days ago, 'Though we cannot say that slavery is struck with an apoplexy, yet we may hope it will die with a consumption.'"[4] Backus, then, joined many other elite, white men of the founding generation who, in principle, opposed slavery while in practice left the horrific institution in place for future generations to contend with.

Although Backus was interested in Baptists everywhere, this was mostly a New England story—as he noted in the title, a *"Church History of New-England."* Although Backus included *"a Concise Account of the Baptists in the Southern Parts of America,"* that account was quite "concise"—mainly due to the lack of sources—just as it was quite white. Backus was impressed with the rise of African American Baptist churches and ministers in the South, but he provided little detail. Above all, then, Backus built his narrative around three overlapping themes:

(1) **The Baptist Heritage in New England**—Backus wanted to prove that colonial American Baptists *had* a history that merited attention, even respect, from all Americans and especially Christians in other denominations. Baptist beginnings, as Backus described them, were inspired and heroic, a drama cast with leading men like Roger Williams, who was driven by a zeal for religious liberty that became legendary. Others followed, too many to mention, although Backus tried. But it was Williams who set the tone as the Baptist witness for liberty, even though he remined a Baptist for only a few months.

(2) **Revivals and Visible Saints**—Baptists not only had a history, but they traced their colonial American roots to *the* origin story that mattered to many Americans: The Puritan migration from England. It was the Baptists, as Backus read them, who were the most faithful heirs of the Puritans. Believers' baptism, perhaps the defining mark of Baptists, was rooted in the Puritan conviction that only serious Christians ("visible saints") should be allowed to join the church. Perfection was impossible but conversion was mandatory. Granted—it was difficult to tell true Christians from hypocrites, but those pursuing church membership should at least provide evidence that Christ had changed them from within. This was a hallmark of Puritan church membership, a crucial requirement for the early Puritans, the founders of the Massachusetts Bay Colony in the early 1630s. Yet later Puritans abandoned these high standards of visible sainthood and church purity—a tragedy in Backus's view, which is why he was glad to see the call for visible sainthood "born

---

[4] As quoted in McLoughlin, *Isaac Backus and the American Pietistic Tradition*, 199. See also, *Proceedings of the Massachusetts Historical Society, 1862–1863* (Boston, MA: John Wilson and Son, 1863), 151–152.

again" in the revivals that later became known as the Great Awakening (or the "First Great Awakening" to distinguish these earlier revivals from revivals that emerged in the early nineteenth century). In his history, therefore, Backus defended the Great Awakening and what we today would call evangelical religion, which Backus believed Baptists were the most faithful proponents of in New England.

(3) **Baptists and the New Nation**—Up through the Revolution and beyond, Baptists demanded religious liberty, served courageously in the Revolutionary War, and exposed the hypocrisy of a nation that claimed to be based on liberty and yet allowed state-funded churches to thrive. At least that was how Backus wrote the history. Also, because of their strong convictions, Baptist life meant struggle, as Baptists were often outsiders, fighting against opposition and yet winning in the competition for adherents. Despite persecution, or perhaps because of it, Baptists grew. In setting the Baptists in opposition to established Congregationalism as well as Universalism, Methodism, and Deism, Backus set in motion Baptist arguments for legitimacy against other churches that would rise to new heights in the nineteenth and twentieth centuries.

This history was important to Backus because he wanted to see the Baptists prosper, not only because he believed Baptist churches were most faithful to scripture, but also because Baptist convictions were important for the world. Backus wanted to raise the Baptist profile in the new nation and, given how rapidly Baptists had already grown, anything seemed possible.

1. The Baptist Heritage in New England

This was the fourth edition of Backus's history, which he had published in several editions with updates and variations, including title changes.[5] The first came off the press during the height of the Revolutionary War in 1777, followed by the second in 1784 soon after the war ended and the third in 1796.[6] By the time he published this edition in 1804, Backus was eighty years old and living in the Early Republic, a period marked by rapid growth in the new nation, growth that brought with it uncertainty. Many Americans had celebrated their revolution and the freedom it brought, but they had also seen in the French Revolution how volatile revolutions could be. Although many Americans did not like it, political parties had formed, with Federalists and Democratic-Republicans vying for power, debating how best to lead the

---

[5] See: Isaac Backus, *A History of New-England, with Particular Reference to the Denomination of Christians Called Baptists.* (Boston, MA: Printed by Edward Draper, at his printing-office in Newbury-Street, 1777).

[6] Backus, *Abridgment of the Church History*, 3.

Historical Introduction

nation into the new century. In religion, evangelicalism surged, but so did deism and radical attacks on Christianity, many of them spearheaded by Thomas Paine's *Age of Reason*.

Understandably, then, the preface to Backus's history reflected the anxieties of the time. How would the nation take shape? Would changes in leadership, especially the presidency, be peaceful? Could the United States be thrown into the kind of chaos Americans saw in the French Revolution?

Apprehension was in the air, but so was promise. It made sense that Backus closed his preface with an argument for the value of history. We needed the past, he believed, for the sake of the present. "In the experience of two centuries," he wrote, "we may see a great variety of different schemes of government that have been tried, which may direct our choice to what is right." Most importantly, the nation needed "to avoid evil ways," which for Backus meant "to guard against all cruelty, deceit and violence."[7]

The relationship between Baptists and the nation was a central theme of this history. It was a relationship that began before the nation, with the English settlers of seventeenth-century New England, whom some later Americans looked back upon as the nation's spiritual founders before the "founding fathers" of the American Revolution. These English immigrants came in waves, with one group, often referred to as the "pilgrims," arriving in 1620 and a larger group, most often called "Puritans," settling the Massachusetts Bay colony in 1630 and beyond.

Despite the different names of "pilgrim" and "Puritan," the two groups had much in common. Both had sailed to North America to escape religious polices in England that did not favor them. As the name indicates, "Puritans" were among the many Protestants of the day who wanted to reform the Church of England, purifying it of its lingering Catholic elements, which they believed had corrupted the Church. Unlike the "pilgrims" who came a few years before them, the Puritans were not "separatists"—they did not believe the Church of England was so corrupt that they had to separate from it. Instead, the Puritans wanted to create a purer church in this "New England," as an example to "old England," showing how best to reform the church.[8]

---

[7] Backus, *Abridgment of the Church History*, 4.

[8] There is almost no end to the books published on Puritanism, both English and American. Excellent books include: Theodore Dwight Bozeman, *To Live Ancient Lives: The Primitivist Dimension in Puritanism* (Chapel Hill, NC: University of North Carolina Press, 1988); Michael P. Winship, *Godly Republicanism: Puritans, Pilgrims, and a City on a Hill* (Cambridge, MA: Harvard University Press, 2012); Perry Miller, *Orthodoxy in Massachusetts, 1630-1650; a Genetic Study* (Cambridge, MA: Harvard University Press, 1933); Perry Miller, *The New England Mind: The Seventeenth Century* (Cambridge, MA: Belknap Press of Harvard University Press, 1939); Harry S. Stout, *The New England Soul: Preaching and Religious*

xiii

Puritans excelled at purity, as the name indicated, and they wanted a church filled with authentic Christians. So, they tightened the standards for church membership. Not only did prospective members have to live a moral life and agree to accept church doctrines and practices, but they also had to give "an account of a change of heart by the work of God's Spirit." Puritans were not naïve—they knew they would never really know that all their members were truly Christians in their hearts. But they wanted to come as close as possible to a pure church, a church comprised of "visible saints."[9]

Although these Puritans traveled to America to escape their enemies back home who mistreated them, they had no intention of tolerating all kinds of people, nor did they advocate religious freedom for everyone. Instead, they wanted a purified church *and* state, meaning a church and state that aligned with their beliefs and followed their rules. Only white, male members of their churches could vote on civil matters, and they wanted church and state working together to promote their agenda, a conviction that brought them into conflict with many outsider groups, including the first Baptists in America. This was the key moment of Baptist beginnings, Backus argued—the time that shaped their identity as a persecuted people who summoned the courage to defy the authorities who had power over them.

In setting the stage for this history, Backus gave a lot of attention to Roger Williams, the most famous and most published seventeenth-century Baptist in New England. Backus did not agree with Williams on everything, and historians have shown how they had different views of religious liberty.[10] But apparently their agreements overwhelmed their disagreements. In the Preface to this final edition of his history, Backus wrote: "Many of the new things in this volume were taken from Winthrop's journal, published in 1790; from the publications of the Historical Society at Boston, and from a book which I borrowed of them, called 'The Bloody Tenet,' of which I know not of another copy in America." This was a book on religious liberty written by Williams, and Backus borrowed heavily from it in this history, showing how he had developed more of an appreciation for Williams, despite his brief time with the Baptists. Backus admired Williams's convictions and his courage.

Culture in Colonial New England (New York: Oxford University Press, 1986); E. Brooks Holifield, *Theology in America: Christian Thought from the Age of the Puritans to the Civil War* (New Haven, CT: Yale University Press, 2003).

[9] Backus, *Abridgment of the Church History,* 25. The classic book on this is Edmund S. Morgan, *Visible Saints: The History of a Puritan Idea* (Ithaca, NY: Cornell University Press, 1963).

[10] McLoughlin, *Soul Liberty*, chapter 12, "Isaac Backus and Thomas Jefferson," pp. 249–269. In this chapter, McLoughlin drew the distinctions between Backus's more pragmatic view of religious liberty from the more principled views of Williams, Jefferson, and Madison.

xiv

Historical Introduction

Williams opposed the Puritan brand of persecution, even though it cost him dearly. Williams "earnestly laboured" against persecution and for "full liberty of conscience in this country," and for that the Puritans "bent all their power against him."[11]

Although some leaders of the Massachusetts Bay Colony liked Williams personally, he disagreed with them on several issues, mostly related to their use of civil power to enforce religious opinions. By 1636, Massachusetts leaders had enough of Roger Williams's views, so they banished him from the Bay Colony. Backus told the story, describing how Williams escaped from the officers before they could arrest him, then made his way south and secured "lands from the Narraganset Indians, where he began the first civil government upon earth that gave equal liberty of conscience." Williams named the place "Providence," because God had protected him as he ran from Puritan authorities. The drama was important here—both to Williams and to Backus. As Williams described his experience, "I was sorely tossed for fourteen weeks, in a bitter winter season, not knowing what bread or bed did mean."[12]

To relate the cruelty Williams endured, Backus turned to the Bible, comparing Williams's banishment to Joseph's capture and enslavement. Joseph's older brothers sold him into slavery, and yet God turned that evil act into a good result. While he was enslaved in Egypt, Joseph worked his way up to a high position in Pharaoh's kingdom, and from there he had power to help the Israelites, even his own family (Genesis 37, 39–43). Likewise, Williams, after his banishment from the Bay Colony, founded Providence and developed good relationships with the Narragansetts. During the Pequot War, Williams's connections with the Narragansetts equipped him for diplomatic work, enabling him to help the colonists, even those who had banished him. As Backus put it, "As God overruled the cruel selling of Joseph to the heathen, as a means of saving the lives of many people; so the banishing of Mr. Williams made him a chief instrument of saving all the English in New-England from destruction."[13]

Backus recorded Williams's diplomatic work during wartime, showing how he risked his life for colonists. As Williams reported, he rowed "all alone in a poor canoe," making his way through storms where he spent three days and nights "with the bloody Pequot ambassadors, whose hands and arms methought wreaked with the blood of my countrymen, murdered and massacred by them on the Connecticut river, and from whom I could not but nightly look for their bloody knives at my own throat also." Despite these threats and

---

[11] Backus, *Abridgment of the Church History,* Preface, 27.

[12] Backus, *Abridgment of the Church History,* 32.

[13] Backus, *Abridgment of the Church History,* 33.

obstacles, Williams prevailed in diplomatic efforts that helped the English colonists to win the war.[14]

In describing the Pequots' behavior in war, Williams and Backus revealed their racism. Williams denied that all Native Americans were savages. Focusing mainly on the Narragansetts, he defended their morality and culture in two books, *Key Into the Language of America* and *Christenings Make Not Christians*. When it came to war with indigenous peoples, however, most English colonists believed God sided with them, and Williams was no exception.[15]

Backus celebrated the victory over the Pequots because it helped to move them out of the way, opening "a wide door for the English to fill the country!"[16] Backus defended these assaults on Native American lands by white settlers, which were part of a horrific ordeal that would kill thousands of native peoples. For Backus, more land for white colonists meant more property and more missionary work. Backus's point in including this episode was a sober one: Despite all Williams did for the colonists in New England, Massachusetts Bay leaders refused to lift his banishment.

Later, Williams assisted in founding "the first Baptist church in America," but within months he had left the Baptist church, convinced that all Christian churches had been corrupted, and that only Christ could reestablish a true church.[17] Although Backus disagreed with Williams's departure from the Baptists, Backus agreed with Williams—and with Puritans in general—that the Catholic Church had corrupted the primitive church founded by the apostles. Many Protestants saw the Catholic Church prophesied in a shocking and misogynistic image: the "great whore" of Babylon described in Revelation 17. As the vision detailed, the "great whore" fornicated with "the kings of the earth." This, they argued, prophesied the alliances between the Pope and several Catholic nations, especially France. The mark of most of these alliances was vicious persecution: The whore was "drunken with the blood of the saints, and with the blood of the martyrs of Jesus" (Revelation 17:6). Eventually, however, the nations that had allied with the whore "shall hate the whore, and shall make her desolate and naked, and shall eat her flesh, and burn her with fire." (17:16). Williams looked forward to this day, and Backus

---

[14] Backus, *Abridgment of the Church History*, 35–36.

[15] See Roger Williams, *Christenings Make Not Christians* (London: Iane Coe, 1645); repr. in *Rhode Island Historical Tracts*, no. 14, ed. Henry Martyn Dexter (Providence, RI: Sidney S. Rider, 1881); Roger Williams, *A Key into the Language of America*, ed. James Hammond Trumball, vol. 1 of *The Complete Writings of Roger Williams* (Providence, RI: Narragansett Club Publications, 1866; repr., New York: Russell & Russell, 1963).

[16] Backus, *Abridgment of the Church History*, 37.

[17] Backus, *Abridgment of the Church History*, 45–46.

Historical Introduction

thought he saw it fulfilled in his time as "the French nation have now taken the riches of the church of Rome to support war and vengeance against her."[18]

Similar anti-Catholic teachings circulated among Protestants throughout much of American history. Backus, Williams, and many others saw the Catholic Church as a main source of religious persecution and false teachings, which then spread to Protestant churches like the Church of England. Anti-Catholicism also influenced the American Revolution as many patriots saw Catholicism as synonymous with tyranny, with the pope the ultimate tyrant. We find an example in the enormously popular *Common Sense* (1776), in which Thomas Paine called colonists to reject all kings, arguing that "monarchy in every instance is the popery of government."[19] Statements like these spread in a nation where Protestants far outnumbered Catholics, causing Anti-Catholic nativism and the overall abuse of Catholics to proliferate throughout American history.

Backus agreed that civil liberty and religious liberty went together, which explained why Roger Williams, the great prophet of religious liberty, was also an early forerunner of ideas that later shaped the American Revolution. To prove the point, Backus quoted Williams's statement: "The sovereign, original, and foundation of civil power lies in the people," and "such governments as are by them erected and established, have no more power, nor for no longer time, than the civil power or people consenting and agreeing shall betrust them with. This is clear, not only in reason, but in the experience of all commonweals, where the people are not deprived of their *natural freedom* by the power of tyrants."[20]

In rejecting Williams's claims, the Bay Colony leaders rejected views that resembled the revolutionary ideas that later shaped the new nation. Even more, the Puritans' mistreatment of Williams set the tone for how New England authorities would persecute Baptists throughout the seventeenth century. Despite all the mistreatment, Baptists prospered, just as Williams did, and he did not let his persecutors get the last word. As he was securing a charter for Providence with the help of friends in Parliament, Williams launched a debate with John Cotton, one of the leading ministers in the Bay Colony. Hardly a mere local affair, this exchange was waged through a series of letters and books that were printed in London. This was a great audience, Williams

---

[18] Backus, *Abridgment of the Church History,* 59.

[19] Thomas Paine, *Common Sense*, Liberty Fund, Online Library of Liberty, https://oll.libertyfund.org/pages/1776-paine-common-sense-pamphlet

[20] Backus, *Abridgment of the Church History,* 59. Backus's quote from Williams is from Roger Williams, *The Bloudy Tenent of Persecution for Cause of Conscience* (Macon, GA: Mercer University Press, 2001), 154–155. This is a reprint edition of Williams's work, which was originally published in London, 1644.

believed, because he wanted Parliament to know what a persecuting and tyrannical place New England had become.[21] The books were long and the titles were priceless, including Williams's famous *Bloudy Tenent of Persecution for Cause of Conscience* (1644), followed by Cotton's response, *The bloudy tenent, washed, and made white in the bloud of the Lambe* (1647), and then Williams's comeback, *The bloody tenent yet more bloody: by Mr Cottons endevour to wash it white in the blood of the lambe.*[22]

The Williams-Cotton debate reflected many conflicting views, including disagreements about the Bible. Cotton and his colleagues used the Old Testament as a political model—Israel was God's chosen nation, and God called them to wage wars against other nations and to enforce both religious and political regulations. Massachusetts Bay Colony did the same, using civil authorities to punish people who disagreed with the legally-established church. Williams responded with amazement and disgust. He granted that God's people in the Old Testament kept religion and the state together, punishing heretics with violence, but that was irrelevant for colonial America because the New Testament had no such commands.[23]

Williams planted his convictions in the colony he founded, naming it "Providence," and adding the word "hope" to the colonial seal. He hoped that God would bless this colony founded on religious liberty.[24] Apparently God blessed the colony with religious diversity, since religious dissenters who could not abide the draconian policies of the Bay Colony fled to Providence. This variety of religious views was fine for Williams, but it scandalized Puritans in Massachusetts who called Providence a gutter of immorality and heresy. Backus denied these claims, arguing that this colony—led by Williams along with John Clarke, Gregory Dexter and others—"held the pure doctrines of grace, and the importance of a holy life, as much as the fathers of the Massachusetts did." And they did so while upholding the lofty standards of religious liberty. In fact, Providence gave birth to liberty, literally, being the home to many great patriots, including General Nathanael Greene, who later

---

[21] On the Williams letter debate against Cotton, see Backus, *Abridgment of the Church History*, 57–63.

[22] Roger Williams, *The Bloudy Tenent, of Persecution, for Cause of Conscience, Discussed, in a Conference between Trvth and Peace. VVho, in All Tender Affection, Present to the High Court of Parliament, (as the Result of Their Discourse) These, (Amoungst Other Passages) of Highest Consideration.* (London, 1644); John Cotton, *The Bloudy Tenent, Washed, and Made White in the Bloud of the Lambe: Being Discussed and Discharged of Bloud-Guiltinesse by Just Defence* (London: Crowne in Popes-Head-Alley, 1647); Roger Williams, *The Bloody Tenent yet More Bloody: By Mr Cottons Endevour to Wash It White in the Blood of the Lambe* (London: Giles Calvert, 1652).

[23] Backus, *Abridgment of the Church History,* 61–63.

[24] Backus, *Abridgment of the Church History,* 65–67.

xviii

Historical Introduction

proved his heroics in the Revolutionary War. Evidently an atmosphere of religious liberty could produce patriotism and courage in its people.[25]

Backus found much of this history valuable because it traced the heroic legacy of early Baptists and their protest for religious liberty. The idea that magistrates had the power to enforce religious convictions was, as Backus said, "the root of all the bloody persecution that ever was in the world."[26] Williams proved this in his words and life, and he was soon joined by other Baptist witnesses for liberty. One of the chief examples came with the ordeal of Obidaiah Holmes and John Clarke, who were arrested and jailed by Massachusetts authorities in July 1651. Backus described Holmes's testimony and description of his whipping at the hands of Massachusetts officers, all the while testifying to his Baptist convictions. "You have struck me as with roses," Holmes said after receiving his thirty lashes, "yet I pray God it may not be laid to your charge."[27]

As he had done with Williams's case, John Cotton of Massachusetts Bay defended the Puritans' punishment of Holmes. This troublemaker, Cotton wrote, "took upon him to baptize"—actually rebaptize—which transgressed "the order and government of our churches" and the colony as well. Cotton also indicated that Holmes had something of a martyr complex. True, the Massachusetts officers whipped him. But the whipping "was more voluntarily chosen by him than inflicted on him." He could have paid the fine and avoided the whipping, and his friends even offered to pay it for him. "But he chose rather to be whipt." Clarke, on the other hand, "was wiser in that point"—he paid the fine and left jail unharmed. Not really, Backus commented. To pay a fine was to admit wrongdoing, which Holmes was unwilling to do. If he had, he would have been dishonest with himself, violating his conscience.[28]

This debate between Puritans and Baptists, between church establishment and disestablishment, ranged over several issues, including the integrity of spirituality. If the state forced people to conform to church laws, did this not increase hypocrisy? Those who did not really believe would fake it, Baptists said. Better to have an unofficial but purer church. Cotton disagreed. It was better to have hypocrites in a colony "than profane persons." After all, "Hypocrites give God part of his due, the outward man, but the profane person giveth God neither outward nor inward man." This was ludicrous, Backus believed—nothing more than a "scheme of compulsion about religion."[29] Where

---

[25] Backus, *Abridgment of the Church History,* 67–68.
[26] Backus, *Abridgment of the Church History,* 69.
[27] Backus, *Abridgment of the Church History,* 71–78; quote is from p. 76.
[28] Backus, *Abridgment of the Church History,* 80–81.
[29] Backus, *Abridgment of the Church History,* 81.

in the Bible did God praise a hypocrite for partial and lukewarm obedience? Far from it. "In the first Christian church God struck two hypocrites dead for lying to the Holy Ghost," Backus said, referring to the story of Ananias and Sapphira from Acts 5. These two so-called Christians offended the Holy Spirit by lying about an offering. "How loud is this warning to all the world against lying and hypocrisy, especially in the affairs of religion!"[30]

John Cotton died two days before Christmas in 1652, shortly after writing this defense of the Puritans' treatment of the Baptists. Despite his disagreements with Cotton, Backus praised him as "a clear preacher of the gospel." As Backus noted, even Cotton's nemesis Roger Williams had called Cotton one "whom I highly esteem and dearly respect," despite their differences.[31]

Examples like this indicate that Backus admired Williams's character and resilience. Just a few months shy of his seventieth birthday, Williams held public debates with the Society of Friends (Quakers) at Newport and Providence. He published a record of the debate in his book, *George Fox digg'd out of his burrowes*—a "dig" at Quaker founder George Fox and English Quaker controversialist Edward Burrough (1676).[32] The Quakers' ideas were dangerous, Backus believed, so he was happy to quote Williams's debate with them. Despite his appeals for religious liberty, Williams did not believe all religions were equally valid, and he rejected Quaker theology. Backus quoted from Williams's statement to the Quakers:

> From my childhood, now above threescore years, the Father of lights and mercies touched my soul with the love of himself, to his only Begotten Son, the true Lord Jesus, to his holy Scriptures, &c. His infinite wisdom hath given me to see the city, court and country, the schools and universities of my native country, to converse with some Turks, Jews, Papists, and all sorts of Protestants; and by books to know the affairs and religions of all countries. My conclusion is, that *Be of good cheer, thy sins are forgiven thee*, Mat. ix. 2, is one of the joyfullest sounds that ever came to poor sinful ears.[33]

This would be one of Williams's final controversies. Upon his death, Backus waxed eloquently on his importance:

---

[30] Backus, *Abridgment of the Church History,* 81–82.

[31] Backus, *Abridgment of the Church History,* 82.

[32] Roger Williams, *George Fox digg'd out of his burrowes* (Boston, MA: John Foster, 1676). On Williams's debates with Quakers, see Backus, *Abridgment of the Church History,* 108–110.

[33] Williams quoted in Backus, *Abridgment of the Church History,* 109. C.f. Williams, *George Fox digg'd*, dedication "To the People called Quakers," page unnumbered.

Historical Introduction

In April...[1683], Mr. Roger Williams was taken to rest, and he hath a large posterity among us to this day. He was honoured of God to be instrumental of founding the first civil government upon earth, since the rise of antichrist, that allowed equal religious liberty, and he was serviceable therein unto the age of 84. And for godly sincerity in public actings, and overcoming evil with good, it is believed no man on earth exceeded him in that age.[34]

This description of Williams set the pattern that Backus followed in praising other Baptist heroes, including John Clarke. All upheld convictions for religious liberty and biblical faith in the face of opposition. This is the Baptist heritage that Backus wanted readers to appreciate during the Early Republic, when the new nation and religion's place in it were facing changes.

2. Revivals and Visible Saints

Backus devoted so much of his history to Roger Williams, John Clarke, and other heroic early Baptists because their witness for religious liberty was needed in his day. Yet he also drew attention to them because they were Baptists, his people, and a people whose presence was challenged, just as it had been a century earlier.

Backus's spiritual journey was like that of many Baptists of his time and place. In August of 1741, during a time of revivalist excitement in Norwich, seventeen-year-old Backus experienced conversion, an event that revivalists were calling the "new birth." At this point Backus became what we would call an "evangelical," a term that would be used more often in the nineteenth century. "Evangelical religion," as historian David Bebbington determined, can be identified by its "special marks": "**conversionism**, the belief that lives need to be changed; **activism**, the expression of the gospel in effort; **biblicism**, a particular regard for the Bible; and what may be called **crucicentrism**, a stress on the sacrifice of Christ on the cross."[35]

---

[34] Backus, *Abridgment of the Church History,* 130.

[35] David W. Bebbington, *Evangelicalism in Modern Britain: A History from the 1730s to The 1980s* (London and New York: Routledge/Taylor & Francis Group, 1989), 16. ProQuest Ebook Central, http://ebookcentral.proquest.com/lib/vand/detail.action?docID=179445. Emphasis added. The literature on evangelicalism is large. Helpful sources include: Gerald R. McDermott, ed., *The Oxford Handbook of Evangelical Theology* (New York: Oxford University Press, 2010); Timothy Larsen and Daniel J. Treier, eds., *The Cambridge Companion to Evangelical Theology*, Cambridge Companions to Religion (Cambridge New York: Cambridge University Press, 2007); Randall Herbert Balmer, *Evangelicalism in America* (Waco, TX: Baylor University Press, 2016); Randall Herbert Balmer, *Encyclopedia of Evangelicalism*, Rev. and expanded ed (Waco, TX: Baylor University Press, 2004); Randall Herbert Balmer, *Blessed Assurance: A History of Evangelicalism in America* (Boston, MA: Beacon Press, 1999).

This definition fits nearly all evangelicals, but as Thomas Kidd pointed out, it also fits some non-evangelicals. Kidd writes, "Missing from Bebbington's definition is early evangelicalism's new attention to the person of the Holy Spirit, particularly in revival. Early American evangelicalism was distinguished from earlier forms of Protestantism by dramatically increased emphases on seasons of revival, or outpourings of the Holy Spirit, and on converted sinners experiencing God's love personally. Both the role of the Spirit and the methods of revival were hotly contested among early American evangelicals."[36]

Backus fit Kidd's description as well. Revival was critical for Backus, and like other evangelicals he found the experience of conversion to be anything but easy. Struggle was everywhere—he fought an inner conflict with sin, and he endured turmoil with and estrangement from religious mentors he respected. Like many Congregationalists attracted to revival, Backus saw tensions between the faith he grew up with and the message of traveling evangelists. Few doubted those conflicts, though some embraced the revivals and others rejected them.[37]

Although the revivals convicted Backus of sin, they left him confused about how to respond to God. As expected, he sought the counsel of his pastor, Rev. Benjamin Lord, who gave a typical response: patience. Live morally, do all the church requires, and await God's presence. This was terrible advice, Backus thought. If the revivals had taught him anything, it was the urgency of salvation.[38] A decision for Christ needed to be made immediately, before it was too late—a point made by countless revival sermons, but never so well delivered than in Jonathan Edwards's classic, *Sinners in the Hands of an Angry God*:

> The God that holds you over the pit of hell, much as one holds a spider, or some loathsome insect, over the fire, abhors you, and is dreadfully provoked; his wrath towards you burns like fire; he looks upon you as worthy of nothing else, but to be cast into the fire; he is of purer eyes than to bear to have you in his sight; you are ten thousand times so abominable in his eyes as the most hateful venomous serpent is in ours. You have offended him infinitely more than ever a stubborn rebel did his prince: and yet 'tis nothing but his hand that holds you from falling

---

[36] Thomas S. Kidd, *The Great Awakening: The Roots of Evangelical Christianity in Colonial America*. (New Haven, CT: Yale University Press), xiv.

[37] Thomas S. Kidd, *God of Liberty: A Religious History of the American Revolution* (Philadelphia, PA: Basic Books, 2010), 47–48, Kindle edition.

[38] McLoughlin, *Isaac Backus*, 11–13

Historical Introduction

into the fire every moment; 'tis to be ascribed to nothing else, that you did not go to hell the last night; that you was suffered to awake again in this world, after you closed your eyes to sleep: and there is no other reason to be given why you have not dropped into hell since you arose in the morning, but that God's hand has held you up; there is no other reason to be given why you han't gone to hell since you have sat here in the house of God, provoking his pure eyes by your sinful wicked manner of attending his solemn worship: yea, there is nothing else that is to be given as a reason why you don't this very moment drop down into hell.[39]

This sermon was exceptional in its terrifying use of imagery, which is one reason it remains widely read. But it was not unusual in its urgency—revival sermons confronted people with their sins and urged them to plead with God for deliverance. Death could come at any moment, and then it would be too late to seek forgiveness.

The experience of the "new birth" did not always come as soon as sinners desired it, which was yet another reason why they should seek it urgently, pleading for it, yearning for its arrival. That's how it was for Backus. Spiritually, he was influenced by his mother, Elizabeth Tracy Backus, who had a renewal of her faith in the summer of 1741, likely through the preaching of James Davenport, an itinerant preacher who copied the style of George Whitefield but was later disciplined for his extreme views. Like his mother, Isaac was influenced by Davenport, among other preachers, and he experienced the "new birth" soon after her experience of renewal. As Isaac described it, after much seeking, God led him to abandon "all trust in myself or any creature, and led me to embrace salvation in His own way." Backus was "mowing alone in the field, August 24th, 1741" when a "divine light" allowed him to see that his life "had been filled up with sin." He found a tree, sat down, prayed, cried, and saw the hopelessness of salvation through his own efforts. Justice meant damnation; he knew it. He placed it "all into his hands, fell at His feet, and was silent and calm before him." Then he saw Christ's "perfect righteousness" and grace, and he was able "to trust Him for salvation."[40]

After he found peace in his soul Backus faced conflict with his home congregation. Rev. Lord embraced the revivals at first, but then he drew back from some of their elements. Eventually Backus determined that Rev. Lord did not support revival, and he doubted that Lord really wanted to cleanse the

---

[39] Jonathan Edwards, "Sinners in the Hands of an Angry God" in *Works of Jonathan Edwards, Volume 22, Sermons and Discourses, 1739–1742*, ed. Harry S. Stout, Nathan O. Hatch, and Kyle P. Farley (New Haven, CT: Yale University Press, 2003), 411–412.

[40] Quoted in McLoughlin, *Isaac Backus*, 14. See also, pp. 9–15.

church from all but "visible saints"—the truly committed and converted members. When he finally left his congregation in 1745, Backus joined a growing number of people who left the established (and legal) Congregational churches to start new, "Separate" (and illegal) congregations. Backus left his parish, moved to Norwich, and helped to start a Separate church there.[41]

This Separate movement among Congregationalists was groundbreaking. It invigorated the Baptist movement in New England, greatly increasing the number of Baptists in the region. Once Separates doubted their Congregationalist churches and left them, it was not a major leap for them to doubt their baptisms, which they had received in these churches. Also, if the church was to be comprised only of converted members, infant baptism was dangerous, because it fooled people into thinking they were in good standing with God even though they may not have experienced the "new birth." Backus resisted this move at first, but he finally embraced Baptist convictions, no doubt influenced by his wife, Susanna Mason Backus, who was raised in a Baptist family in Rehoboth. By 1756, he was in Middleboro, Massachusetts, helping to start a Baptist church that he would pastor for the rest of his life.[42]

None of this would have happened if Backus had not embraced the revivals, but he did embrace them, becoming a revivalist preacher and defender. Theologically, Backus resembled Jonathan Edwards, a man Backus called "The excellent Mr. Edwards."[43] Edwards figured prominently in Backus's history. He described the revivals in Northampton, Massachusetts, as Edwards narrated them in his famous *A Faithful Narrative of the Surprising Work of God* (1737), which, as Backus reported, "was printed in England as well as America, and caused great joy to many," although even greater joys and greater revivals were to come.[44]

Backus's history is a valuable, firsthand account of the revivals and the controversies they caused. Historians have examined these revivals extensively, some crediting them with great influences on society—even

---

[41] McLoughlin, *Soul Liberty*, 251; Kidd, *Liberty*, 47–48.

[42] The classic book on Separatism is, C. C. Goen, *Revivalism and Separatism in New England, 1740–1800: Strict Congregationalist and Separate Baptists in the Great Awakening*, (New Haven, CT: Yale University Press, 1962). But see the excellent analysis of the Great Awakening in New England, including Separatism: Douglas L. Winiarski, *Darkness Falls on the Land of Light: Experiencing Religious Awakenings in Eighteenth-Century New England*. (Chapel Hill, NC: Published for the Omohundro Institute of Early American History and Culture, Williamsburg, Virginia, by the University of North Carolina Press, 2017). See also, McLoughlin, *Isaac Backus*, 64–69; Kidd, *Liberty*, 47–49.

[43] Backus, *Abridgment of the Church History,* 181.

[44] Backus, *Abridgment of the Church History,* 160; Jonathan Edwards, "Faithful Narrative" in *The Great Awakening*, ed. C. C. Goen (New Haven, CT: Yale University Press/WJE Online Vol. 4), 96-211.

Historical Introduction

postulating that the Great Awakening helped to bring on the American Revolution. Others have downplayed the revivals and their influences. Yale historian Jon Butler famously claimed that the Great Awakening was a "fiction," contending that the revivals, while important in certain regions, were exaggerated by later writers into a massive, intercontinental event.[45]

From Backus's perspective, the revivals could scarcely have been exaggerated. He could hardly contain his excitement in describing their effects:

> Religion was much revived at Boston, Northampton, and other places in the fall and winter [of 1741]; and in the two years following, the work spread through most parts of New-England, New-York, New-Jersey, and Pennsylvania, beyond all that was ever known before in America. Several ministers, who were converted before, were now greatly quickened, and spent much of their time in travelling and preaching in various parts of the land. Others, who had been blind guides before, were now spiritually enlightened, and heartily joined in this great work....Religious meetings, and religious conversation, engaged the attention of a great part of the people in most parts of the land. A reformation of life, confessing their former faults, and making restitution for injuries done; were evident in many places; and a vast number of all ages, made a profession of religion, and joined to the several churches where they lived.[46]

Yet Backus's experience as a Baptist had taught him that God's work encountered resistance, and God's people often suffered persecution. Sure enough, once the revivals increased in intensity and frequency, controversy erupted, as "a great majority of the ministers and rulers through the land disliked this work, and exerted all their powers against it." Unfortunately, a few revival preachers had given critics too much ammunition—there were "many imperfections" in some revivals and their preachers, and these needed to be corrected or all the good the revivals were doing would be extinguished.[47]

Again, Backus turned to Jonathan Edwards, the most critical defender of the revivals, praising Edwards's sermon, *Distinguishing Marks of a Work of the Spirit of God* (1741), preached at Yale. As Backus wrote, this sermon "was printed and spread through the nation, and was much esteemed." In it, Edwards "well distinguished between the marks of a true work of God, and all false appearances of it."[48]

---

[45] Jon Butler, "Enthusiasm Described and Decried: The Great Awakening as Interpretive Fiction," *Journal of American History* 69, September (1982): 305–325.

[46] Backus, *Abridgment of the Church History,* 164–165.

[47] Backus, *Abridgment of the Church History,* 165.

[48] Backus, *Abridgment of the Church History,* 165.

Of special concern for Backus was the revivals' most famous critic, Boston minister Charles Chauncy (1705–1787) and especially his *Seasonable Thoughts on the State of Religion in New England*.[49] As Backus observed, Chauncy "spends about three hundred pages upon what he calls, 'things of a bad and dangerous tendency, in the late religious appearances in New-England.'"[50] For example, Chauncy targeted itinerant preaching, made famous by George Whitefield, the greatest revival preacher of the day and a true international celebrity. Whitefield, who had been ordained in the Church of England, joined John and Charles Wesley in the beginnings of the Methodist movement at Oxford. From there, he exploded on the scene, headlining tours in which he preached to crowds of over twenty thousand people. Both in England and in the colonies, people flocked to see Whitefield, who held them in rapt attention in outdoor services, often in open fields and towns.

Whitefield's traveling evangelism astounded onlookers, including Benjamin Franklin, but it alarmed critics of revival, including Chauncy, who quoted several scriptures to argue against itinerant preaching. Yet none of these scriptures, in Backus's opinion, had any relevance to the issue. In fact, traveling preachers had been important to the spread of Christianity from the beginning—"travelling preaching hath often been blessed for the good of souls in every age, and in every country where the gospel has come," Backus wrote.[51]

Chauncy lashed out at revivalists who claimed that some area ministers were not even true Christians. Presbyterian Gilbert Tennent had put it best in his ruckus-raising sermon, "On the Danger of an Unconverted Ministry" (1740). Not surprisingly, this infuriated established ministers, and Chauncy was one of them. But he had no cause to complain, Backus wrote, because both churches and ministers *had* grown to be less serious about conversion, beginning with the Puritan churches of the previous century. Granted—Backus had disagreements with the early Puritan settlers of New England, especially their denial of religious liberty to those who disagreed with them, including Baptists. But he did admire their demand that all church members be "visible saints" who were able to testify to their conversion experiences. This was a Puritan innovation and a good one, because it required all full members of the church to give evidence that they had been truly converted. Of course, there would always be weeds hidden within the wheat—false

---

[49] Charles Chauncy, *Seasonable Thoughts on the State of Religion in New England, A Treatise in five Parts* (Boston, MA: Rogers and Fowle, 1743), v–vi.

[50] Backus, *Abridgment of the Church History,* 168.

[51] Backus, *Abridgment of the Church History,* 169.

xxvi

Historical Introduction

Christians hidden among true believers—but at least the Puritan churches upheld high standards for spirituality.[52]

But it did not last. Over time, New England churches turned away from this requirement, which led to a decline in seriousness about conversion and true spirituality, Backus believed. A major warning sign appeared in 1662, when a synod "introduced a half way covenant" to deal with spiritual decline. Many adults in the churches, who had been baptized as infants, had never fulfilled the requirement of church membership by testifying to their conversion experience. Something was wrong; people were not converting as they once did. What was to be done? If Puritans remained true to their standards, there would be fewer church members, and the churches would have grown smaller, in part because these adults who were not church members could not have their children baptized. The "half way covenant" tried to solve this problem by allowing these non-members to be "half way" members so that they could have their children baptized in the church. "This was pleasing to many," Backus wrote, "while others thought it to be an apostasy from the first principles of the country; and the controversy about it, in various shapes, has continued ever since."[53]

Backus did not mince words; he was one of those who thought the "half way covenant" was "an apostasy from the first principles of the country," and he believed the declension moved on from there, as churches grew listless and less spiritually fervent. The revivals attempted to counter that, but Chauncy was one of many critics who resisted, mainly because he did not believe people needed to provide evidence of conversion to join the church. It was no wonder Chauncy opposed revivals – he was part of the problem, in Backus's view, one of those who had led in in the spiritual decline from high standards set by the early Puritans.[54]

With the opposition of Chauncy and others, revivals were in peril, which meant true religion was under attack, Backus believed. Agreed—there were problems with the revivals, but overall they were God's work. Some even speculated that the revivals could be part of God's preparations for the millennium—the thousand-year reign of Christ. Along these lines, Backus included a quote from Edwards's *Some thoughts concerning the present revival of religion in New-England* (1742), which warned that ministers who attacked

---

[52] Backus, *Abridgment of the Church History,* 162–165. Note that Backus spelled the name "Gilbert Tennant," but the standard spelling is "Tennent."

[53] Backus, *Abridgment of the Church History*, 95. An older but classic treatment is Robert G. Pope, *The Half-Way Covenant: Church Membership in Puritan New England* (Princeton, NJ: Princeton University Press, 1969).

[54] Backus, *Abridgment of the Church History*, 95, 169–170.

the revivals could be attacking God's plan, and these ministers could be under threat of judgement from God. Backus's long quote from Edwards concluded with the following:

The times of Christ's remarkably appearing in behalf of his church, and to revive religion, and advance his kingdom in the world, are often spoken of in the prophecies of Scripture, as times wherein he will remarkably execute judgment on such ministers or shepherds, as do not feed the flock, but hinder their being fed, and so deliver his flock from them, as Jeremiah xxiii. Ezekiel xxxiv. Zech. x. Isaiah xlvi. &c. "How solemn are these considerations!" Backus exclaimed.[55]

Both Edwards and Backus believed in church purity; all members should be "visible saints." This conviction led Edwards to reject the "open communion" policies of his predecessor and grandfather Solomon Stoddard, a pastor who was beloved by many and a legend in his own time. Stoddard allowed anyone to take the Lord's Supper, even if they could not testify to an experience of conversion, because he believed the practice of communion could help move people to salvation. The Lord's Supper could be "a converting ordinance," Stoddard thought.[56]

As Backus described, Edwards tolerated Stoddard's views for "fifteen years in that way, until he was fully convinced that it was contrary to the word of God; and he also found that gospel discipline could not be practised in such a way." Edwards would pay the price for breaking with Stoddard's lenient form of church discipline: "No sooner was his change of mind discovered, in 1744, than most of his people were inflamed against him, and never would give him a hearing upon the reasons of his change of sentiments; but they were resolute to have him dismissed." Edwards even wrote an extensive defense of his position, although most of his church members "would not read his book."[57]

If they had bothered to read it, they would have seen this critical statement, which Backus quoted:

that baptism, by which the primitive converts were admitted into the church, was used as an exhibition and token of their being visibly

---

[55] Edwards as quoted in Backus, *Abridgment of the Church History*, 173. The quote may be found with minor variations in the Yale edition of Edwards's works: Edwards, *Some Thoughts Concerning the Revival*, in *Works of Jonathan Edwards, Volume 4, Great Awakening*, ed. C. C. Goen (New Haven, CT: Yale University Press, 1970), 376-377. Backus's views on revivalism and conversion were similar to Edwards's views. See Noll, *America's God*, 150.

[56] For detail and background, see: George M. Marsden, *Jonathan Edwards: A Life* (New Haven, CT: Yale University Press, 2003), 345–56. See also chapter 7.

[57] Backus, *Abridgment of the Church History*, 181.

Historical Introduction

regenerated, dead to sin, and alive to God. The saintship, godliness and holiness of which, according to Scripture, professing Christians and visible saints do make a profession and have a visibility, is not any religion and virtue that is the result of common grace, or moral sincerity (as it is called) but *saving grace*.

Backus knew Edwards was not a Baptist, nor did he intend to become one. Yet, in Backus's view, Edwards's theology of church purity implied believer's baptism. As Mark Noll wrote, "Backus thought he was understanding the implications of Edwards's theology better than Edwards himself."[58]

Edwards would suffer for his convictions, just as many Baptists did. Eventually, as Backus wrote:

> Mr. Edwards was *separated* from the flock he dearly loved. Thus one of the best men in our land was rejected from his place and employment, only for coming into the belief that a profession of saving faith was necessary in all who came into communion in the church of Christ. But as this was evidently a good cause, so God was with him in it, so that he afterwards wrote a book which opened the true nature of the liberty of the will of moral agents [Edwards's *Freedom of Will*], beyond any thing that ever was published in latter ages; and that and many other works of his are still greatly esteemed in Europe, as well as America. He was very useful in the ministry, until he died President of New-Jersey College, March 22, 1758, in his 56th year.[59]

Backus also defended George Whitefield. When the famous evangelist returned to New England in 1744, Backus reported that "such opposition appeared against [Whitefield], as never was seen before against any minister of the gospel in our land." Harvard College printed a statement against Whitefield, and so did several ministerial associations. By February of 1745 Yale College had joined the revolt against Whitefield, claiming that he was scheming to have all the respected ministers in the area thrown out and replaced with outsiders. "This was so opposite to truth," Backus wrote, insisting "that all his life was evidently spent in labouring for the conversion and edification of precious souls, while he left the building and government of churches to

---

[58] Backus pointed out that Edwards supported this statement with "Rom. ii. 29. vi. 1–4. Phil. iii. 3. Col. ii. 11, 12."—and added that "many others have been made Baptists by the same Scriptures, and the same ideas from them." Backus, *Abridgment of the Church History*, 181–182. The Edwards quote in the Yale edition of his works can be found in *An Humble Inquiry into the Rules of the Word of God, in Works of Jonathan Edwards, Volume 12, Ecclesiastical Writings*, ed. David D. Hall (New Haven, CT: Yale University Press, 1994), 196. See also Noll, *America's God*, 150; McLoughlin, *Isaac Backus*, 3-4.

[59] Backus, *Abridgment of the Church History,* 182.

others." Granted, once people "were brought to a saving knowledge of Christ," it would be difficult for them to accept "teachers who were strangers to him," as evidently many ministers were in New England.[60]

There was no greater defender of the revivals than Backus, therefore, and he framed his defense in the form of a history, connecting the Baptists with the best elements of the Puritan tradition. By doing so, he placed Baptists at the forefront of evangelicalism in revolutionary America.

3. Baptists and the New Nation

The American Revolution transformed Backus's world. It seemed miraculous that an assemblage of mostly inexperienced soldiers from the colonies, living on the edge of the frontier, could fight a war and win their independence from the mighty British Empire. Suddenly the idea of serving a king, which everyone had taken for granted just a few years earlier, seemed preposterous for many colonists. They had imbibed republican ideas from Thomas Paine's *Common Sense* and other sources—they even found them in the Bible—and so they believed Jefferson's statement from the Declaration of Independence: "That all men are created equal; that they are endowed by their Creator with certain unalienable rights; that among these are life, liberty, and the pursuit of happiness."[61] Of course the white men who believed this did not apply it to African Americans or to women, and Americans would point out that hypocrisy for years to come.

Backus published his history just as the new nation was coming to terms with its founding. These were the important years of the Early Republic (1780–1830). Republican convictions for liberty mixed with revivalism, and together they stimulated evangelical growth in the new nation. Baptists were in the forefront of this rising evangelicalism, but they were not alone, beset as they were on all sides by critics and challengers from other religious movements.

Baptists felt right at home with the language of liberty that saturated the American Revolution. Religious liberty had been a rallying cry for Baptists

---

[60] Backus, *Abridgment of the Church History,* 183.

[61] Declaration of Independence, Avalon Project, Yale Law Library, https://avalon.law.yale.edu/18th_century/declare.asp On the Bible and republicanism, see James P Byrd, *Sacred Scripture, Sacred War: The Bible and the American Revolution* (New York: Oxford University Press, 2013); N. Perl-Rosenthal, "The 'Divine Right of Republics': Hebraic Republicanism and the Debate Over Kingless Government in Revolutionary America," *The William and Mary Quarterly* 66, no. 3 (July 2009): 535–564; Eran Shalev, *American Zion: The Old Testament as a Political Text from the Revolution to the Civil War* (New Haven, CT: Yale University Press, 2013); Eran Shalev, "'A Perfect Republic': The Mosaic Constitution in Revolutionary New England, 1775–1788," *The New England Quarterly* 82, no. 2 (2009): 235–263.

Historical Introduction

since their beginnings, as evidenced by Backus's narrative of Williams, Clarke, and others from the previous century. Much to Backus's frustration, many patriots who fought the British to defend their political liberties balked on religious liberty. They held firm on established churches in the colonies, taxing Baptists and others to support state churches. Liberty was liberty—political or religious, Backus insisted. A people could not stand for liberty in politics while enforcing tyranny in religion. This was hypocrisy, Backus thought, pure and simple. He made this point before the war began, insisting that "many who are filling the nation with the cry of LIBERTY and against oppressors [in Parliament] are at the same time themselves violating the dearest of all rights, LIBERTY OF CONSCIENCE." This was no more than "taxation without representation," which was as wrong in religion as it was in politics.[62] In this way Backus was one of those Baptists, who, as Mark Noll stated, became adept at "employing the rhetoric of the Revolution's leaders against those leaders themselves."[63]

Backus engaged many religious controversies in revolutionary America, including the proposal to assign an Anglican bishop in the colonies. This was a dangerous move, colonists believed, because they knew that bishops usually defended the power of kings at all costs. On this point Backus found himself agreeing with none other than Charles Chauncy. In 1768, Chauncy published a book of more than two hundred pages, arguing that an Anglican bishop in America would threaten the colonists' religious liberty. Backus's history included a long quotation from Chauncy's book, including: "We are in principle against all civil establishments in religion, and as we do not desire any establishment in support of our own religious sentiments or practice, we cannot reasonably be blamed, if we are not disposed to encourage one in favor of the Episcopal Colonists."[64]

This was amazing, Backus asserted, because Chauncy was one of the staunchest defenders of Congregational establishments in New England. Now he was contradicting himself—Chauncy protested the British attempt to put a bishop in America, claiming that it would be a dangerous establishment of religion, and yet Chauncy had no problem with his Congregationalist church living off tax money from all the people in the colony, whether they were Congregationalist or not.

---

[62] Quoted in McLoughlin, *Isaac Backus*, 122; Noll, *America's God,* 151; Original source: Backus, *A Seasonable Plea for Liberty of Conscience Against Some Late Oppressive Proceedings Particularly in the Town of Berwick* (Boston, MA: 1770).

[63] Noll, *America's God*, 151.

[64] As quoted in Backus, *Abridgment of the Church History,* 201. C.f. Charles Chauncy, *The Appeal to the public answered, in behalf of the non-Episcopal churches in America* (Boston, MA: Kneeland and Adams, 1768), 152.

Chauncy would deny this accusation, as would other elite ministers in New England, declaring that these were two different systems, and that their establishments of the Congregationalist Church in the New England colonies were not "real establishments." Yet they were, Backus insisted, because they included the "three principles" that were "the foundation of all worldly establishments that ever were made under the name of Christianity." The first principle was "infant baptism, which lays bands upon children before they can choose for themselves." The next principle was "the supporting of religious teachers by force, by the power of the magistrate." The last was granting "ministers a power of office which the people cannot give nor take away." Adding insult to injury, Backus linked Congregationalists with Roman Catholics: "The church of Rome, and the church of England, were built and are now upheld entirely by these three principles: and the Congregational churches that are established by law in the Massachusetts and Connecticut, hold each of them fast."[65]

And there they were – three principles of state-supported, forced religion that Baptists fought against. But these principles were not just anti-Baptist; they were anti-republican, Backus believed. They violated the convictions for liberty that undergirded the American Revolution. Even if one did not care about religion, there were political reasons to ban favoritism to a particular church in the state. Just think about the money, Backus said, "The costs of Legislatures to make laws about worship, parishes and ministers, is a main part of the expenses of all governments who go in that way." Then there was the reality that "Religious pretences [sic] have caused the most of the wars that have been in the world, under the name of Christianity; and the expenses which are occasioned by wars, are as much as half of the support of government in Europe and America." When the state involved itself in legislating religion, the results were often not only expensive but violent.[66]

One would think that such arguments would play well in revolutionary America, but Backus encountered substantial opposition. Old habits died hard; there was much invested in legal church establishments, and neither politicians nor ministers would give them up without a fight. One conflict occurred in 1774, when Backus protested church establishments before the Continental Congress. John and Samuel Adams rejected Backus' appeal.

---

[65] Backus, *Abridgment of the Church History*, 202–203.

[66] Backus, *Abridgment of the Church History,* 203. As Mark Noll argues, Backus used republican political arguments when he needed to, but the source of his ideas was theological, not political. He was a revivalist Calvinist; his ideas about liberty flowed from this identity. True freedom came only from God; it was impossible without God's saving grace that transformed the will. Noll, *America's God*, 151.

Historical Introduction

Dissenters did not suffer much due to the church establishment, they argued. It was only a matter of a little money—no great persecution. Backus reported John Adams's statement that one "might as well expect a change in the solar system, as to expect they would give up their establishment."[67]

There was also a war to fight. The Revolutionary War did not directly affect Backus. He did not fight in it—he was 51 when the war started in 1775—and there were no battles near his town of Middleborough. But the war held deep meaning for him. The war, as Backus saw it, was God's providence at work, ridding the nation of tyrannical religion as well as tyrannical politics.[68] Throughout the war and afterwards, Backus presented Baptists as true patriots, willing to fight for the liberty of the colonies, even though leaders of these colonies had mistreated them. It had been so bad for Baptists that some had accepted Britain's support against colonial oppression. Yet these Baptists would not support the British in the war, Backus insisted. The Baptists, "though they had received relief from the British court, several times, yet they saw that this was done for political ends, by men who now aimed to bring all America into bondage."[69]

> The Revolutionary War was a time of revolutionary growth for Baptists. As Backus reported, the power of spiritual weapons was such, that God again revived his work in 1779, and it prevailed so far for three years, as greatly to increase the old Baptist churches, and to form above thirty new ones in New-England, beside many more in the southern parts of America. And as pure religion is directly against all offensive wars, and fills the people of God with an earnest desire and pursuit of justice and equity, this revival had a great influence in procuring the peace of 1783.[70]

A bold statement, but Backus believed it: Baptists and the revivals they supported had helped to end the war.

Once patriots had defeated the British—a feat many had thought impossible—they had another major task ahead of them that seemed almost as incredible: Establishing a new nation. It would need to have a centralized power—a federal authority—but it would also need to protect the rights of individual states. Some thought the nation needed a written constitution; others feared that a constitution would give too much power to a centralized

---

[67] Isaac Backus, *A History of New England, With Particular Reference to the Denomination of Christians Called Baptists. Second Edition, with Notes. By David Weston* (Newton, MA: Backus Historical Society, 1871), 202. C.f. Kidd, *Liberty*, Kindle ed., 171.

[68] McLoughlin, *Isaac Backus*, 136–138.

[69] Backus, *Abridgment of the Church History*, 206.

[70] Backus, *Abridgment of the Church History*, 216.

government, which would create yet another tyrannical ruler. These concerns were at play when the Constitutional Convention was held in Philadelphia in 1787.

The resulting Constitution had to be ratified by the states, which meant convincing various constituents in the states to support it. By this time Baptists had grown numerous enough to be taken seriously in politics. If enough Baptists rejected the Constitution in some states, they could jeopardize its ratification. And many Baptists did oppose the Constitution because it said nothing about guaranteeing religious liberty to Baptists who refused to support the state-endorsed churches.

In Virginia, James Madison learned quickly that he needed to lobby for the Baptist vote. He eventually secured it, but only by promising to endorse an amendment to the Constitution that would safeguard religious liberty. We do not know for sure, but Madison may have negotiated with well-known Baptist evangelist John Leland, who had traveled extensively from New England to the South, preaching both the gospel of salvation and the Baptist gospel of religious liberty.[71]

Baptists in Virginia also trusted in the word of George Washington, who wrote a letter "To the United Baptist Churches of Virginia" in May 1789, assuring them that:

> If I could have entertained the slightest apprehension that the Constitution framed in the Convention, where I had the honor to preside, might possibly endanger the religious rights of any ecclesiastical Society, certainly I would never have placed my signature to it; and if I could now conceive that the general Government might ever be so administered as to render the liberty of conscience insecure, I beg you will be persuaded that no one would be more zealous than myself to establish effectual barriers against the horrors of spiritual tyranny, and every species of religious persecution—For you, doubtless, remember that I have often expressed my sentiment, that every man, conducting himself as a good citizen, and being accountable to God alone for his religious opinions, ought to be protected in worshipping the Deity according to the dictates of his own conscience.[72]

---

[71] Backus includes a lot of information about Leland, a fascinating evangelist and Baptist. For his writings, see: John Leland and L. F. Greene, *The Writings of the Late Elder John Leland: Including Some Events in His Life* (New York: Printed by G.W. Wood, 1845).

[72] *The Papers of George Washington Digital Edition* (Charlottesville, VA: University of Virginia Press, Rotunda, 2008). Canonic URL: https://rotunda-upress-virginia-edu.proxy.library.vanderbilt.edu/founders/GEWN-05-02-02-0309 [accessed 25 May 2021]. See also Kidd, *Liberty*, 223; Backus, *Abridgment of the Church History,* 224–225.

Historical Introduction

This was wonderful for Baptists. George Washington was the most respected leader in colonies and in the new nation, and he praised the Baptists in his letter. As Backus quoted Washington:

> While I recollect with satisfaction that the religious Society of which you are Members, have been, throughout America, uniformly, and almost unanimously, the firm friends to civil liberty, and the persevering Promoters of our glorious revolution; I cannot hesitate to believe that they will be the faithful Supporters of a free, yet efficient general Government. Under this pleasing expectation I rejoice to assure them that they may rely on my best wishes and endeavors to advance their prosperity.[73]

In New England, Backus agreed to support the Constitution because it had no religious "test" or requirement for one to hold office. Other colonies worried that if there were no religious test, they could be stuck with officeholders who were not even Protestant, perhaps even Catholic—a great fear for many colonists. That was not Backus's concern. He and other Baptists had lived under Protestant establishments long enough to know that they could be as tyrannical as any kingdom.[74]

Backus, like Leland and many other Baptists, celebrated the First Amendment, which stated:

> Congress shall make no law respecting an establishment of religion, or prohibiting the free exercise thereof; or abridging the freedom of speech, or of the press; or the right of the people peaceably to assemble, and to petition the Government for a redress of grievances.[75]

At last Baptists had a broad statement against church establishments, even though it pertained only to the federal government, not the individual states. Backus protested against Connecticut and Massachusetts, states that continued their church establishments "to this day. And so all the evils that worldly establishments have ever produced, ought to be considered as a warning to them."[76]

---

[73] *The Papers of George Washington Digital Edition* (Charlottesville, VA: University of Virginia Press, Rotunda, 2008). Canonic URL: https://rotunda-upress-virginia-edu.proxy.library.vanderbilt.edu/founders/GEWN-05-02-02-0309 [accessed 25 May 2021]. See also Backus, *Abridgment of the Church History,* 224–225.

[74] Kidd, *Liberty* 224.

[75] The Constitution of the United States, The Avalon Project, Yale Law School, https://avalon.law.yale.edu/18th_century/rights1.asp#1 Note that Backus quoated a slightly different form of it in his *Abridgment of the Church History,* 225.

[76] Backus, *Abridgment of the Church History,* 225.

Not only were Baptists wrestling with religious establishments, but they also dealt with the religious diversity and competition of the time. The Early Republic was an era of revolution and revival, and both forces gave new energy to religious innovation. New religious movements, and new so-called prophets emerged everywhere, and they competed with existing denominations. Amid this competitive religious marketplace, Backus became the major defender of Baptists in New England. He wrote nearly 40 religious tracts and many sermons, mainly, as William McLoughlin summarized, against "four major threats—the Shaker movement, the Universalists, the Methodists, and the Freewill Baptists."[77]

Among these, the Methodists would become the Baptists' most serious rivals. Initially Methodists encountered several disadvantages in competing with Baptists in New England. First, Methodists had a terrible reputation because their founder, John Wesley, had spoken out against the Revolutionary War. So, Methodists were disloyal "Tories" who could not be trusted, many Americans believed. Second, Methodists arrived late in New England. They came to the area in the 1790s, where they faced Baptists who had been there longer. Third, Methodists gained a reputation for uneducated, traveling preachers who claimed that all Christians should strive to be perfect. Many misunderstood what John Wesley meant by "perfection," but the mere mention of the idea shocked Calvinistic New Englanders who believed that one could never fully overcome sin in this life.[78]

Connected with this perfectionist belief was the Methodists' Arminianism, which Backus attacked, criticizing Wesley for claiming that "Christ died equally for all mankind," not for the elect only. Here Backus claimed that Methodists forgot the words of the New Testament about divine election:

> "If ye were of the world, the world would love his own; but because ye are not of the world, but I have chosen you out of the world, therefore the world hateth you." John xv. 19. He chose, or *elected* them out of the world, and so they are elect according to the foreknowledge of God the Father, through sanctification of the Spirit unto obedience, and sprinkling of the blood of Jesus Christ. 1 Peter, i. 2. God the Father hath chosen us in Christ, before the foundation of the world, that we should be holy, and without blame before him in love. Eph. i. 3, 4. He chose them that they *should be holy,* and not as they become holy in conversion. If our conversion and holiness were the cause of God's electing us, our salvation would be of works, and not of grace; and this

---

[77] McLoughlin, *Isaac Backus*, 170
[78] McLoughlin, *Isaac Backus*, 179.

Historical Introduction

would also exclude all men from hope, who see that they are wholly under sin, and have naturally no good thing in them.[79]

And there was no perseverance of the saints for Wesley. Those saved could backslide and lose their salvation. All these ideas offended Backus's Calvinist convictions.[80]

Methodists did some good in the world, Backus admitted—"Many have doubtless been reformed by their means, and some converted; but they readily receive awakened persons to communion, without a profession of regeneration. Hereby church and world are as really bound together, as they were in old worldly establishments."[81]

The Methodist challenge to Baptists—and to Calvinism—would only strengthen over time. The Methodist movement proclaimed itself to be a church at the 1784 "Christmas Conference" in Baltimore. From then on, their circuit rider preachers, led by bishop Francis Asbury, scoured the new nation. Asbury set the example, traveling thousands of miles by horseback, shunning property and the comforts of life, and demanding that those under his charge do the same. The effort contributed to the Methodists' expansion, as did the Methodist growth among African Americans under the leadership of people like Richard Allen, first bishop of the African Methodist Episcopal Church. By the middle of the nineteenth century, various Methodist groups would claim about one million adherents—double the number of the Baptists, who were the second largest denomination.[82]

When Backus published his history, Baptists faced obstacles, both from remaining church establishments in New England and from various other denominations, all of whom competed for adherents. Still, he concluded his history on an optimistic note because revivals were surging through the new nation. Backus included documentation, inserting letters into his text that described dramatic revivals and listing statistics on baptisms from state to state. He added details about Baptist leaders in the South, especially white evangelists John Leland (who was sometimes in the South), Shubael Stearns, and Daniel Marshall. Lacking from Backus's account is much detail on the

---

[79] Backus, *Abridgment of the Church History,* 219; McLoughlin, *Isaac Backus*, 177.

[80] McLoughlin, *Isaac Backus*, 177.

[81] Backus, *Abridgment of the Church History,* 219.

[82] Daniel Walker Howe, *What Hath God Wrought: The Transformation of America, 1815–1848*, The Oxford History of the United States (New York: Oxford University Press, 2007), 176; Bret E. Carroll, *The Routledge Historical Atlas of Religion in America*, Routledge Atlases of American History (New York: Routledge, 2000), 64. See also John Wigger, "Francis Asbury and American Methodism," in *The Oxford Handbook of Methodist Studies*, eds. James E. Kirby and William J. Abraham (New York and London: Oxford University Press, 2011), 53–62.

development of African American Baptist churches in the South, although he did observe that "A great many Negroes in those parts have been converted and baptized, and some of them have been called to preach the gospel."[83] Specifically, Backus described George Liele's successes preaching and baptizing many people in Savannah, Georgia and then Jamacia, where "he had 350 members in his church in 1791." In addition, Backus reported on Andrew Bryan's leadership of "a large negro church in Savannah, Georgia."[84]

In addition to key individuals, Backus also praised Baptists' efforts to organize themselves, much as other denominations were doing. Some Baptists guarded the local churches' power to control their own affairs, so they were suspicious of denominational power structures like conventions, associations, and missionary societies. The Warren Association of Baptist Churches, which Backus helped to establish, was instituted upon strict principles because Baptists had seen how "very cruel and oppressive" ministerial associations had been in New England. If properly controlled, however, associations could be invaluable, and the Warren Association was a key example. "They refuse to hear and judge of any personal controversy in any of their churches, or to intermeddle with the affairs of any church which hath not freely joined with them." By various ways, then, the Warren Association helped its churches without compromising local church control. Baptists associations, and Baptist churches, seemed to be springing up everywhere. As Backus was pleased to report, "we have thirteen associations in New-England, in which are 312 churches, and 23638 members, where there were but nine Baptist churches in 1700, and but five more in all America."[85]

When Backus published this edition of his history, he saw the world changing all around him. A new nation, built on ideas of liberty, was thriving, and society was being transformed, and that included the churches. A few years after Backus wrote, Washington Irving published his famous story, *Rip Van Winkle*, telling of how a somewhat idle man named Rip slept for years and awoke to what seemed like a new world. That story was popular because many people felt that way. Changes had come quickly.[86]

Like countless Christians, Backus reacted to these changes by reflecting on scripture, particularly the Book of Revelation and other apocalyptic texts. From them, he drew teachings of promise and warning. He saw promise in

---

[83] Backus, *Abridgment of the Church History,* 257.

[84] Backus, *Abridgment of the Church History,* 257.

[85] Backus, *Abridgment of the Church History,* 259–261.

[86] Gordon S Wood, *Empire of Liberty: A History of the Early Republic, 1789–1815*, The Oxford History of the United States (Oxford; New York: Oxford University Press, 2009). See "Introduction: Rip Van Winkle's America."

Historical Introduction

the Baptists, and like John Leland, he also saw promise in the presidency of Thomas Jefferson. Though hardly evangelical in his religious beliefs, Jefferson believed in the Gospel of religious liberty. As Backus wrote in praise of Jefferson:

> A man was elected into that office [president] in 1801, who is for equal liberty to all the nation. And if the Holy Scriptures are well regarded, we shall be the happiest people upon earth; for they shew that every man, who is fit for a ruler, is like good trees and vines, which yield sweet fruits to all around them, without injuring anyone; and that tyrants are like the bramble, which would set the whole community on *fire*, and burn up the best characters in it, if they stood in the way of their gratifying their own lusts of pride and covetousness. Judges ix. 7-15.[87]

Of course, Backus was wrong about Jefferson: This slaveholding president was not "for equal liberty to all the nation," and many Americans would emphasize the hypocrisy of a slaveholder who proclaimed "that all men are created equal." In 1802, approximately two years before Backus published the final edition of his *Abridgment of the Church History*, a journalist named James Callender published a report that Jefferson had an enslaved "concubine" named "Sally." This rumor circulated for years. It has now been confirmed by many leading historians, supported by DNA evidence, that Jefferson fathered children with Sally Hemings, an enslaved woman who had no power—legally or otherwise—to say no to sexual intercourse with him.[88] We do not know what—if anything—Backus knew or thought about Jefferson and Sally Hemings, but there was no secret that Jefferson was a slaveholder. Despite this fact, Backus believed Jefferson would support liberty over tyranny because, as previously noted, Backus was less concerned about slavery than he was about church-state establishments and, on that score, Jefferson supported his agenda.

Backus's agreements with Jefferson only went so far. Both rejected any state establishments of religion, but they disagreed on the role Christianity should play in the nation. As William McLoughlin stated, "Isaac Backus…believed in separation of church and state, but he was also among those who thought the United States was and should be a Christian nation. That would be true as soon as all those outside the churches were persuaded to become

---

[87] Backus, *Abridgment of the Church History,* 264.

[88] See: Annette Gordon-Reed, *Thomas Jefferson and Sally Hemings: An American Controversy* (Charlottesville, VA: University Press of Virginia, 1997); Annette Gordon-Reed, *The Hemingses of Monticello: An American Family*, 1st ed (New York: W.W. Norton & Co, 2008); "The Life of Sally Hemings," https://www.monticello.org/sallyhemings/

members. Religious liberty would create an open marketplace for preaching the various forms of Christianity and, in his opinion, the United States would ultimately be a Baptist nation, for the Bible says that 'the Truth is great and shall prevail.'" In contrast, Jefferson rejected the idea of a Christian nation.[89]

The hope for religious liberty in the nation, as Backus saw it, lay in obedience to the scriptures and their teachings against church establishments and religious persecution. "Language cannot describe our times more exactly, than it was thus done by God, near eighteen hundred years ago…. The best churches that ever supported their ministers by force, had no more than *a form* of godliness; and all men have denied the *power* of it, who have denied that the laws and Spirit of Christ were entirely sufficient to support his ministers, without any arm of flesh in the case."[90]

Backus concluded his history with an apocalyptic warning against ungodliness and religious persecution. Like Roger Williams more than a century before him, he believed that the battle between good and evil, a spiritual warfare that encompassed the scriptures, reflected the battle between religious liberty and bloody persecution. In the end, as in the end of the Book of Revelation, God would take revenge on evil empires and "their *bloody* gains," and finally "heaven and earth will rejoice to see his truth and justice glorified."[91]

---

[89] McLoughlin, *Soul Liberty*, 249, 259.
[90] Backus, *Abridgment of the Church History,* 270.
[91] Backus, *Abridgment of the Church History,* 271.

AN

ABRIDGMENT

OF THE

Church History

OF

NEW-ENGLAND,

FROM 1602 TO 1804.

CONTAINING A VIEW OF THEIR

PRINCIPLES AND PRACTICE, DECLEN-
SIONS AND REVIVALS, OPPRES-
SION AND LIBERTY.

WITH A

CONCISE ACCOUNT OF THE BAPTISTS IN THE
SOUTHERN PARTS OF AMERICA,

AND A

CHRONOLOGICAL TABLE of the WHOLE,

BY ISAAC BACKUS, A.M.

PASTOR OF A CHURCH IN MIDDLEBOROUGH.

Published according to Act of Congress.

BOSTON:

PRINTED FOR THE AUTHOR, BY E. LINCOLN.

SOLD BY MANNING & LORING, NO. 2, CORNHILL, AND BY E. LINCOLN, WATER-STREET.

1804.[1]

---

[1] This version of Backus's history has been transcribed from the 1804 edition by James P. Byrd and Alex Ayris with the assistance of a scanned copy of the original in PDF format. Original text is possession of William Brackney: 12.5 mm x 21.5 mm,72 p, leatherbound.

PREFACE.

THE experience of mankind, from age to age, gives the best light to direct our ways of any human means; and the record of the word of God is our only sure guide to eternal life. Comparing spiritual things with spiritual, under the influence of the Holy Spirit, is the way to bring us to that happy end; and though the writings of all uninspired men are imperfect, yet by comparing their various accounts together, we may gain much instruction from them about the accomplishment of prophecy, and many other things.

These things were much upon my mind in early life, especially about the history of my own country. And when the knowledge of experimental religion was given me, above threescore years ago, it increased my attention to these things. But when some of our chief ministers requested me to engage to write our history, in 1771, the greatness of the work, and the difficulty of obtaining the necessary materials, were great objections in my way. Yet their importunity prevailed; and I spent much of my time in going to, and searching of the records of the old colonies of Plymouth, the Massachusetts, Rhode Island, Connecticut, and of the United Colonies, which last are at Plymouth. I also searched many other records and papers, as well as books of various kinds, and inquired of intelligent persons, to get all the light I could from every quarter. And our first volume was published in 1777, the second in 1784, and the third in 1796; and I never heard of any thing published against the work, though I desired that it might be corrected.

4   PREFACE.

As several things have come to light of late, that I had not before, and my ability for writing is continued to old age,* I have thought it to be duty to reduce the most useful things into one volume, with a concise view of our southern States, as well as to bring the history down to the present time. And as writers are often incorrect in their dates, I have paid much attention to that subject; and have given an exact table of events, according to what light I could gain, following the old style, until the new took place in 1752.

Many of the new things in this volume were taken from Winthrop's journal, published in 1790; from the publications of the Historical Society at Boston, and from a book which I borrowed of them, called "The Bloody Tenet," of which I know not of another copy in America. The accounts of our southern States were collected partly when I was in North Carolina and Virginia, in 1789, and partly from other sources of intelligence. And in the experience of two centuries, in this great country, we may see a great variety of different schemes of government that have been tried, which may direct our choice to what is right, and to avoid evil ways; especially to guard against all cruelty, deceit and violence. These things are humbly presented to the public, by their aged friend,

ISAAC BACKUS.

MIDDLEBOROUGH, August 30, 1804.

* Eighty on January 20, 1804.

CHRONOLOGICAL TABLE OF CONTENTS,
With some things not before mentioned.

1602	THEIR first church formed	9
1606	They become two -	10
1608	Both go to Amsterdam * -	ibid
1609	One goes to Leyden -	ibid
1610	Robinson defends them - -	11,23,64
1613	Disputes against Arminians	12
1617	They consult about removing	13
1620	Excellent advice given ...	14
	They come to Cape Cod—Plant Plymouth	19,20
1621	Many die there - - -	ib.
	But Indians are friendly ...	ib.
1623	Relief in distress.—New-Hampshire begun	21

1625	Robinson dies - -	ib
1628	Their debts paid—Salem begun	22,24
1629	More come over -	22
	Massachusetts charter - - -	24
1630	Plymouth charter—Their church order	22,23
1630	Boston planted -	25
1631	Church governs the world	ib.
	Williams comes over - -	28
1633	Also, Cotton and Hooker ...	26
	Williams goes to Salem	28
1634	New oath imposed	29
1635	All to take it—Williams against it	30
	Lands taken from Salem	ib.
	Windsor planted .	26
1636	Lands restored	31
	Williams banished—Plants Providence	32
	Does great service to many	34
	Church order at Boston	26,40,66
	Reasons of it	33,39
	Hartford planted	26
1637	Pequot war—But soon over	36,37
	Confusion at Boston—A synod called	40
	Some banished—Connecticut more mild	41,26,42
1638	Rhode Island begun—New-Haven also	43,37
	Harvard College founded	
	Providence government	45
1639	Province of Maine granted	
	Baptist church at Providence—Baptists elsewhere	45,46
1640	Coddington's changes	44,70
1641	Account of Knollys	47
1642	Pawtuxet difficulties	51
1643	The colonies confederate	52
	Gorton and others confined	53
	Miantenimo killed	54
	Williams went to England	47,56
1644	A number banished	54
	Williams gets a charter	56

CHURCH HISTORY OF NEW ENGLAND

	Exposeth persecution -	58–61,69
	Boston law against Baptists	48
1645	They sent an agent to England	122
1646	Severity pleaded for—Others for pure liberty	63, 64
1647	Providence colony—A view of their leaders	65, 67
	Extracts from Cotton	49, 58, 60
	—and Hooker	68, 141
1648	Owen for liberty—Others for force	62, 69
1649	Winthrop a good ruler --	70
1650	Some for oppression	69, 71
1651	Cruelty at Boston	72,74
	—A good testimony there	22
	Warwick sufferings -	84, 88
1652	Baptist testimonies	72-77
	—Letters about them	78-81
	Johnson	33, 37, 55, 83, 84
	Cotton dies - -	82
1653	Light about baptism—and about England	83, 86
1655	Williams prevails here -	88
1656	The Massachusetts requited	89
	Quakers come over -	90
1657	Bradford against persecution	ibid
1658	Quakers described	91
1659	Some are hanged	93
1660	Conscience pleaded for it	92
1661	Great cruelty in England -	94
1662	Injustice about colony lines	106
	Settled afterwards - -	107
1663	Swansea church formed -	95
1665	Also one in Boston, who suffer much -	96, 97
1667	Neal spake for them	98
1668	Yet they were banished—Cause of it	100
1669	Moving letters from England	101–104
1670	Divisions about them	101,111
1671	Another Baptist church	113
1672	A dispute with Quakers -	108
1673	Some Baptists join them	110

1673	Clarke's character—His faith	113,114
1676	His death -	116
	Indian war	117–121
	Christian Indians described - -	122–124
1677	Baptists still oppressed -	125
1679	They increase -	127
1680	Their friends in England favour them	128
1682	Piscataqua affairs	129
1683	Williams dies	130
1684	Charter vacated	ibid
1686	Great cruelties here - - - -	131
1688	Mather goes to England—his mind is changed	132
1691	New charter given -	133
1692	The world above the church—Boston not so	134
1697	Declensions described	136
1700	More of it—Testified against	137,173
1701	Episcopal scheme	138,201
1705	Attempts for lordly power	138
1708	Connecticut got it	139
1709	Churches corrupted *	145
1710	Norwich case	142, 187
1714	Queen removed in mercy	138
1715	Lordly power attempted again	143
1716	Again condemned	144
1718	Boston ordination	146
1720	Baptist's liberality	147
1721	Revivals of Religion—Comer converted	152, 153
1722	Dartmouth oppressed	149
1723	Increase Mather dies	150
1725	Ministers try for more power	ibid
1726	Inconsistent therein	ibid
1727	Great earthquake	160
1728	Pharaoh imitated	151
1729	Many were imprisoned	ibid
1731	Baptist ministers settled	156
1732	A new Baptist church	155
1734	Two ministers die	156

1735	Another church formed	ibid
	A great work at Northampton	160
1738	Callender dies	157
	Of Congregational churches	158
1740	Low state of religion	161
	But it was greatly revived	162
1741	It spread far	163
	Nature of the work -	164
1742	Laws against it	167
	Edwards for it -	165,173
1743	Chauncy against it	168
	Condemns himself	170
	Finley persecuted	172
1744	Violence against the work	174,175, 177
	Divisions caused by it	177,178, 180
1745	A new church formed	177
	Whitefield abused	183
1746	Robbins much more	185
	Separate ordinations	178
1748	Ministers lose by it	186
1749	Cruel laws suspended	ibid
1750	Edwards cruelly rejected	182
1751	He is useful elsewhere	ibid
1752	Imprisonment for taxes	188,189, 207
1754	Opposition abates	193
1755	Another earthquake	197
1756	The Baptists increase	191,192,194, 196
1758	Wallingford division	194,196
1759	Episcopal scheme	197
1761	More Baptist churches	ibid
1762	Religion again revived	ibid
1763	It spreads far	198
1764	A Baptist college begun, on liberal principles -	199

1765	Haverhill church begun -	200
1767	The tea act passed—Episcopalians stir	200,201
1768	Chauncy inconsistent	202,213
1770	Establishments described - - - -	203
1771	A drunkard favoured -	204
1772	Universalism	205
1774	Religion revived again-New attempts for liberty	205,209
1775	A cruel war came on	211
1 776	Union and plenty in it - -	ibid
1777	An army captivated -	
1778	Pepperell riot -	212
	Quakers divided—Baptists united	213
1779	Baptists falsely accused—Oppression continued by it 214	
1780	Conscience pleaded for it	215
	Christ's kingdom described -	216
	Baptist churches increase	
1781	Another army captivated	
1782	Peace proposed	
1783	It is established -	223
	Yet ministers claimed a power from England -	217
	And accuse us falsely -	ibid
1784	Methodism described—And other bishops -	218,220
1785	Oppression continued - - -	218
1786	Liberty in Virginia	222
1787	New constitution formed - -	223
1788	It is adopted -	ibid
	Ministers inconsistent - -	224
1789	Liberty more secured - - - -	225
1790	Eastern and western revivals - -	226,227
1791	Manning dies—but has good successors -	229
1793	Ministerial power opened - -	230
1795	New oppressions	232
1796	Others kind - - -	234
1798	New revivals -- - - -	235
1799	The work extends far -	239
1800	Virginia shares in it -	241
1801	Vast numbers baptized -	242

CHURCH HISTORY OF NEW ENGLAND

1802	A book against it—Remarks thereon;	242,243
	Account of South-Carolina—Pennsylvania—New-Jersey—-North-Carolina—Virginia—Georgia—New-York—Kentucky	247–258
	Associations described - - - -	259
1804	Number of Baptists in the United States	261
	Late revivals -	262
	Their likeness to the fathers of New-England	ibid
	How infant baptism originated -	ibid
	Happy change in our government -	264
	The latter day glory	268

A
Church History
OF
NEW-ENGLAND.

CHAP. I.

Their first church formed.—They divide into two.— They remove to Amsterdam.—One goes to Leyden.—They increase to three hundred.—Part of them come to America.—Here many of them die.—Yet the rest are prospered.—Robinson dies in Holland.—Yet more come over.—Their charter given.—Their church order.

THE light of Revelation, and the superstitions and persecutions of the church of England, were the causes of the first planting of New-England. A number of people near the borders of the counties of York, Nottingham and Lincoln, were so much convinced of the corruptions of the church of England, that they withdrew from her in 1602, and formed another church, in which they covenanted together, to walk in all the ordinances and commandments of God, according to the light he had given, or should give them out of his holy word. But for so doing they were cruelly persecuted by the ruling powers of the national church. Yet they increased so much in about four years, as

to divide into two churches; and this increased the resentment of their enemies so much, that they removed to Amsterdam in 1608. One of these churches had the aged Mr. Richard Clifton and Mr. John Robinson for their pastors; but Clifton died at Amsterdam.* And as contentions had broken out in the other church, Mr. Robinson and his people removed to Leyden in 1609, though to their temporal disadvantage. There they lived in peace and harmony, and increased to three hundred communicants.

This caused much uneasiness in the church of England, and many things were published against them. Mr. Richard Bernard of Nottinghamshire, in particular, wrote a large book against them, which Mr. Robinson answered in 1610; and he observes, that because one Bolton, in the early part of the reign of Queen Elizabeth, formed a church in a way of separation from the church of England, which persecution brought him to renounce, and afterwards to hang himself; and Robert Brown, a minister of that church, came out and formed several separate churches, and yet turned back again into the national church, Mr. Bernard brought these instances as arguments against all who separated from them. Upon which Robinson said, "The universal apostasy of all the bishops, ministers, students in the universities, yea, of the whole church of England in queen Mary's days (a handful in comparison excepted) might more colourably be urged by the papists against Mr. Bernard, than some few instances against us. The fall of Judas, an apostate, of Nicolas one of the seven deacons, and of Demas, one of Paul's special companions in the ministry, sufficiently teach us that there is no cause so holy, nor calling so excellent, as not to be subject to the invasion of painted

* Prince's Chronology, page 254.

1610.]　　　　　　　　OF NEW-ENGLAND.　　　　　　　　11

hypocrites.* And as Mr. Bernard referred to many evils in the primitive churches, as a plea that the church of England might be a true church of Christ, notwithstanding all her corruptions, Robinson says, "It is true that the apostles mentioned them, but always with utter dislike, severe reproof, and strict charges to reform them. Rom. xvi. 17, 1 Cor. v. 1 Thess. v. 14. 2 Thess. iii. 6. 1 Tim. vi. 5. Rev. ii. 14—16, 20. But how doth this concern you? Though Paul and all the apostles with him; yea, though Christ himself from heaven should admonish any of your churches to put away any person, though never so heretical or flagitious, you could not do it."† "Your prelates govern, or rather reign, but teach not; your parish priests teach so much as they dare for fear of their imperious lords, but they govern not."‡ "Nothing hath more advanced the throne of antichrist in former days, nor doth more uphold it at this day, than the people's discharging themselves of the care of public affairs in the church, on the one side, and the priests and prelates arrogating all to themselves, on the other."|| "And I doubt not but Mr. Bernard, and a thousand more ministers in the land (were they secure of the magistrate's sword, and might they go on with good licence) would wholly shake off their canonical obedience to their ordinaries, and neglect their citations and censures, and refuse to sue in their courts, for all the peace of the church, which they commend to us for so sacred a thing."§

This remark was plainly verified in the vast numbers who afterwards came over to New-England, who did not separate from the national church before they came away. The follow-

* Robinson, page 53–55.
† Robinson, page 82.   ‡ 359. || 204.
§ Robinson, page 14.

A CHURCH HISTORY.   [CH. I.

ing account may give us some idea of his views of gospel doctrines. James Arminius, a professor of divinity in the university of Leyden, died there in 1609; but the opinions he had advanced have caused much controversy ever since. It was so sharp at Leyden in 1612, between the two professors in their university, that few of the disciples of the one would hear the other; but Mr. Robinson, though he preached thrice a week, and wrote sundry books, beside many other labours, yet went constantly to hear them both, whereby he was grounded in the controversy, and saw the force of all their arguments. And in 1613, Episcopius set forth sundry Arminian theses at Leyden, which he would defend in public against all opposers; upon which Polyander, and the chief preachers of the city, desired Mr. Robinson to dispute against him. But being a stranger, he was loath to engage: Yet the other telling him, that such was the ability and expertness of the adversary, that truth was in danger of suffering if he would not help them, he at length yields; and when the day came, he defended the truth and foiled the opposer, so as to put him to an apparent nonplus in a great and public audience. The same he does a second and a third time, upon like occasions; which caused many to praise God, and highly to esteem Mr. Robinson.*

Thus it appears that Mr. Robinson was a firm believer of those doctrines which are called Calvinism, while he was earnest for allowing all men liberty of conscience; and that the contrary behaviour of many was not owing to that plan of doctrine, but to other causes. For the rulers in Holland held firmly to that doctrine, and yet they established such religious liberty as was not then enjoyed in any other part of Europe. But though their religious

* Prince's Chronology, p. 36, 38.

1613.]   OF NEW-ENGLAND.   13

privileges were great, yet many other things caused Mr. Robinson and his people to desire a removal to a better country. For most of them had been bred to husbandry, which they had not advantages to follow in Holland; and the language and manners of the Dutch were not agreeable to them; and their little regard to the sabbath, and other religious duties, were offensive to them; and the climate of the country was not favourable to their health, but their children were oppressed with labour and disease, so as to abate the vigour of nature in early age; neither could they be willing to lose their interest in the English nation, and the government thereof, if they could obtain liberty of conscience from thence. And they believed that if they could have such liberty granted them in America, many would remove thither, who would enlarge the English dominions, and also spread the light of the gospel among the heathen. They therefore sent two agents to England in 1617, to petition for such liberties and privileges. And having received some encouragement from the Council there, who had the care of the American affairs, Mr. Robinson and Elder Brewster wrote to them these encouraging considerations. "1. We verily believe and trust that the Lord is with us; to whom and whose service we have given ourselves in many trials, and that he will graciously prosper our endeavours according to the simplicity of our hearts. 2. We are well weaned from the delicate milk of our mother country, and inured to the difficulties of a strange land. 3. The people are, for the body of them, industrious and frugal, we think we may safely say, as any company of people in the world. 4. We are knit together as a body, in a most strict and sacred bond and covenant of the Lord; of the violation whereof we make great conscience, and by virtue whereof we hold ourselves straitly tied to all care of each other's good, and of the whole. 5. It

14   A CHURCH HISTORY   [CH. I

is not with us, as with other men, whom small things can discourage, and small discouragements cause to wish ourselves at home again."*

Herein they were not mistaken, as will soon appear; for though contentions in said council, and other things, delayed their proceedings for three years, and they could not obtain a promise of liberty of conscience in this country, but only that the king would connive at them, and not molest them, if they carried peaceably, "yet, casting themselves on the care of Providence, they resolved to venture." But as they could not obtain help enough, from the merchant adventurers in England, to carry over half of their society at first, Mr. Robinson was obliged to stay with the majority in Holland, while elder Brewster came with the rest to America. And before they came away Mr. Robinson gave them this solemn advice. Said he, "We are now to part asunder, and the Lord knoweth whether I shall live to see your faces again: but whether he hath appointed it or not, I charge you before God and his blessed angels, to follow me no further than I have followed Christ. And if God shall reveal any thing to you by any other instrument of his, be as ready to receive it as ever you were to receive any truth by my ministry; for I am very confident that the Lord has more truth and light yet to break forth out of his holy word. Here he took occasion to bewail the state and condition of the reformed churches, who were come to a period in religion, and would go no further than the instruments of their reformation. As for example, the Lutherans could not be drawn to go beyond what Luther saw; for whatever part of God's will he had further imparted and revealed to Calvin, they will rather die than embrace it. And so you see the Calvinists, they stick where he left

* Prince, p. 51, 52.

1620.]   OF NEW-ENGLAND.   15

them, a misery much to be lamented; for though they were precious shining lights in their times, yet God has not revealed his whole will to them. And were they now living, they would be as ready and willing to embrace further light, as that they had received. And here I must put you in mind of our church covenant, wherein we promise and covenant with God and one another, to receive whatsoever light or truth that shall be made known to us from his written word. But withal I exhort you to take heed what you receive for truth, and well to examine and compare it with other Scriptures before you receive it; for it is not possible that the christian world should come so lately out of such thick antichristian darkness, and that full perfection of knowledge should break forth at once.*"

And after an affectionate parting, Mr. Robinson, on July 27, 1620, sent them the following letter :

"*Loving Christian Friends*,
"I do heartily, and in the Lord salute you, as being those with whom I am present in my best affections, and most earnest longing after you, though I be constrained for awhile to be bodily absent from you: I say constrained; God knowing how willing, and much rather than otherwise, I would have borne my part with you in this first brunt, were I not by strong necessity held back for the present. Make account of me in the mean time as a man divided

in myself, with great pain (and as natural bonds set aside) having my better part with you: and although I doubt not but in your godly wisdoms you both foresee and resolve upon that which concerneth your present state and condition, both severally and jointly; yet have I thought it but my duty to add some further spur of provocation unto them who run already, if not because you need it,

* Winslow against Gorton, p. 97, 98.

16 A CHURCH HISTORY [CH. I.

yet because I owe it in love and duty. And first, as we are daily to renew our repentance with our God, especially for our sins known, and generally for our unknown trespasses; so doth the Lord call us in a singular manner, upon occasions of such difficulty and danger as lieth upon you, to both a narrow search and careful reformation of your ways in his sight, lest he, calling to remembrance our sins forgotten by us, or unrepented of, take advantage against us, and in judgment leave us to be swallowed up in one danger or other. Whereas, on the contrary, sin being taken away by earnest repentance, and the pardon thereof from the Lord sealed up to a man's conscience by his Spirit, great shall be his security and peace in all dangers, sweet his comforts in all distresses, with happy deliverance from evil, whether in life or death.

"Now next after this heavenly peace with God and our consciences, we are carefully to provide for peace with all men, what lieth in us, especially with our associates; and, for that watchfulness must be had, that we neither at all in ourselves do give, no, nor easily take offence being given by others. Wo be to the world for offences; for although it be necessary, considering the malice of Satan and men's corruptions, that offences come, yet wo unto the man, or woman either, by whom the offence cometh, saith Christ, Mat. xviii. 7. And if offences in the unseasonable use of things in themselves indifferent be more to be feared than death itself, as the apostle teacheth, 1 Cor. ix. 15. how much more in things simply evil, in which neither the honour of God, nor love to man is thought worthy to be regarded! Neither yet is it sufficient that we keep ourselves by the grace of God from giving offence, except withal we be armed against taking of them when they are given by others; for how imperfect and lame is the work of grace in that person, who wants charity to cover a mul-

1620.] OF NEW-ENGLAND. 17

titude of offences! as the scripture speaks. Neither are you to be exhorted to this grace, only upon common grounds of Christianity, which are, that persons ready to take offence either want charity to cover offences, or duly to weigh human frailties; or lastly, are gross though close hypocrites, as Christ our Lord teacheth, Mat. vii. 1—3. As indeed, in my own experience, few or none have been found who sooner give offence, than such as easily take it; neither have they ever proved sound and profitable members in societies, who have nourished this touchy humour. But besides these, there are divers motives provoking you above others to great care and conscience of this way; as first, there are many of you strangers, as to the persons so to the infirmities of one another, and so stand in need of more watchfulness this way, lest when such things fall out in men and women as you expected not, you be inordinately affected with them, which doth require at your hands much wisdom and charity for the covering and preventing of incidental offences that way. And lastly, your intended course of civil community* will minister continual occasion of offence, and be as fuel for that fire, except you diligently quench it with brotherly forbearance. And if taking offence causelessly or easily at man's doings, be so carefully to be avoided, how much more heed is to be taken that we take not offence at God himself! which we certainly do, so oft as we murmur at his providence in our crosses, or bear impatiently such afflictions wherewith he is pleased to visit us. Store up therefore patience against the evil day; without which we take offence at the Lord himself in his holy and just works. There is a fourth thing carefully to be provided for; viz. That with your com-

* For seven years their affairs were managed in one common stock.

A CHURCH HISTORY

mon employments you join common affections truly bent upon the general good, avoiding as a deadly plague of both your common and special comforts, all retiredness of mind for proper advantage, and all singularly affected every manner of way; let every man repress in himself, and the whole body in each person, as so many rebels against the common good, all private respects of men's selves, not sorting with the general convenience. And as men are careful not to have a new house shaken with violence, before it be well settled, and the parts firmly knit; so be you, I beseech you, brethren, much more careful that the house of God (which you are) be not shaken with unnecessary novelties, or other oppositions at the first settling thereof.

"Lastly, whereas you are to become a body politic, using civil government among yourselves, and are not furnished with special eminency above the rest, to be chosen by you into office of government; let your wisdom and godliness appear, not only in choosing such persons as do entirely love, and will promote the common good; but also in yielding unto them all due honour and obedience in their lawful administrations; not beholding in them the ordinariness of their persons, but God's ordinance for your good; not being like the foolish multitude, who honour the gay coat more than either the virtuous mind of the man, or the glorious ordinance of the Lord; but you know better things, and that the image of the Lord's power and authority, which the magistrate beareth, is honourable in how mean persons soever; and this duty you may the more willingly, and ought the more conscionably to perform, because you are (at least for the present) to have them for your ordinary governors, which yourselves shall make choice of for that work.

1620.]   OF NEW-ENGLAND.   19

"Sundry other things of importance I could put you in mind of, and of those before mentioned in more words; but I will not so far wrong your godly minds, as to think you heedless of these things, there being also divers among you so well able both to admonish themselves and others of what concerneth them. These few things, therefore, and the same in a few words, I do earnestly commend to your care and conscience, joining therein with my daily incessant prayers unto the Lord, that he who made the heavens, and the earth, and sea, and all rivers of water, and whose providence is over all his works, especially over all his dear children for good, would so guide and guard you in your ways, as inwardly by his Spirit, so outwardly by the hand of his power, as that both you, and we also, for and with you, may have after matter of praising his name, all the days of your and our lives. Fare you well in him in whom you trust, and in whom I rest, an unfeigned well-wisher to your happy success in your hopeful voyage.
JOHN ROBINSON."*

This they received at Southampton in England; and these excellent instructions had lasting influence upon their posterity. Two ships had been provided to carry them to America, but after failing twice, and turning back, one of them was left, and the other sailed from Plymouth, September 6, and landed on Cape Cod, November 11. And as this was northward of where they had any patent, they drew a covenant for their civil government, which was signed before they landed by John Carver, William Bradford, Edward Winslow, Isaac Allerton, William Brewster, Miles Standish, John Alden,

Samuel Fuller, and thirty three more, their whole number being 101 souls. Mr. Carver was chosen their governor; and they had

* Morton, page 7–10,

20   A CHURCH HISTORY   [CH. I.

a tedious time to find out a place to settle in; but on December 16, 162[0], the ship came into the harbour which they called Plymouth, and then they had to build themselves habitations, in a cold winter season, without any friend to help them. They intended to have gone to Hudson's river, but the Dutch had hired the master of the ship deceitfully to prevent it; though God meant it for their good; for the Indians were numerous there, while there were none here. A great sickness a few years before had laid this place desolate, and had swept off most of the Indians for forty miles round, so that those who remained were glad of their help against the Narragansets, where the sickness did not reach; and here were fields ready cleared for them, who had no cattle to help them till several years after.

How wonderful, are the works of God! Yea, and his judgments are a great deep; for by reason of their long voyage, and the difficulties of the winter following, without good accommodations, near half of their company died in six months, among whom was governor Carver and his wife. Yet the survivors were wonderfully supported, and the chief sachem of the Indians in these parts came to Plymouth in March, 1621, and entered into a friendly covenant with them, which lasted all their days. Afterwards some friends in England wrote to them, and said, "we are still persuaded, you are the people that must make a plantation, and erect a city in those remote places, when all others fail."* And they will be remembered to the latest posterity.

Massassoit, the sachem who had made a league with them, having found out a plot which was laid against the English in the spring of 1623, by some Indians in the Massachusetts Bay, informed

* Historical Society, vol. 3, page 33.

1628.]   OF NEW-ENGLAND.   21

our fathers of Plymouth of it, and advised them to cut off a few leaders in it, whom he named, which they did, and so the plot was entirely crushed.* Such a scarcity also came upon them in that year, that they had no bread at Plymouth from the time of their planting until their corn was grown; but they

CHURCH HISTORY OF NEW ENGLAND

lived upon fish, deer, fowls and ground nuts. And to add to their trials, a great drought came on with heat, from the third week in May to the middle of July, so that their corn withered as if it were dead; and a ship which they had long expected did not arrive, but they thought they saw signs of its being wrecked on the coasts. This was distressing indeed; but their authority set apart a day of fasting and prayer to seek help from their God, and they found it was not in vain; for though the former part of the day was clear and hot, yet before their exercise was over the clouds gathered, and distilled next morning in gentle showers, and so; for fourteen days together, which revived their corn and other fruits, so that they had a plentiful harvest. And soon after, the ship which they expected arrived, and another in a few days, wherein came sixty of their friends.† And they never had such scarcity afterwards.

Mr. Robinson and the most of his people were detained in Holland, until, after a short sickness, he died there on March 1, 1625, in the fiftieth year of his age, greatly lamented by his people both there and here. His family came over afterwards, and his son Isaac lived to be above ninety years old, and left male posterity in the county of Barnstable. The company of adventurers in England would not be at the expense of conveying these and others from Leyden, and yet demanded the pay for their former expenses. Therefore in 1628, their friends here engaged to do it, when William Brad-

* Prince, 129–133.
† Ibid, page 137–139.

22   A CHURCH HISTORY   [CH. I.

ford, Miles Standish, Isaac Allerton, Edward Winslow, William Brewster, John Howland, John Alden, and Thomas Prince, with four friends in London, after having the trade of this colony secured to them, undertook to pay the debts of the colony in England, which were eighteen hundred pounds sterling, and also to bring those friends over.* And in August 1629, thirty-five families arrived at Plymouth, from Leyden, the transporting of whom cost five hundred and fifty pounds sterling, besides supporting of them above a year more, till they had a harvest of their own, all which was freely given them.† A wonderful instance of Christian generosity.

On January 13, 1630, the Council for New-England gave a patent to William Bradford and his associates and assigns of all that part of New-England between Cohasset rivulet towards the north, and Narraganset river towards the south, the western ocean towards the east, and between a straight line directly extending up into the main land toward the north from the mouth of Narraganset river, to the utmost bounds of a country in, New-England, called Pacanokit, alias Swamset, westward, and another straight line extending directly from the mouth of Cohasset river towards the west, so far into the main land westward as to the utmost limits of the said Pacanokit or Swamset extend; and also a tract of land extending fifteen miles wide on each side of Kennebeck river, &c.|| and this continued a distinct government until 1692. In 1621, they chose a governor and one assistant with him; in 1624, they chose five assistants; and in 1633, they chose a governor and seven assistants, and continued that number as long as they remained a distinct government.

* Historical Collections at Boston, 1794, p. 61.
† Prince, p. 168, 192.
|| Prince, p. 196, 197.

1630.]   OF NEW-ENGLAND.   23

As to the government of the Church, they held the power to be in each particular Church, to receive and exclude members, and to choose and ordain officers, though they would act in fellowship with sister churches. As to officers, they held to having pastors, ruling elders and deacons. Their ruling elders were to have the gifts of public teachers, but not to administer the ordinances of baptism and the holy supper. Such was Mr. William Brewster, from their first coming to this land, until he died in 1644. They also held that every brother in the church might improve his gifts in public teaching, if he had gifts that could edify the brethren, to whom they were to be subject. Some of their proofs for it were these: One apostle says, "he that prophesieth, speaketh unto men to edification, and exhortation, and comfort. And ye may all prophesy one by one, that all may learn, and all may be comforted." 1 Cor. xiv. 3, 31. And another says, "As every man hath received the gift, even so minister the same one to another, as good stewards of the manifold grace of God. If any man speak, let him speak as the oracles of God; if any man minister, let him do it as of the ability which God giveth; that God in all things may be glorified through Jesus Christ." 1 Peter, iv. 10, 11.* Though they took much pains, yet they never obtained a pastor here, until Mr. Ralph Smith came over with the Salem company in 1629, and not being wanted there, he came that year to Plymouth, and was their pastor about six years.

* Robinson against Bernard, p. 235.

CHAP. II.

A Church settled at Salem.—Governor Winthrop comes over with their charter.—Church and State united.—Williams banished.—His great service in the Pequot war.—A synod at Cambridge.—A new court called, who punished many whom the synod had condemned.

AFTER our fathers at Plymouth, through great dangers and difficulties, had prepared the way, many who disliked the corruptions and oppressions in the Church of England made preparations for a removal into this country. Mr. John White, a minister at Dorchester in England, prevailed with a number of wealthy men to write over to Roger Conant and others, who were scattered in different places, to repair to Cape Ann, and they would send over money and goods to assist them in planting and fishing; and they did so with success. And on March 19, 1628, the Council for the affairs of New-England sold to a number of men, their heirs and associates, that part of New-England which lies between lines drawn three miles north of every part of Merrimack river, and three miles south of every part of Charles river and the Massachusetts bay, and extending west from the Atlantic ocean to the south sea. And they sent over Mr. John Endicot as governor of said people, who made Salem to be their chief town; and on March 4, 1629, king Charles granted the Massachusetts charter, including all the lands before described, to be holden of him and his heirs and successors. And Mr. Francis Higginson and Samuel Skelton, with two other ministers and above three hundred persons with them, came over to Salem, and gathered a church, and ordained these two ministers on Aug. 6, 1629, and also a ruling elder; and they received

the right hand of fellowship from the church of Plymouth the same day.* So early did they join with those here, whom many had censured for separating from the church of England in their native country.

And on June 12, 1630, governor Winthrop arrived at Salem; and about fifteen hundred people came over that year, bringing the Massachusetts charter with them, and the churches of Boston, Dorchester, and Watertown, were soon formed and organized like Salem, as Charlestown also was in 1632. At first they received members by a general declaration of their faith, and the discovery of a regular walk; but they afterwards required of each one an account of a change of heart by the work of God's Spirit. Mr. John Wilson was the first pastor of the church of Charlestown and Boston, who was ordained, with a ruling elder and two deacons, August 27, 1630. Governor Winthrop says, "We used imposition of hands, but with this protestation by all, that it was only a sign of election and confirmation, not of any intent that Mr. Wilson should renounce his ministry he received in England."† But he afterwards informs us, that when a minister had resigned his pastoral charge of any church, he was then "no minister," by the received determination of their churches; and also that they did not allow any elders to lay on hands in ordinations, but those who were of the church where the ordination was.‖ But in 1648 that liberty was granted in their platform.

The General Court at Boston, May 18, 1631, made a law that no man should hereafter be admitted as a freeman, to have a vote in their government, but a member in some of their churches. On Sept. 4, 1633, arrived a ship, in which

* Prince, p. 83, 190, 191.
† Journal, p. 20.‖Page 227, 268.

26   A CHURCH HISTORY   [CH. II

came John Cotton, Thomas Hooker, and Samuel Stone, ministers, and John Haynes, afterwards governor of the Massachusetts, and then of Connecticut. Mr. Cotton was soon settled in the ministry at Boston, where he had as much influence, both in the civil and ecclesiastical affairs of the country, as any one man therein, for near twenty years, till he died. But Mr. Hooker could not agree with him in some things of great importance, though he did in others. Hooker and Stone settled first at Cambridge, and then removed with many others to Hartford, in 1636, and were leaders in the colony of Connecticut, where men were received to be freemen who were not members of their churches. They also held that none had a right to bring their children to baptism but communicants, while Cotton was for others doing it, if they were not scandalous. And he was for carrying the power of councils higher than Hooker would.

Governor Winthrop gives the following account of the manner of their forming churches, and receiving members into them, which was soon established. It was, that where a church was designed to be gathered, their chief rulers and ministers must be convened, and those who were to be the first members of the church were to tell their experiences before them, and have their approbation, or else they were not to proceed. Of this he relates the

CHURCH HISTORY OF NEW ENGLAND

following example. In 1635, the most of the church in Dorchester, with their minister, removed up, and planted Windsor, and began the colony of Connecticut; in which year Mr. Richard Mather came over and settled in Dorchester. And on April 11, 1636, many rulers and ministers met there for the purpose of forming a new church; but it was not done, because the most of those who intended to be members were thought not meet at present to be the foundation of a church, because they had built their hopes of salvation upon un-

1633.]   OF NEW-ENGLAND.   27

sound grounds, viz. "Some upon dreams and ravishes of spirit by fits; others upon the reformation of their lives; others upon duties and performances, &c. wherein they discovered three special errors. 1. That they had not come to hate sin because it is filthy, but only left it because it is hurtful. 2. That by reason of this they had never truly closed with Christ, (or rather Christ with them) but had made use of him only to help the imperfection of their sanctification and duties, and not made him their sanctification, wisdom, &c. 3. They expected to believe by some power of their own, and not only and wholly from Christ." These are the views that governor Winthrop had of Christian experiences, and of how churches should be gathered. And satisfaction was gained the fall after, when a church was gathered there.*

Perhaps he, and many rulers and teachers among them, were as wise and pious men as any who ever undertook to establish religion upon earth by human laws, enforced by the sword of the magistrate; and the evils which they ran into ought to be imputed to that principle, and not to any others which they held that were agreeable to the gospel. But as their persecutors in England were then exerting all their influence to bring these people again under their power in religious matters, they took such measures to defend themselves as cannot be justified; and as Mr. Roger Williams earnestly laboured to prevent those measures, and to promote the establishment of full liberty of conscience in this country, they bent all their power against him.

According to his own account, and good information from others, he was born in Wales in 1599, and he had the early patronage of the famous Sir Edward Coke; was educated at the university of

* Winthrop, page 98, 105.

28   A CHURCH HISTORY   [CH. II.

Oxford, and was introduced into the ministry in the church of England. But he soon found that he could not in conscience conform to many things in their worship; therefore he came over to this country, and arrived at Boston in February 1631; and in April he was called to preach at Salem; but as he had refused to commune with the church at Boston, and objected against the oaths which they took when they came out of England, and the force in religious affairs which they exercised here, the court at Boston wrote to Salem against him, upon which he went to Plymouth, where he preached above two years, and was highly esteemed by governor Bradford and others. Mr. Prince supposed that he had taken the oath of a freeman at Boston in May 1631, because a man of his name is upon their records in that month; but this was an evident mistake, and I found a Roger Williams upon their records the fall before this minister came to America. As these colonies had received the grant of American lands from the kings of England, Mr. Williams wrote his thoughts against it while he lived at Plymouth, which some liked, and others did not; and as Mr. Skelton was sick at Salem, Williams was invited there to preach in his place, and he obtained a dismission in the summer of 1633, and preached there till Skelton died, August 2, 1634, after which he was ordained in Salem. He had spoken against the meeting of ministers by themselves, once a fortnight, fearing that it might grow in time to a presbytery or superintendency over the churches;* and greater difficulties soon followed.

Their charter gave them no power to make any laws contrary to the laws of England, and they had sworn to act accordingly; yet when they met at Boston, May 14, 1634, before they elected their

* Winthrop, p. 57.

1634.]   OF NEW-ENGLAND.   29

officers, the assembly passed an act which said, "It was agreed and ordered, that the former oath of freemen shall be revoked, so far as it is dissonant, from the oath of freemen hereunder written, and that those that received the former oath shall stand bound no further thereby, to any intent or purpose, than this new oath ties them that now take the same.

The oath of a freeman.

I A. B. being by God's providence an inhabitant and freeman in this Commonweal, do freely acknowledge myself to be subjected to the government thereof, and therefore do here swear by the great and dreadful name of the everliving God, that I will be true and faithful to the same, and will accordingly yield assistance and support hereunto with my person and

CHURCH HISTORY OF NEW ENGLAND

estate as in equity I am bound, and will also truly endeavour to maintain and preserve all the liberties and privileges thereof; submitting myself to the wholesome laws and orders made and established by the same. And further, that I will not plot nor practise any evil against it, nor consent to any that shall so do; but will truly discover and reveal the same to lawful authority now here established, for the speedy preventing thereof. Moreover I do solemnly bind myself in the sight of God, that when I shall be called to give my voice touching any such matters of this state wherein freemen are to deal, I will give my vote and suffrage as I shall judge in mine own conscience may best conduce and tend to the public weal of the body, without respect of persons or favour of any man; so help me God in the Lord Jesus Christ."

And it appears that they never acted any more in the name of the kings of England, until after 1660. And what a stretch of arbitrary power was this! Yet men might still choose whether they would take this oath or not, if they would be con-

30   A CHURCH HISTORY   [CH. II.

tent not to be freemen. But when they met again, March 4, 1635, they enacted, "That every man of or above the age of sixteen years, who hath been or shall hereafter be resident within this jurisdiction by the space of six months, (as well servants as others) and not infranchised, shall take the oath of residents, before the governor, deputy governor, or two of the next assistants, who shall have power to convent him for that purpose; and upon his refusal, to bind him over to the next court of assistants, and upon his refusal the second time to be punished at the discretion of the court. It is ordered that the freeman's oath shall be given to every man of or above the age of sixteen years, the clause for election of magistrates only excepted."

Now as this act was to bind all, Mr. Williams openly preached against it at Salem, for which the governor and assistants convented him before them on April 30; but he refused to retract what he had done, and Mr. Cotton says, "The court was forced to desist from that proceeding."* Indeed he calls it the first of these acts, but governor Winthrop shews it to be the second.‡ And because of it, they at their meeting in May took away some land from Salem, by an act which said, "The land betwixt the Clift and the Forest river, near Marblehead, shall for the present be improved by John Humphrey, Esq.; and as the inhabitants of Marblehead shall stand in need of it, the said John Humphrey shall part with it, the said inhabitants allowing him equal recompence for his labour and cost bestowed thereupon; provided, that if in the mean time the inhabitants of Salem can satisfy the court that they have a true right unto it, that then it shall belong unto the inhabitants thereof." And how was that satisfaction to be given? Why they gave up Mr. Williams in the fall after, and when

* Tenet washed, part second, page 29. ‡ Journal, page 80.

the court met, March 3, 1636, they said, "It was proved this court that Marbleneck belongs to Salem."

Thus it stands upon their records, though Mr. Cotton pretends that Salem only petitioned for land in May, 1635; instead of their having some taken from them, until they gave him up. That act of taking land from them, appeared so evil to Mr. Williams and his church, that they wrote letters of reproof to the churches where those rulers belonged; upon which their rulers and ministers met in July, and gave Williams notice that he should be banished if he did not give them satisfaction; and Salem church yielded so much to them, that he left preaching to them in August. And when the court met in September, governor Winthrop says, "Mr. Endicot made a protestation in justification of the letters formerly sent from Salem to other churches against the magistrates and deputies, for which he was committed, but the same day he came and acknowledged his fault, and was discharged."* He afterwards acted at the head of their government in hanging the quakers; but as Williams remained stedfast, their records say,

"Whereas Mr. Roger Williams, one of the elders of the church of Salem, hath broached and divulged divers new and dangerous opinions against the authority of magistrates, as also writ letters of defamation both of the magistrates and churches here, and that before any conviction, and yet maintaineth the same without any retraction; it is therefore ordered, that the said Mr. Williams shall depart out of this jurisdiction within six weeks now next ensuing, which if he neglect to perform, it shall be lawful for the governor and two magistrates to send him to some place out of this juris-

* Journal, page 84, 86.

diction, not to return any more without leave from the court."

As he did not go, they sent for him to come to Boston in January, 1636, but he sent an excuse for not coming; upon which they sent an officer

CHURCH HISTORY OF NEW ENGLAND

to take him, and to convey him on board a ship bound for England; but when the officer got to Salem, he had been gone three days.* He first went to the place since called Rehoboth; but governor Winslow wrote to him, that he was then within Plymouth colony, but if he would only go over the river, he would be out of it, and be as free as themselves. And he readily did so, and obtained a grant of lands from the Narraganset Indians, where he began the first civil government upon earth that gave equal liberty of conscience. Though before he obtained it, he says, "I was sorely tossed for fourteen weeks, in a bitter winter season, not knowing what bread or bed did mean."† And from a view of the great things which God had done for him, he called the place PROVIDENCE.

The nature of true liberty of conscience was very little understood then in the world. And as God had brought the people here, out of an Egyptian bondage, and given them a good land, they imagined that they ought to imitate the children of Israel, in punishing the wicked, and in establishing an holy government in this great country. And from hence, they who opposed such a great and good work, appeared to them exceedingly criminal. A noted man, who was then active among them, thought that Christ called them, not only to assist in building up his churches, but also in pulling down the kingdom of antichrist; and that he said to them, "You are not set up for tolerating times, nor shall any of you be content with this, that you

* Journal, page 92.
† Historical Society, vol. I. page 276.

1636.]   OF NEW-ENGLAND.   33

are set at liberty, but take up your arms, and march manfully on till all opposers of Christ's kingly power are abolished. Have you not the blessedest opportunity put into your hands that ever any people had? Then fail not in prosecution of the work, for your Lord hath furnished you with able pilots, to steer the helm in a godly, peaceable, civil government also; then see that you make choice of such as are sound both in profession and confession, men fearing God and hating bribes; whose commission is not limited to the commands of the second table, but they are to look to the rules of the first also; and let them be sure to put on Joshua's resolution and courage, never to make a league with any of these seven sectaries. [1] The Gortonists, who deny the humanity of Christ, and most blasphemously and proudly profess themselves to be personally Christ. 2. The Papists, who with almost equal blasphemy and pride prefer their own merits and works of supererogation as equal with Christ's invaluable death and sufferings. 3. The Familists, who depend upon rare revelations, and forsake the sure revealed word of Christ. 4. The Seekers, who deny the churches and ordinances of Christ. 5. Antinomians, who deny the moral law to be the rule of Christ. 6. Anabaptists, who deny civil government to be proved of Christ. 7. The Prelacy, who will have their own injunctions submitted unto in the churches of Christ."*

Here we may plainly learn the cause why Mr. Williams was treated so cruelly. But as God overruled the cruel selling of Joseph to the heathen, as a means of saving the lives of many people; so the banishing of Mr. Williams made him a chief instrument of saving all the English in New-England from destruction. For he had obtained much knowledge of the Indian language, and friendship

* Johnson, page 7, 8.

34   A CHURCH HISTORY   [CH. II.

with them, when a war was ready to break out with the most powerful nation in the land. Of this a concise view was given, by governor Trumbull and the general court of Connecticut, in 1774, in answer to a query from England, to know by what title they held their lands. Upon it, they said, "The original title to the lands on which the colony was first settled, was at the time the English came hither, in the Pequot nation of Indians, who were numerous and warlike; their country extended from Narraganset to Hudson's river, and over all Long-Island. Sassacus, their great Sagamore, had under him twenty six sachems: he injuriously made war upon the English; he exercised despotic dominion over his subjects; he with all his sachems and people were conquered, and made tributaries to the English. The war being ended, considerations and settlements were made with such sachems and people as remained, who came in and received full contentment and satisfaction."*

Some Indians up Connecticut river had been so much oppressed by Sassacus, that they came down to Plymouth and Boston, so early as 1631, to get some of the English to go up and settle there.† And they afterwards went up to trade there several times, before they planted Windsor, and began a fort at Saybrook, in 1635, and Hartford in 1636. But the Pequots killed several men, from time to time, until they murdered John Oldham, near Block Island, because they went to trade that way. Mr. Williams began at Providence in the spring of 1636, just before Oldham was killed, the news of which they first received from him at Boston, July 26; upon which the governor there wrote

CHURCH HISTORY OF NEW ENGLAND

to him to use all his influence with the Narragansets, to obtain their help against the Pequots. This he did so expeditiously, as to return their an-

* Said answer, page 4.   † Winthrop, p. 25.

1636.]   OF NEW-ENGLAND.   35

swer July 30. Messengers were then sent to the Narragansets, who returned to Boston with a favourable answer on August 13. An army was then sent round by water, to revenge the death of Oldham, and to try to bring the Pequots to terms; but they returned without success.* Upon a sight of their danger, the Pequots sent directly to the Narragansets, with whom they had been at war several years, and desired that they would make peace with them, and for all to join together, and to drive the English out of the country; saying, "If you should help the English to subdue us, you would thereby make way for your own ruin; and we need not come to open battle with them, but only fire their houses, kill their cattle, and lie in wait and shoot them as they go about their business, and they will soon be forced to leave the country, and the Indians not be exposed to much hazard."†

What policy was here! and what would the English have done, if they had sent Williams out of the country as they intended? But a kind Providence prevented it, and he now wrote an account of these things to Boston; upon which they sent to him, to do his utmost for their relief; and he says, "The Lord helped me immediately to put my life in my hand, and, scarce acquainting my wife, to ship myself all alone in a poor canoe, and to cut through a stormy wind with great seas, every minute in hazard of life, to the sachem's house. Three days and nights my business forced me to lodge and mix with the bloody Pequot ambassadors, whose hands and arms methought wreaked with the blood of my countrymen, murdered and massacred by them on Connecticut river, and from whom I could not but nightly look for their bloody knives at my own throat also. But God wonder-

* Winthrop, p. 103–105.
†Preface to Mason's History, page 4.

36   A CHURCH HISTORY   [CH. II

fully preserved me, and helped me to break to pieces their design, and to make, promote and finish, by many travels and charges, the English league with the Narragansets and Mohegans against the Pequots.["]* He prevailed with Miantenimo, the chief sachem of the Narragansets, to come to Boston in October, and to covenant with them to war against the Pequots till they were subdued; and they sent a copy of it to Mr. Williams, who could best interpret it to him.†

Uncas, the sachem of the Mohegans, who lived between New-London and Norwich, had revolted from the Pequots a little before, and now joined against them; and the colonies agreed to raise an army against them in the spring.

But the Pequots were too early for them, and sent an army up the river in April, and killed several, and captivated others; upon which Connecticut raised an army of ninety English, and an hundred Mohegan Indians, who went down to Saybrook, where captain Underhill joined them with nineteen men, upon which twenty of the others were sent back, and then the army sailed to the Narraganset bay, under the command of captain John Mason of Windsor. After they landed, many of the Narragansets joined them, and they marched over Powcatuck river, and encamped in the night; but the Narragansets were so much afraid of the Pequots, that they all forsook the English, and the Mohegans went behind them. Yet captain Mason and his men assaulted Mistick fort in Stonington, a little before day, May 26, 1637, and by fire and sword destroyed six or seven hundred Pequots, in about an hour, when only seven were captivated, and about seven escaped; while he had but two men killed, and twenty wounded.‡ Sassacus was at another fort, where

*Historical Society, vol. i. p. 277. † Winthrop, p. 109, 110.
‡ Mason's History, page 10.

1636.]   OF NEW-ENGLAND.   37

some of his own men were for killing him, because he had caused this dreadful war; but others pleaded for him, though they all concluded to flee over Connecticut river. After which general Stoughton came up with 120 men, and Mason and part of his men joined him, and they pursued the Pequots beyond New-Haven, and Sassacus fled to the Mohawks, who cut off his head, and informed the English of it. So many Pequots were slain or captivated, that the rest sued for peace, which was granted upon condition of their quitting their name, and former habitations, and being dispersed among the Mohegans and Narragansets, who should pay an annual tribute for them, while others were servants to the English.

CHURCH HISTORY OF NEW ENGLAND

All this was accomplished in about six months, as appears by the journal of governor Winthrop, the history of captain Mason, and other accounts; and Indian sachems came to Boston in 1638, from all the country, as well as from Long-Island, to express their gratitude to the English for this victory, as governor Winthrop informs us. And captain Mason says in his history, that they had but about two hundred and fifty men in all Connecticut, when the war began, and they were in the midst of those enemies. How wonderful then was their victory, which opened a wide door for the English to fill the country! Governor Eaton and Mr. Davenport, who came over in the time of the war, went and planted New-Haven, in 1638, and began another colony, who allowed none to be freemen but communicants in their churches. About three thousand people came over that year; and it was computed that from 1628 to 1643, about 21200 persons came over here;* and very few of them had separated from the church of England before they came away. This fully verified what

* Johnson, p. 31.

38   A CHURCH HISTORY   [CH. II.

Mr. Robinson said, twenty years before Boston was planted; and it shews how men are influenced in religious matters by the government which they are under.

An act of justice now towards the Indians, served greatly to confirm their friendship. For four young men ran away from Plymouth, and meeting with an Indian near Providence, with a rich pack upon his back, they murdered him for it, and then fled to Rhode Island. Mr. Williams informed Governor Winthrop of it, who advised him to write to Plymouth about it, which he did, and they sent to Rhode Island, and caught three of them, and hanged them at Plymouth. And though some might think it strange, that three English should be executed for one Indian, yet none can tell how many lives this saved afterwards.

Yet all the great services which Mr. Williams did for the Massachusetts, could not prevail with them to take off his sentence of banishment, though Governor Winthrop was for it. A fear of their enemies in England had a great hand in this; for on April 28, 1634, King Charles gave a commission to archbishop Laud, and eleven men more, to revoke all the charters which he had given to these colonies, and to make such new constitutions and laws as they thought meet for them; and also to displace their governors and other officers, and to appoint others in their room; to impose tithes for the clergy, and to punish all those who disobeyed them, with fines, imprisonment or death. And though Governor Winslow was sent over their agent, and got this commission revoked, yet Laud caused him to be imprisoned in London seventeen weeks, for teaching sometimes at Plymouth, and for marrying people as a magistrate, which Laud called an invasion of the ministerial office.* And

* Historical Society, vol. iv. page 119, 120.

1637.] OF NEW-ENGLAND. 39

to guard against such tyranny, was of great importance. Another reason was, that they expected to obtain so much power here, as to give a wound to antichrist in other countries. For a man who was well acquainted with their views, speaking of the man of sin, says, "Mr. John Cotton, among others, hath diligently searched for the Lord's mind herein, and hath declared some hidden blow to be given to this blood thirsty monster; but the Lord Christ hath inseparably joined the time, means, and manner of this work together."*

The planting of this country, and the great things which God hath done here, has evidently given much light to Europe, and weakened the power of antichrist there; but the use of force in religious affairs, has been so far from weakening that enemy, that his main strength lies therein. But the Massachusetts still went on in that way, and on March 3, 1636, they said, "This court doth not nor will hereafter approve of any such companies of men, as shall henceforth join in any way of church fellowship, without they shall first acquaint the magistrates, and the elders, of the greater part of the churches of this jurisdiction, and have their approbation herein. And further it is ordered, that no person, being a member of any church which shall hereafter be gathered without the approbation of the magistrates and the greater part of the said churches, shall be admitted to the freedom of this commonwealth.'' And when they met at Boston, May 25, 1636, Henry Vane, Esq. was chosen governor, and John Winthrop, deputy governor; and he and Dudley were elected to be a standing council for life, and the governor for the time being was to be their president. Endicot was also chosen a counsellor for life the next year;

* Johnson, page 230.

40 A CHURCH HISTORY [CH. II.

CHURCH HISTORY OF NEW ENGLAND

for which their charter gave no right, and no others were ever elected so among them. Five rulers and three ministers were also now appointed, "To make a draught of laws which may be the fundamentals of this commonwealth, and to present the same to the next General Court; and it is ordered that in the mean time the magistrates and their associates shall proceed in the courts, to hear and determine all causes according to the laws now established; and where there is no law, then as near the laws of God as they can."

So that when their laws were made, their judges were to act thereby in religious affairs, instead of the laws of God. But what followed among them may be a warning to all after ages, against confounding church and state together in their government. For disputes and divisions about grace and works, between their chief rulers and ministers, came on in Boston, and spread through all the country to a great degree. A fast was appointed on account of it, on January 19, 1637; but Mr. Wheelwright then preached a sermon which increased their difficulties, for which he was called before their General Court, March 9, who dismissed him for the present; and when they met May 17, after a sharp contention, Mr. Winthrop was again chosen Governor, and Mr. Vane was left out of office, and the case of Wheelwright was again deferred. A synod of ministers from all the colonies met at Cambridge, August 30, and sat three weeks, and drew up a list of eighty errors which they said were held in the country; and then the General Court met September 26, and again dismissed Mr. Wheelwright, and dissolved the house of deputies, and called another for November 2, 1637. Such an instance as never was here before or since, of electing the house of deputies twice in one fall. The house they dissolved

1637.]   OF NEW-ENGLAND.   41

had 26 deputies, and the new one 31, only eleven of whom were in that which was dissolved.

And now they had a majority to punish those whom the synod had condemned; and they went on to banish John Wheelwright, William Aspinwall, Ann Hutchinson, and others, and to disarm 76 men, 58 of whom were of Boston. Of these Mr. Wheelwright and some others went and planted Exeter in New-Hampshire, and were dismissed and recommended to form a church there, from the church in Boston;* though Mr. Williams was excommunicated by the church in Salem, after he had been banished by the Court, for things that Governor Winthrop judged to be less dangerous than the other was guilty of.† Wheelwright was banished for what they judged to be sedition and contempt of their government, and Williams for denying that they had any right to make laws, and enforce them with the sword in religious affairs. Wheelwright afterwards made a slight confession to them, and was restored to favour, but Williams never retracted his opinion about liberty of conscience, therefore they never would restore him. And how many have there been ever since, who have been more earnest for the use of force in religious affairs, than for the peace and good order of civil government! but wise men learn much by the mistakes of others. Mr. John Haynes was Governor of the Massachusetts in 1635, and pronounced the sentence of banishment on Williams; but he removed to Hartford in the spring of 1637, where he afterward said to Williams, "I think I must confess to you, that the most wise God hath provided and cut out this part of his world, for a receptacle and refuge for all sorts of consciences. I am now under a cloud, and my

* Belknap's New-Hampshire, vol. i. page 37.
† Hutchinson's Collections, page 71.

brother Hooker, with the Bay, as you have been; we have removed from them thus far, and yet they are not satisfied."* This confirms what was before said of the difference between the Massachusetts and Connecticut governments.

In September, 1638, the Massachusetts made a law to compel all the inhabitants in each town to pay an equal proportion towards the support of religious ministers, though none had a vote in choosing them but communicants in their churches. And they then made another law, which said, "That whosoever shall stand excommunicated for the space of six months, without labouring what in him or her lieth to be restored, such person shall be presented to the court of assistants, and there proceeded with by fine, imprisonment, banishment, or farther for the good behaviour, as their contempt and obstinacy upon full hearing shall deserve." But this act was so high and glaring that it was repealed the next year. In the mean time, as adultery was a capital crime by the law of Moses, a law to punish it with death was made at Boston, in 1631, and three persons were banished for it in 1638, and a man and a woman were hanged for it in 1644.

* Historical Society, vol. i. p. 280.

CHAP. III.

Rhode Island planted.—Their first government.—Providence upon another plan.—The Baptist church there.—Their sentiments spread.—Account of Knollys.—A law against the Baptists.—And writings also.— Men in England against them.—The case of Gorton and his company.—Indians against them.—They are banished, but obtain relief from England.—Williams obtains a charter: and writes against persecution, and Cotton against him.—Owen for him.—These colonies for severity; but Robinson for liberty.

WHEN such cruelty was exercised at Boston, Mr. John Clarke, his brother Joseph, and many others concluded to remove away; and when they came to Providence, Mr. Williams advised them to go to the Island of Aquidnet; and he went with them to Plymouth, to inquire whether they claimed it or not; and finding that they did not, many went there, and signed a covenant on March 7, 1638, in which they said, "We whose names are underwritten, do here solemnly, in the presence of JEHOVAH, incorporate ourselves into a body politic, and as he shall help, will submit our persons, lives and estates, unto our Lord Jesus Christ, the King of kings, and Lord of lords, and to all those perfect and most absolute laws of his, given us in his holy word of truth, to be guided and judged thereby.——William Coddington, John Clarke, William Hutchinson, John Coggshall, *William Aspinwall*, *Thomas Savage*, William Dyre, William Freeborne, Philip Sherman, John Walker, Richard Carder, William Baultsone, *Edward Hutchinson*, *Edward Hutchinson, junior*, Samuel Wilbore, John Sanford, John Porter, Henry Bull."
[Note: The following verses are set aside in the margin next to the previous quotation:] Exodus, xxxiv. 3, 4. 2 Chron. xi. 3. 2 Kings, xi. 17.

44   A CHURCH HISTORY   [CH. III.

This I copied from their records. Those whoso names are in *Italic* afterwards went back, and were reconciled to the Massachusetts; and most of the others were of note on the Island, which they called Rhode Island. Their covenant to be governed by the perfect laws of Christ as a body politic, seemed to be preferable to the scheme of the Massachusetts; yet as they could not find laws to govern such a body in the New Testament, they went back to the laws of Moses, and elected a judge and three elders, to rule them. And an assembly of their freemen, on January 2, 1639, said, "That the judge, together with the elders, shall rule and govern according to the general rules of the word of God, when they have no particular rule from God's word, by the body prescribed as a direction unto them in the case." But on March 12, 1640, they changed their plan of government, and elected a governor, deputy governor, and four assistants; and they went on till they disfranchised four men, and suspended others from voting in their elections; afterwards Mr. Williams went over to England, and obtained a charter which included them in his government.

He had procured a deed of Rhode Island for them, from the Narraganset sachems, on March 24, 1638; and another to himself of Providence, the same day. He and a few friends had been there for two years before; and when he had obtained a deed of the town, he gave a deed to Stukely Westcoat, William Arnold, Thomas James, Robert Cole, John Green, John Throckmorton, William Harris, William Carpenter, Thomas Olney, Francis Western, Richard Waterman, Ezekiel Holliman, and such others as the major part of them should admit into fellowship and vote with them.

To these he gave a right in the town freely; but they who were received afterwards, were to pay him thirty shillings a piece. And they were Chad Brown, William Field, Thomas Harris, William

1639.]   OF NEW-ENGLAND.   45

Wickenden, Robert Williams, Richard Scott, William Renolds, John Field, John Warner, Thomas Angell, Benedict Arnold, Joshua Winsor, Thomas Hopkins, Francis Weeks, &c. They all signed a covenant, which said,

"We whose names are underwritten, being desirous to inhabit in the town of Providence, do promise to submit ourselves in active or passive obedience to all such orders or agreements as shall be made for public good of the body in an orderly way, by the major consent of the present inhabitants, masters of families, incorporated together into a township, and such others whom they shall admit unto the same, *only in civil things*." And I found a record afterward, which said, "It was agreed that Joshua Verin, upon breach of covenant, or restraining liberty of conscience, shall be withheld from liberty of voting till he shall declare the contrary." He retrained his wife from going to meeting as often as she desired; and upon this act against him he removed away, as their records shew.

And the men who were for such liberty, soon formed the first Baptist church in America. Mr. Williams had been accused before of embracing principles which tended to anabaptism; and in March, 1639, he was baptized by one of his brethren, and then he baptized about ten more. But in July following, such scruples were raised in his mind about it, that he refrained

CHURCH HISTORY OF NEW ENGLAND

from such administrations among them.* Mr. Williams discovers in his writings, that as sacrifices and other acts of worship were omitted by the people of God, while his temple lay in ruins; and that they were restored again by immediate direction from Heaven, so that some such direction was necessary to restore the ordinances of baptism and the supper, since the desolation of the church in mystical Babylon.†

* Winthrop, p. 174, 183.   † Reply to Cotton, p. 107.

46   A CHURCH HISTORY   [CH. III.

But these cases are far from being parallel; for the altar of God in one place, in the land of Canaan, was the only place where acceptable sacrifices could then be offered; while the Christian church is not confined to any place, but Christ is with his saints wherever they meet in his name; and he says to his ministers, Go ye and teach all nations, baptizing them in the name of the Father, and of the Son, and of the Holy Ghost; teaching them to observe all things whatsoever I have commanded you: and lo, I am with you always, even unto the end of the world, Amen. Mat. xviii. 20. xxviii. 19, 20. And these promises belong only to the children of God, in the way of observing all his commandments, let them be ordained by whom they may. As the priests who could not find a *register* of their lawful descent from Aaron were put from the *priesthood*; so those who are *born again* are the only *priesthood* whom Christ owns under the gospel. Ezra ii. 62. 1 Peter i. 23. xi. 9.

After Mr. Williams left that church in Providence, they chose Mr. Thomas Olney for their pastor, and he served them in that office until he died, in 1682; and through many trials and changes they have continued ever since, and are now a flourishing church. Others had much labour about baptism in these times. Mr. Charles Chauncy preached at Plymouth above two years, and they would fain have settled him with Mr. Reyner, their other minister; but he believed that gospel baptism was dipping, and that sprinkling for baptism was not *lawful*, as their records shew. He therefore went to Scituate, where he practiced the dipping of infants.* He was afterwards president of the college at Cambridge. Governor Winthrop also says, "The lady Moody, a wise and anciently religious woman, being taken with the er-

* Winthrop, p. 200, 251.

1641.]   OF NEW-ENGLAND.   47

ror of denying baptism to infants, was dealt with by many of the elders and others, and admonished by the church of Salem, whereof she was a member; but persisting still, and to avoid further trouble, she removed to the Dutch against the advice of all her friends. Many others infected with anabaptism, removed thither also." They went to the west part of Long Island, where Mr. Williams went in 1643, and made peace between the Indians and the Dutch, and then sailed for England.*

Mr. Hanserd Knollys was a minister in the church of England for nine years, and then he was so cruelly persecuted therein, that he came over to Boston in the spring of 1638; but their rulers called him an Antinomian, and would not suffer him there; therefore he went to Dover on Piscataqua river, where he preached near four years, and then returned to England, and arrived in London in December, 1641. As the war broke out there the next year, liberty for various opinions was caused thereby, and he became a Baptist, and gathered a church in London, where he often had a thousand hearers. He baptized Mr. Henry Jessy, an eminent minister in that city, and was one who signed the Baptist confession of faith in 1643, which was as clear in the doctrines of the gospel, as was that of the divines at Westminster; a copy of which Mr. Crosby has given at the end of the first volume of his history. He also informs us that Mr. Knollys continued a faithful pastor of his church in London, through great changes and sufferings, until he died in peace, September 19, 1691, aged 93 years. And though many things were published against him here, yet Dr. Mather says, "He had a respectful character in the churches of this wilderness."† And Mr. John Clarke was a preacher of the gospel at Newport, until he form-

* Winthrop, p, 273, 298, 299.   † Magnalia, Book iii. p. 7.

48   A CHURCH HISTORY   [CH. III.

Ed a Baptist church there in 1644, which has continued by succession ever since. But the Massachusetts were so much afraid of the spread of their principles, that they made a law in November that year, which said,

"Forasmuch as experience hath plentifully and often proved, that since the first rising of the Anabaptists, about 100 years since, they have been the incendiaries of the commonwealths, and the infectors of persons in main matters of religion, and the troublers of churches in all places where they have been, and that they who have held the baptizing of infants unlawful, have usually held other errors or heresies together therewith, though they have (as other heretics use to do) concealed the same till they spied out a fit advantage and opportunity to vent them, by way of question or scruple; and whereas divers of this kind have, since our coming to New-England, appeared amongst ourselves, some whereof (as others before them) denied the ordinance of magistracy, and the lawfulness of making war, and others the lawfulness of magistrates, and their inspection into the breach of the first table; which opinions, if they should be connived at by us, are like to be increased amongst us, and so must necessarily bring guilt upon us, infection and trouble to the churches, and hazard to the whole commonwealth; it is ordered and agreed, that if any person or persons, within this jurisdiction, shall either openly condemn or oppose the baptizing of infants, or go about secretly to seduce others from the approbation or use thereof, or shall purposely depart the congregation at the ministration of the ordinance, or shall deny the ordinance of magistracy, or their lawful right and authority to make war, or to punish the outward breaches of the first table, and shall appear to the court wilfully and obstinately to continue therein, after due time and means of conviction, every such person or persons shall be sentenced to banishment."

1643.]   OF NEW-ENGLAND.   49

Thus denying infant baptism was made a cause of banishment, by men who knew that many who did so, did not hold the errors mentioned in this law. And Mr. Cotton said in those times, "they do not deny magistrates, nor predestination, nor original sin, nor maintain free-will in conversion, nor apostacy from grace; but only deny the lawful use of the baptism of children, because it wanteth a word of commandment and example, from the Scripture. And I am bound in 40hristian love to believe, that they who yield so far, do it out of conscience, as following the example of the apostle, who professed of himself and his followers, We can do nothing against the truth, but for the truth. But yet I believe withal, that it is not out of love to the truth that Satan yieldeth so much, but rather out of another ground, and for a worse end. He knoweth that now, by the good hand of God, they are set upon purity and reformation; and now to plead against the baptism of children upon any of those Arminian and Popish grounds, as those above named, Satan knoweth they would be rejected. He now pleadeth no other arguments in these times of reformation, than may be urged from a main principle of reformation, to wit, That no duty of God's worship, nor any ordinance of religion, is to be administered in his church, but such as hath a just warrant from the word of God. And by urging this argument against the baptism of children, Satan transformeth himself into an angel of light."*

Here we may see that Mr. Cotton knew the Baptists among them were not such as are described in the above law; though his charity about them was, that they were deceived by the devil, in pleading plain Scripture against infant baptism, which hath no precept nor example for it in the

* Cotton on baptism, 1647, p. 3.

50   A CHURCH HISTORY   [Ch. III.

word of God. And another minister near him, in writing then against the Baptists, ranks them with our first mother Eve, and says, "*Hath God said it?* was the old serpentine insinuation to blind and beguile, and to corrupt first the judgment in point of warrant of this or that practice."* As if a calling in question a custom of men, which is not named in the word of God, was as criminal and dangerous as a disputing the authority and truth of his express command. Of this every one must judge for himself. The Presbyterian assembly of divines at Wesminster now denied liberty to their Congregational brethren in England, to have gathered churches there, distinct from their parish churches and said to them, "This liberty was denied by the churches of New-England, and we have as just ground to deny it as they: this desired forbearance is a perpetual drawing away from churches under the rule; for upon the same pretence, those who scruple infant baptism may withdraw from their churches, and so separate into another congregation; and so in that, some practice may be scrupled, and they separate again."† Such is the effect of the use of force in religious affairs. And it now caused much trouble to the Massachusetts, from men who were really very corrupt in doctrines.

Samuel Gorton had considerable knowledge of the Hebrew and Greek languages, which he made use of to corrupt the word of God. He held the coming and sufferings of Christ to be within his children, and that he was as much in this world at one time as another; or that all which we read about him is to be taken in a mystical sense, which he called spiritual sense. And of the visible church, he says, "Pharisaical interpreters, who erect churches as true churches of God, that admit of

* Cobbet on baptism, p. 8.
† Crosby, vol. i. page 186, 187.

1643.]   OF NEW-ENGLAND.   51

CHURCH HISTORY OF NEW ENGLAND

decay, and falling from God in whole, or any part thereof, are they who have deceived and undone the world from the foundation thereof unto this day, and are the proper witches of the world, which the Scripture intends." Again he says, "They can strain out the gnat of dipping into, or sprinkling with water in the entrance into their church." And he says, "Antichrist is not to be confined to any one particular man or devil, but every one of that spirit is the original and proper inlet of sin, and inundation of God's wrath into the world, 1 John ii. 18, 22. Neither is the disposition, office and authority of the Son of God, confined and limited to one man; but every one that is of that spirit, hath that royal prerogative or set in him to be the Son of God, even so many as believe in that name." John i. 12.*

And his practice was no better than his principles. For he came over to Boston in 1636, where he caused considerable trouble, and then did the like at Plymouth, from whence he went to Newport, and behaved so there, that they inflicted corporeal punishment upon him. He then went and bought some land near Pawtuxet river, in the south part of Providence, in January 1641; but such contention soon arose among neighbours there, about earthly things, that they came armed into the field to fight; but Mr. Williams interposed and pacified them for the present, and then wrote to Boston for advice and help. This was not granted from thence, unless they would come under the Massachusetts government. And as difficulties continued great in that place, four men went from Pawtuxet to Boston, in September 1642, and submitted themselves and their lands under that government; and then their rulers wrote to Gorton and others to come to Boston, and answer to the

* Antidote against Pharisaical teachers, page 42, 60, 61.

52   A CHURCH HISTORY   [CH. III.

complaints of these men. But they were so far from going, that they wrote a long letter, containing a mystical paraphrase upon their writing, and many provoking sentences against said rulers, and their religious principles and conduct, and a refusal to go, dated November 20, 1642, signed by twelve men. And to get out of their reach, these men went over the river, and bought the lands at Shawomet, of the Indians, and received a deed of it, January 12, 1643, signed by Miantanimo and Pumham.

In May following the General Court at Boston sent men into those parts; and finding that Gorton and his company were gone out of what they called their jurisdiction, they got Pumham and Socononco, two Indian sachems, to come to Boston in June, and to submit themselves and their lands unto their government; and then to enter a complaint against Gorton and his company, that they had taken away their lands, by the influence of Miantanimo, who forced Pumham to sign the deed, as they said, though he would not receive any of the pay for it. Upon which the Governor and one Assistant wrote to Gorton and his company to come to Boston, and answer to these complaints; and they sent to Miantanimo also to come to Boston for the same end. But Gorton and his company sent a long and provoking letter, and refused to go. Miantanimo went down and justified his sale of those lands, and said those sachems were his subjects, or rulers under him. And it appears by many writings, that he was a man of the greatest powers of mind, and of the greatest influence among the Indians of almost any one in the land, which caused the English to be greatly afraid of him.

After much consultation, commissioners from New-Haven, Connecticut, Plymouth and the Massachusetts, met at Boston in September, and signed articles of confederation, for mutual assistance

1643.]   OF NEW-ENGLAND.   53

and defence; that two commissioners from each colony should meet once a year, or oftener if necessary, to order the general affairs of all, while the internal government of each should be as before. And the Massachusetts declared that Shawomet was within Plymouth colony, and called upon them to relieve the Indians there, whom they said Gorton's company had oppressed; but rather than attempt it, they gave up all the right they had there to the Massachusetts, and the other commissioners assented to it.

The Massachusetts then put their government into a posture of war, and sent three officers, and forty armed soldiers to Shawomet, and brought Gorton and a number of his company to Boston by force. They also brought away about eighty head of their cattle, to pay the cost of this expedition. And when they had got these men there, they left the affair about lands, and tried them for their lives, upon a charge of heresy and blasphemy: but a small majority saved their lives for that time; and they enacted that Samuel Gorton, John Weeks, Randal Holden, Robert Potter, Richard Carder, Francis Weston, and John Warner, should be confined in seven of their chief towns, during the pleasure of the court, to work for their living, and not to publish their errors nor to speak against the government, each upon pain of death. Some others had smaller punishments.

In the mean time war had broken out between the Narragansets and the Mohegans, in which Uncas prevailed, and took Miantanimo prisoner, and carried him to Hartford, and left him in the hands of the English, at his own

CHURCH HISTORY OF NEW ENGLAND

request; and when the commissioners met at Boston in September, they debated about what they should do with him; and though they could not see any right they had to put him to death, yet they feared that if he was set at liberty it would be very dangerous to them-

54   A CHURCH HISTORY   [CH. III.

selves, and therefore they delivered him to Uncas, for him to execute him without torture, which he did.* Thus one evil leads on to others, like the breaking forth of waters.

For the confinement of Gorton and his company did no good to them, and it caused uneasiness to many of their own people; and therefore when the General Court met at Boston, March 7, 1644, they passed an act, which said, "It is ordered that Samuel Gorton and the rest of that company, who stand confined, shall be set at liberty; provided that if they or any of them shall, after fourteen days after such enlargement, come within any part of our jurisdiction, either in the Massachusetts, or in or near Providence, or any of the lands of Pumham and Socononco, or elsewhere within our jurisdiction, then such person or persons shall be apprehended, wheresoever they may be taken, and shall suffer death by course of law; provided also, that during all their continuance in our bounds inhabiting for the said time of fourteen days, they shall be still bound to the rest of the articles of their former confinement, upon the penalty therein expressed."

Thus it stands upon their records. And one of the officers who brought them to Boston, says, "To be sure there be them in New-England, that have Christ Jesus and his blessed ordinances in such esteem, that, the Lord assisting, they had rather lose their lives, than suffer them to be thus blasphemed, if they can help it. And whereas some have favoured them, and endeavoured to bring under blame such as have been zealous against their abominable doctrines; the good God be favourable unto them, and prevent them from coming under the like blame with Ahab. Yet they remain in their old way; and there is somewhat to be considered in it,

* Winthrop, page 262, 295, 303, 305, 306.

1644.]   OF NEW-ENGLAND.   55

to be sure, that in these days, when all look for the fall of antichrist, such detestable doctrines should be upheld, and persons suffered, who exceed the beast himself for blasphemy; and this to be done by those that would be counted reformers, and such as seek the utter subversion of antichrist."*

This history was finished in 1652; and it discovers the sincerity of the actors in those measures, which now appear very strange. And if any men had a right to use force with others about religious affairs, perhaps these were as pious men as ever did so, as I observed before. But nothing serves more to prejudice sinful men against the truth, than injurious treatment from those who teach it; which Gorton and his company have evidenced even to this day. For when they were released, they went to Rhode-Island, and from thence over to the Narragansets, where they procured a deed from the Indians of all their people and lands, which they re-signed over to the king of England, and appointed Gorton and others as their agents, to carry the same to him, dated April 19, 1644. And they went over to England with it, and there published an account of their sufferings at Boston; and though the king could not help them, yet they obtained an order from the Parliament to the Massachusetts, to allow them to enjoy the lands which they had purchased, and to remove any obstructions that they had put in the way of it. And as the earl of Warwick was their great friend in this affair, they called their town Warwick. And Gorton taught his doctrines there for many years; and the effects of them, and of the persecutions which these men suffered, with the general nature of sin, have caused a large part of their posterity to neglect all religion to this day; others of them have become professors of religion, but not in the Congregational way.

* Johnson's Hist. page 187.

56   A CHURCH HISTORY   [CH. III.

When Mr. Williams saw how things went here, and that some light opened in England, he went there in the spring of 1643, and published a Key to the language and customs of the Indians in our country; which the Historical Society at Boston reprinted in 1794. And as Sir Henry Vane, who was Governor at Boston in the time of the Pequot war, was now a member of Parliament, and had a great regard for Mr. Williams, he used his great influence in procuring a charter for him, "Bordering northward and northeast on the patent of the Massachusetts, east and southeast on Plymouth patent, south on the ocean, and on the west and northwest by the Indians called Narragansets; the whole tract extending about twenty five miles, unto the Pequot river and country; to be known by the name of "the incorporation of Providence plantations in the Narraganset bay, in New-England." It gave

CHURCH HISTORY OF NEW ENGLAND

them power to form their own government, elect all their officers, and to make all their laws, as near the laws of England as they could. This charter was dated March 14, 1644, and was signed by Robert Warwick, Philip Pembroke, Say and Seal, Philip Wharton, Arthur Haslerig, Cornelius Holland, Henry Vane, Samuel Vassel, John Rolle, Miles Corbet and William Spurstow.

With this they sent a letter to the rulers and other friends in the Massachusetts, saying, "Taking notice, some of us of long time, of Mr. Roger Williams his good affections and conscience, and of his sufferings by our common enemies and oppressors of God's people the prelates; as also of his great industry and travel in his printed Indian labours in your parts, the like whereof we have not seen extant from any part of America, and in which respect it hath pleased both houses of Parliament freely to grant unto him and friends with him a free and absolute charter of civil government for these

1644.]   OF NEW-ENGLAND.   57

parts of his abode; and withal sorrowfully resenting, that amongst good men, our friends, driven to the ends of the earth, exercised with the trials of a wilderness, and who mutually give good testimony each of other, as we observe you do of him, and he abundantly of you; there should be such a distance. We thought it fit upon divers considerations, to profess our great desires of both your utmost endeavours of nearer closing, and of ready expressing of these good affections, which we perceive you bear each to other, in the actual performance of all friendly offices; the rather because of those bad neighbours you are like to find too near you in Virginia, and the unfriendly visits from the west of England and from Ireland;* that howsoever it may please the Most High to shake our foundations, yet the report of your peaceable and prosperous plantations may be some refreshing to your true and faithful friends."†

Mr. Williams arrived at Boston with this letter, in September 1644, and they let him pass on to Providence; but they never took off his sentence of banishment, nor ever allowed of the validity of the charter of his own civil government until 1656. And we are now to see the cause of it more fully. For Mr. Williams published a book in London that year, which opened the evil of their conduct, beyond any thing he had done before. The title of it is, "The bloody tenet of persecution for the cause of conscience." It appeared to Mr. Cotton to be of so dangerous tendency to them, that he published an answer to it in 1647, which he called, "the bloody tenet washed, and made white in the blood of the Lamb." But Williams replied to it in 1652, and called it, "The bloody tenet yet

* Places that were then in the king's party, but were soon after brought under the parliament.
† Winthrop, p. 356.

58 A CHURCH HISTORY [CH. III.

more bloody, by Mr. Cotton's endeavour to wash it white." And I will give a few extracts from these writings.

A prisoner in London wrote some reasons against persecution, which one Hall of Roxbury obtained, and sent it to Mr. Cotton, and he wrote an answer to it. But as Mr. Hall was not satisfied therewith, he sent it to Mr. Williams, who now published the whole controversy. The prisoner first brought the case which Christ has stated, of the children of his kingdom, and the children of the devil, appearing by their fruits in the field of the world, when he said, "Let both grow together until the harvest." Mat. xiii. 30, 38. And the prisoner said, "the reason seems to be, because they who are *tares*, may hereafter become *wheat;* they who are blind, may hereafter see; they who resist him, may hereafter receive him; they who are now in the devil's snare, and averse to the truth, may hereafter come to repentance; they who are now blasphemers and persecutors, as Paul was, may in time become faithful as he did; they who are now idolaters, as the Corinthians once were, may hereafter become true worshippers, as they did; 1 Cor. vi 9; they who are *no people* of God, nor under *mercy*, may hereafter become his people, and obtain mercy. 1 Peter ii. 10."*

Now, though these things are very plain, yet Mr. Cotton went on for more than forty pages, before he came to the case in hand, which the prisoner said in few words, "Tares are antichristians or false Christians."† And when Mr. Cotton came to this, he said, "It is not the will of Christ that antichrist, and antichristianity should be tolerated in the world, until the end of the world. For God will put it into the hearts of faithful princes (as they have given their kingdoms to the beast, so)

* Bloody tenet, p. 2.   † Bloody tenet, p. 44.

1644.] OF NEW-ENGLAND. 59

in fulness of time to hate the whore, to leave her desolate and naked, and to burn her flesh with fire. Rev. xvii. 16, 17."* Mr. Williams had before said,

CHURCH HISTORY OF NEW ENGLAND

"This hating and desolating and making naked and burning, shall not arise by way of *ordinance*, warranted by the institution of Christ Jesus; but by way of *providence*, when (as it useth to be with whores and their lovers) the church of Rome and her great lovers shall fall out; and, by the righteous vengeance of God upon her, drunk with the blood of the saints, these mighty fornicators shall turn their love into hatred, which shall make her a poor naked whore, torn and consumed."† But Mr. Cotton passed this over in silence.

Now if we take the word flesh here to mean riches, it is well known that the king of France did the most to enrich the Pope, of any king upon earth; and the French nation have now taken the riches of the church of Rome to support war and vengeance against her, above all others in the world. And is not this according to that prophecy?

Of civil government, Mr. Williams says, "The sovereign, original, and foundation of civil power lies in the people; and it is evident that such governments as are by them erected and established, have no more power, nor for no longer time, than the civil power or people consenting and agreeing shall betrust them with. This is clear, not only in reason, but in the experience of all commonweals, where the people are not deprived of their *natural freedom* by the power of tyrants."‡ Yea, the experience of all America, in her deliverance from the tyranny of Britain, confirms this truth. And as to religion, Mr. Williams says, "Persons may with less sin be forced to marry whom they cannot love,

* Tenet washed, p. 42, 43.
† Bloody tenet, p. 246.
‡ Ibid, tenet, p. 137.

60   A CHURCH HISTORY   [CH. III.

than to worship where they cannot believe.["]* And I find no answer to this.

Mr. Cotton was so far from thinking that he was a persecutor, that he said, "It is not lawful to prosecute any, until after admonition once or twice; and so the apostle directeth, and giveth the reason, that in fundamental points of doctrine or worship, the word of God is so clear, that he cannot but be convinced in conscience of the dangerous error of his way, after admonition once or twice, wisely and faithfully dispensed. And then if any one persist, it is not out of conscience, but *against his conscience*, as the apostle saith. Titus iii. 10, 11." Upon which Williams says, "Titus, unto whom these directions were written, was no minister of the civil state, armed with the material sword, who might inflict punishments upon the bodies of men, by imprisonments, whipping, fines, banishment and death. Titus was a minister of the gospel, armed only with the spiritual sword of the word of God, and such spiritual weapons as were mighty through God to the calling down strong holds; yea, every high thought of the highest head and heart in the world, I Cor. x. 4."* And he observes that the charges and exhortations which Christ gave to his ministers, are now applied to civil magistrates in this affair. But upon this Mr. Cotton says,

"Look the answer through, and you shall find not one of the charges or exhortations given to ministers, ever directed by the answerer to civil magistrates: the falsehood of the discusser in this charge upon the answerer is palpable and notorious." And yet in this book he says, "the good that is brought to princes and subjects by the due punishment of apostate seducers, idolaters and blasphemers, is manifold. 1. It putteth away evil from the people, and cutteth off a gangrene, which

* P. 14.3.   † Bloody tenet, p. 36.

1644.]   OF NEW-ENGLAND.   61

would spread to further ungodliness, Deut. xiii. 5. 2 Tim. ii. 16—18.   2. It driveth away wolves from worrying and scattering the sheep of Christ; for false teachers be wolves. Mat. vi. 15. Acts xx. 29. And the very name of wolves holdeth forth what benefit will redound to the sheep, by either killing them, or driving them away."*

If any man will take the pains to examine Mr. Cotton's book well, he will find that his main arguments are taken from scriptures which belong to the church, and not to the state. And that passage in the epistle to Titus, about a heretic, condemned of himself, is referred to from one end of his book to the other. And it is implied in the sentence of banishment, passed against Mr. Williams, where he is condemned for writing letters against their rulers, "before any conviction." This idea the court evidently took from Mr. Cotton, who had great influence in their government. And as Williams denied that Christ had appointed the civil sword as a remedy against false teachers, Cotton said, "It is evident that the civil sword was appointed for a remedy in this case, Deut. xiii. And appointed it was by that angel of God's presence, whom God promised to send with his people, as being unwilling to go with them himself. Exod. xxxiii. 2, 3. And that angel was Christ, whom they tempted in the wilderness. 1 Cor. x. 9. And therefore it cannot truly be said, that the Lord Jesus never appointed the civil sword for a remedy in such case; for he did expressly appoint it in the Old Testament; nor did he ever abrogate it in the New. The reason of the law, which is the life of the law, is of eternal force and equity in all ages, Thou shalt surely kill him, because he hath sought to thrust thee away from the Lord thy God, Deut. xiii. 9, 10. This reason is

* Tenet washed, page 88, 137, 138.

62   A CHURCH HISTORY   [CH. III.

of moral, that is, of universal and perpetual equity, to put to death any apostate seducing idolater, or heretic, who seeketh to thrust away the souls of God's people, from the Lord their God."*

From hence Williams called his reply, "The bloody tenet yet more bloody, by Mr. Cotton's endeavour to wash it white;" from which many extracts are made, in the first volume of our History; and also an extract from Dr. Owen, who said, "He who holds the truth may be confuted, but he cannot be convinced but by the truth. That a man should be said to be convinced of a truth, and yet that truth not shine in upon his understanding, to the expelling the contrary error, to me is strange. To be convinced is to be overpowered by the evidence of that, which before a man knew not. I once knew a scholar invited to a dispute with another man, about something in controversy in religion; in his own, and in the judgment of all the bystanders, the opposing person was utterly confuted: and yet the scholar, within a few months, was taught of God, and clearly convinced, that it was an error which he had maintained, and the truth which he opposed; and then, and not till then, did he cease to wonder, that the other was not convinced by his strong arguments, as he before had thought. To say a man is convinced, when either from want of skill and ability, or the like, he cannot maintain his opinion against all men, is a mere conceit. That they are obstinate and pertinacious is a cheap supposal, taken up without the price of a proof. As the conviction is imposed, not owned, so is this obstinacy: if we may be judges of other men's obstinacy, all will be plain; but if ever they get uppermost, they will be judges of ours."†
This the great Dr. Owen published in London, the year

* Ibid, p. 66, 67.
† Folio collection of his tracts, p. 312.

1646.]   OF NEW-ENGLAND.   63

after Mr. Cotton's book came out there. But it was so little regarded here, that violent methods were still pursued in this country, though against the minds of many.

When the commissioners of the united colonies met at New-Haven, September 9, 1646, they said, "Upon serious consideration of the spreading nature of error, the dangerous growth and effects thereof in other places, and especially how the purity and power both of religion and civil order is already much complained of, if not wholly lost in part of New-England, by a licentious liberty granted and settled, whereby many, calling off the rule of the word, profess and practise what is good in their own eyes; and upon information of what petitions have been lately put up in some of the colonies, against the good and straight ways of Christ, both in the churches and in the commonwealth, the commissioners, remembering that these colonies, for themselves and their posterity, did unite into this firm and perpetual league, as for other respects, so for mutual advice, that the truth and liberties of the gospel might be preserved and perpetuated, thought it their duty seriously to commend it to the care and consideration of each General Court within these united colonies, that as they have laid their foundations and measured the house of God, the worship and worshippers, by the rod God hath put into their hands, so they would walk on and build up (all discouragements and difficulties notwithstanding) with undaunted heart and unwearied hand, according to the same rules and patterns; that a due watch be kept at the doors of God's house, that none be admitted as members of the body of Christ, but such as hold forth effectual calling, and thereby union with Christ the head; and that those whom Christ hath received, and enter by an express covenant to observe the laws and duties of that spiritual corporation; that baptism, the seal

64   A CHURCH HISTORY   [CH. III.

of the covenant, be administered only to such members and their immediate seed; that Anabaptism, Familism, Antinomianism, and generally all errors of like nature, which oppose, undermine and slight either the Scriptures, the Sabbath, or other ordinances of God, bring in and cry up unwarrantable revelations, inventions of men, or any carnal liberty under a deceitful colour of liberty of conscience, may be duly and seasonably suppressed; though they wish as much forbearance and respect may be had of tender consciences seeking light, as may stand with the purity of religion and peace of the churches."

CHURCH HISTORY OF NEW ENGLAND

But the commissioners from Plymouth did not concur with this act. They had not lost the impression of the instructions which they received before they came to America; which said, "As the kingdom of Christ is not of this world, but spiritual, and he a spiritual king, so must the government of this spiritual kingdom under this spiritual king needs be spiritual, and all the laws of it. And as Christ Jesus hath, by the merits of his priesthood, redeemed as well the body as the soul;* so is he by the sceptre of his kingdom to rule and reign over both; unto which Christian magistrates, as well as meaner persons, ought to submit themselves; and the more Christian they are, the more meekly to take the yoke of Christ upon them; and the greater authority they have, the more effectually to advance his sceptre over themselves and their people, by all good means. Neither can there be any reason given why the merits of saints may not as well be mingled with the merits of Christ, for the saving of the church, as the laws of men with his laws, for the ruling and guiding of it. He is as absolute and as entire a king as he is a priest, and his people must be as careful to preserve the dignity of the one, as to enjoy the benefit of the other.†"

* John xviii. 36. 1 Cor. vi. 20.
† Robinson against Bernard, p. 38.

1647.]   OF NEW-ENGLAND.   65

CHAP. IV.

Plan of Williams' government; and of the churches in the Massachusetts.—Cambridge platform.—Williams on national confusion.—Coddington does hurt to his own colony.—Winthrop dies.—Clarke and Holmes suffer at Boston.—Williams and Clarke go to England, and expose such doings there.—Letter about it from thence.—Cotton dies.—Infant baptism opposed at Cambridge.—Williams and Clarke opposed in England, and yet prevail.—Williams returns and is President here; and prevails in his colony.—Quakers come over and behave provokingly, and four of them were hanged.

THE severities, that were exercised in the other colonies, caused many of different opinions to remove into Providence colony, where they could have full liberty; and this made it more difficult for them to agree upon their plan of government. But on May 19, 1647, they met at Portsmouth, and elected a President, as their chief ruler, and an Assistant from each of the towns of Providence, Portsmouth, Newport and Warwick; and they were to be Judges in executive courts, and to keep the peace. But six representatives from each town were to make their laws, which were to be sent to each town, to be established or disannulled by the major vote of all their freemen. Mr. Williams was their Assistant for Providence; but such difficulties arose in the colony, that he drew a covenant in December following for all to sign who would, wherein they say, "That government held forth through love, union and order, though by few in number and mean in condition, yet hath by experience withstood and overcome mighty opposers; and above all, the several unexpected deliverances

66 A CHURCH HISTORY [CH. IV.

of this poor plantation, by that mighty Providence who is still able to deliver us, through love, union and order; therefore being sensible of these great and weighty premises, and now met together to consult about our peace and liberty, whereby our families and posterity will still enjoy these favours; and that we may declare unto all the free discharge of our conscience and duties, whereby it may appear upon record that we are not wilfully opposite, nor careless and senseless, and so the means of our own and others' ruin and destruction; and especially in testimony of our fidelity and affection unto one another here present, we promise unto each other to keep unto the ensuing particulars." And so went on to lay down excellent rules of conduct, in order to remove their difficulties.

The name Providence, which Mr. Williams gave both to his town and colony, and the word HOPE, in their public seal, with the figure of an ANCHOR therein, were designed to hold forth the HOPE that he had in God, that he would succeed the great work that he was engaged in, of establishing a civil government upon the principles of true freedom to soul and body. This appears plain in many of his writings. But as they now appeared to be weak, and to have divisions among them, the Massachusetts still refused to own them as a distinct government, and tried all they could to bring them under their power, which they thought was a holy government; and to continue it so, Governor Winthrop says,

"Two churches were appointed to be gathered, one at Haverhill and the other at Andover, both upon Merrimack river. They had given notice thereof to the magistrates and elders, who desired, in regard of their remoteness and scarcity of housing there, that the meeting might be at Rowley, which they assented unto; but being assembled, most of those who

CHURCH HISTORY OF NEW ENGLAND

were to join, refused to declare how God had carried on the work of grace in them,

1647.]   OF NEW-ENGLAND.   67

because they had declared it formerly in their admission into other churches; whereupon the assembly broke up without proceeding." This was in the fall of 1644.* Their strictness of government, both in church and state, did much towards restraining of immoralities among them; so much that Mr. Hugh Peters, who came over to Boston in 1635, and travelled and laboured much in this country, until he went back upon the turn of times in England, where he became very famous, gave an extraordinary character of New-England. When the Parliament had conquered all the king's forces in England, they kept a day of thanksgiving for it, April 2, 1646, and Peters preached a sermon before the Parliament, the Westminster assembly of divines, and the corporation of the city of London, to whom he said, "I have lived in a country, where for seven years I never saw a beggar, nor heard an oath, nor looked upon a drunkard."† This he said to urge them into like measures with the Massachusetts.

But a greater sight now appears before the world, than was then so much extolled. For the scheme which they so much admired, has long since been broken and dissolved; and the principles which were then despised and persecuted, are now become the glory of America. Roger Williams, John Clarke, Joseph Clarke, Thomas Olney, Gregory Dexter, Samuel Hubbard, and many others in that little colony, held the pure doctrines of grace, and the importance of a holy life, as much as the fathers of the Massachusetts did; and they established the first government upon earth, that gave equal liberty, civil and religious, which is now enjoyed in the most parts of America. General Greene also, the second military character in our revolutionary war, sprang from one of the first

* Winthrop, p. 356.
† Peters' Sermon, p. 44.

68   A CHURCH HISTORY   [CH. IV.

planters of Providence. These things shew how great men have been mistaken, and that we ever should judge of things by the light of revelation, and not take any men as our guides, further than they appear to walk in that light.

Many books were brought from England about this time, but none were more disagreeable to the fathers of the Massachusetts, than those which were written against infant baptism, and for liberty of conscience. Several extracts from those writings have already been given. And the public records at Boston, in 1646, shew that controversies about infant baptism were a chief cause of their calling a synod, to compose a platform of government for their churches. Ministers were called from all their colonies to assist in this work. But Mr. Hooker of Hartford died before they met, on July 7, 1647. A book of his was printed in London, after his death, in which he says, "Children, as children, have no right to baptism; so that it belongs not to any predecessors, either nearer or further off, removed from the next parents, to give right of this privilege to their children."* And when the synod met in 1648, and composed their platform, which was approved by their general court, the majority of them agreed with him in this, though Mr. Cotton would have extended it further. And though he, and their churches in general, had allowed no elders to lay on hands in ordination, but the elders of the church in which the pastor was ordained; yet they now said, "In churches where there are no elders, and the church so desire, we see not why imposition of hands may not be performed by the elders of other churches." In this I think they were right; but when they say, "If any church, one or more, shall grow schismatical, rending itself from the communion of

* Survey of church discipline, part iii. 13.

1648.]   OF NEW-ENGLAND.   69

other churches, or shall walk incorrigibly or obstinately in any corrupt way of their own, contrary to the rule of the word; in such case the magistrate is to put forth his coercive power, as the matter shall require;* here I must enter my dissent, because this principle is the root of all the bloody persecution that ever was in the world.

Mr. Williams observes, that the attempts for a reformation in England, by the power of the magistrate, filled their country with blood and confusion for an hundred years. For says he, "Henry the seventh leaves England under the slavish bondage of the Pope's yoke. Henry the eighth reforms all England to a new fashion, half papist, half protestant. King Edward the sixth turns about the wheels of state, and works the whole land to absolute protestantism. Queen Mary succeeding to the helm, steers a direct contrary course, breaks in pieces all that Edward wrought, and brings forth an old edition of England's reformation, all popish. Mary not living out half her

CHURCH HISTORY OF NEW ENGLAND

days (as the prophet speaks of bloody persons) Elizabeth (like Joseph) is advanced from the prison to the palace, and from the irons to the crown; she plucks up all her sister Mary's plants, and sounds a trumpet, all protestant. What sober man is not amazed at these revolutions!"†

Yet as all those revolutions were made by rulers who were not comparable to the godly magistrates and ministers here, they regarded not the warnings of men whom they thought to be deceived. And a writ was sent from Boston, to cite men in the midst of Providence colony, to come to Boston to answer to complaints that were entered there, dated June 20, 1650; which writ is recorded at Providence. Not only so, but when Mr. Coddington was elected President of his colony, May 16, 1648, he refus-

* Platform, cap. ix. xvii.
† Bloody Tenet, p. 197.

70   A CHURCH HISTORY   [CH. IV.

ed to serve, because William Dyre had commenced an action against him about some lands; and in September after he went and tried to get Rhode-Island to be received into confederacy with the united colonies; and as that scheme failed, he went to England, in the year 1651, and obtained a commission for himself to be Governor of that island, separate from the rest of the colony, when he had the deeds of the whole island in his own hands. This caused such a fire of contention among them, that one man was condemned by a vote of the town of Newport, and was carried out and shot to death in their presence. How they were relieved will appear hereafter.

Governor Winthrop was an excellent ruler, until he died, March 26, 1649, in his 62d year. He kept a journal of remarkable events in his colony, from 1630, until near his end. Hubbard, Mather and Prince, made great use of it in their histories. But the first volume of it was published entire in 1790, as it never was before. It gives the clearest account of dates, principles and motives of actions in their government, of any work that ever was published. By it we may learn that he was for milder measures with dissenters from their worship, than the majority of their rulers and ministers were; and though they drew him into greater severities than he desired, yet near his end, when Mr. Dudley desired him to sign an order to banish a person for heterodoxy, he refused, saying, "We have done too much of that work already."* He spent a large part of his great estate in promoting the plantation of his colony, though he met with much ungrateful treatment therein; but his eldest son went over

56

and procured Connecticut charter, and was Governor of that colony until he died, in 1676. These were great honours for one family.

* Belknap's Biography, vol. ii. p. 356.

1649.]   OF NEW-ENGLAND.   71

Mr. John Clarke was an Assistant and the Treasurer of Rhode Island colony in 1649; but that could not secure him from cruel persecution in the Massachusetts two years after, with Mr. Obadiah Holmes, who sprang from a good family in England. When Holmes came over first to this country, he joined to the church in Salem, and was dismissed from thence to the church in Rehoboth, under the ministry of Mr. Samuel Newman. With them he walked about five years, and then he withdrew from Newman, because he had assumed a presbyterial power over the church. Soon after, he and some others became Baptists, upon which Newman excommunicated them, and then got them presented to the court of Plymouth, June 4, 1650. And when they came there, they found that one letter was sent to the court against them from Rehoboth, another from Taunton, a third from most of the ministers in Plymouth colony, and a fourth from the court at Boston, all urging sharp dealings with them. But Governor Bradford and his court only charged them to desist from their separate meeting at Rehoboth, and adjourned their case to October court, when they were dismissed without any punishment. Such was then the government of Plymouth colony. But how different was that of the Massachusetts! There Mr. Clarke and two of his brethren went to visit an old brother of theirs at Lynn, beyond Boston, where they arrived July 19, 1651, and held worship with him the next day, which was the Lord's day. But Mr. Clarke could not get through his first sermon before he and his friends were seized by an officer, and carried to a tavern, and to the parish worship in the afternoon; and at the close of it Clarke spake a few words, and then a magistrate sent them into confinement, and next day to Boston prison. And on July 31, they were tried before the court of Assistants, by whom Clarke was

72   A Church History   [CH. IV.

fined twenty pounds, Holmes thirty, and John Crandal five, or each to be well whipt. When Judge Endecot gave this Sentence against them, he said, "You go up and down, and secretly insinuate things into those that are weak, but you cannot maintain it before our ministers; you may try and dispute with them." Therefore Mr. Clarke wrote from the prison to the court, and proposed a fair dispute upon his principles with any of their ministers. And upon their asking what said principles were, he said,

"I testify that Jesus of Nazareth, whom God hath raised from the dead, is made Lord and Christ; this Jesus I say is Christ; in English, the anointed one; hath a name above every name; he is the anointed Priest, none to or with him in point of atonement; the anointed Prophet, none to him in point of institution; the anointed King, who is gone unto his Father for his glorious kingdom, and shall ere long return again; and that this Jesus Christ is also Lord, none to or with him by way of commanding and ordering, with reference to the worship of God, the household of faith, which being purchased with his blood as a priest, instructed and nourished by his Spirit as a prophet, do wait in his appointments, as he is the Lord, in hope of that glorious kingdom, which shall ere long appear. 2. I testify that baptism, or dipping in water, is one of the commandments of the Lord Jesus Christ, and that a visible believer, or disciple of Christ Jesus (that is, one who manifesteth repentance towards God, and faith in Jesus Christ) is the only person that is to be baptized or dipped with that visible baptism or dipping of Jesus Christ in water, and also that visible person that is to walk in that visible order of his house, and to wait for his coming the second time in the form of Lord and King, with his glorious kingdom, according to promise; and for his sending down, in the time of

1651.]   OF NEW-ENGLAND.   73

his absence, that Holy Ghost, or Holy Spirit of promise, and all this according to the last will and testament of that living Lord, whose will is not to be added to or taken from. 3. I testify or witness, that every such believer in Christ Jesus, that waiteth for his appearing, may in point of liberty, yea, ought in point of duty, to improve that talent his Lord hath given him, and in the congregation may ask for information to himself; or if he can, may speak by way of prophecy for the edification, exhortation and comfort of the whole; and out of the congregation at all times, upon all occasions, and in all places, as far as the jurisdiction of his Lord extendeth, may, yea ought to walk as a child of light, justifying wisdom with his ways, and reproving folly with the unfruitful works thereof; provided all this is shewn out of a good conversation, as James speaks, with meekness of wisdom. 4. I testify, that no such believer, or servant of Christ Jesus, hath any liberty, much less authority from his Lord, to smite his fellow servant, nor with outward force, or arm of flesh to constrain, or restrain his conscience, nor his outward man for conscience sake, or worship of his God, where injury is not offered to any, person, name or estate of others, every man being such as shall appear before the judgment seat of Christ, and must give an account of himself to God; and therefore ought to be fully persuaded in his own mind for what he undertakes, because he that doubteth is damned if he eat, and so also if he act, because he doth not eat or act in faith, and what is not of faith is sin."*

When he had given this plain testimony, there was a talk that Mr. Cotton would dispute him upon it; but after consulting together, Cotton declined, and Clarke was released from prison, to be

* Clarke's Narrative, p. 9, 10.

A CHURCH HISTORY [CH. IV.

gone out of their colony as soon as possible. Crandal also was released with him; but as Holmes had been one of them, they resolved to make him a public example. He was therefore confined until September, and then was brought out to be punished in Boston; and two magistrates, Nowel and Flint, were present to see it done severely. Mr. Holmes, after giving the previous exercises of his own mind, says,

"I desired to speak a few words, but Mr. Nowel answered, It is not now a time to speak; whereupon I took leave, and said, Men, brethren, fathers and countrymen, I beseech you to give me leave to speak a few words, and the rather because here are many spectators to see me punished, and I am to seal with my blood, if God give strength, that which I hold and practise in reference to the word of God, and the testimony of Jesus. That which I have to say in brief is this, although I am no disputant, yet seeing I am to seal with my blood what I hold, I am ready to defend by the word, and to dispute that point with any that shall come forth to withstand it. Mr. Nowel answered, now was no time to dispute; then said I, I desire to give an account of the faith and order which I hold, and this I desired three times; but in comes Mr. Flint, and saith to the executioner, Fellow, do thine office, for this fellow would but make a long speech to delude the people; so I being resolved to speak, told the people, that which I am to suffer for is the word of God, and testimony of Jesus Christ. No, saith Mr. Nowel, it is for your error, and going about to seduce the people; to which I replied, Not for error, for in all the time of my imprisonment, wherein I was left alone, my brethren being gone, which of all your ministers came to convince me of error? And when upon the Governor's words, a motion was made for a public dispute, and often renewed upon fair terms,

1651.]   OF NEW-ENGLAND.   75

and desired by hundreds, what was the reason it was not granted? Mr. Nowel told me, it was his fault who went away and would not dispute; but this the writings will clear at large. Still Mr. Flint calls to the man to do his office; so before, and in the time of his pulling off my clothes, I continued speaking, telling them that I had so learned that for all Boston I would not give my body into their hands thus to be bruised upon another account, yet upon this I would not give the hundredth part of a *wampum peague, to free it out of their hands; and that I made as much conscience of unbuttoning one button, as I did of paying the thirty pounds in reference thereunto. I told them moreover, that the Lord having manifested his love towards me, in giving me repentance towards God, and faith in Christ, and so to be baptized in water by a messenger of Jesus, in the name of the Father, Son, and Holy Spirit, wherein I have fellowship with him in his death, burial and resurrection, I am now come to be baptized in afflictions by your hands, that so I may have further fellowship with my Lord, and am not ashamed of his sufferings, for by his stripes am I healed. And as the man began to lay the strokes upon my back, I said to the people, though my flesh should fail, and my spirit should fail, yet God would not fail; so it pleased the Lord to come in, and to fill my heart and tongue as a vessel full, and with an audible voice I break forth, praying the Lord not to lay this sin to their charge, and telling the people that now I found he did not fail me, and therefore now I should trust him forever who failed me not; for in truth, as the strokes fell upon me, I had such a spiritual manifestation of God's presence, as I never had before, and the outward pain was so removed from me, that I could well bear it, yea, and

* The sixth part of a penny.

76   A CHURCH HISTORY   [CH. IV.

in a manner felt it not, although it was grievous, as the spectators said, the man striking with all his strength, spitting in his hand three times, with a three corded whip, giving me therewith thirty strokes. When he had loosed me from the post, having joyfulness in my heart, and cheerfulness in my countenance, as the spectators observed, I told the magistrates, You have struck me as with roses; and said moreover, although the Lord hath made it easy to me, yet I pray God it may not be laid to your charge.

"After this many came to me, rejoicing to see the power of the Lord manifested in weak flesh; but sinful flesh takes occasion hereby to bring others into trouble, informs the magistrates hereof, and so two more are apprehended as for contempt of authority; their names are John Hazel and John Spur, who came indeed and did shake me by the hand, but did use no words of contempt or reproach unto any. No man can prove that the first spake any thing; and for the second, he only said, Blessed be the Lord; yet these two, for taking me by the hand, and thus saying, after I had received my punishment, were sentenced to pay forty shillings, or to be whipt. Both were resolved against paying their fine: nevertheless, after one or two days imprisonment, one paid John Spur's fine, and he was released; and after six or seven days imprisonment of brother Hazel, even the day when he should have suffered, another paid his, and so he escaped, and the next day went to visit a friend about six miles from Boston, where he fell sick the same day, and within ten days he ended this life. When I was come to the prison, it pleased God to stir up the heart of an old acquaintance of mine, who with much tenderness, like the good Samaritan, poured oil into my wounds, and plastered my sores; but there was present information given of what was done, and inquiry made who was the sur-

1652.]   OF NEW-ENGLAND.   77

geon, and it was commonly reported he should be sent for; but what was done, I yet know not. Now thus it hath pleased the Father of mercies to dispose of the matter, that my bonds and imprisonment have been no hinderance to the gospel; for before my return, some submitted to the Lord, and were baptized, and divers were put upon the way of inquiry; and now being advised to make my escape by night, because it was reported that there were warrants forth for me, I departed; and the next day after, while I was on my journey, the constable came to search at the house where I lodged; so I escaped their hands, and by the good hand of my heavenly Father brought home again to my near relations, my wife and eight children, the brethren of our town and Providence having taken pains to meet me four miles in the woods, where we rejoiced together in the Lord. Thus have I given you, as briefly as I can, a true relation of things; wherefore, my brethren, rejoice with me in the Lord, and give all glory to him, for he is worthy, to whom be praise forevermore, to whom I commit you, and put up my earnest prayers for you, that by my late experience, who trusted in God and have not been deceived, you may trust in him perfectly: wherefore, my dearly beloved brethren, trust in the Lord, and you shall not be ashamed nor confounded. So I rest, yours in the bond of charity,

OBADIAH HOLMES.*

"Unto the well beloved John Spilsbury, William Kiffen, and the rest that in London stand fast in the faith."

This was carried to England, and published there in 1652; upon which Sir Richard Saltonstall, who was an early magistrate in the Massachusetts, when

---

* Clarke p. 17–23.

---

78   A CHURCH HISTORY   [CH. IV.

Boston was first planted, but was now in London, wrote to the ministers of Boston, and said:

"Reverend and dear friends, whom I unfeignedly love and respect,

"It doth not a little grieve my spirit to hear what sad things are reported daily of your tyranny and persecution in New-England; that you fine, whip and imprison men for their consciences. First, you compel such to come into your assemblies as you know will not join with you in worship, and when they shew their dislike thereof, or witness against it, then you stir up your magistrates to punish them for such (as you conceive) their public affronts. Truly, friends, this practice of compelling any in matters of worship to do that whereof they are not fully persuaded, is to make them sin, for so the apostle tells us, Rom. xiv. 23; and many are made hypocrites thereby, conforming in their outward man for fear of punishment. We pray for you, and wish your prosperity every way; hoped the Lord would have given you so much light and love there, that you might have been eyes to God's people here, and not to practise those courses in a wilderness, which you went so far to prevent. These rigid ways have laid you very low in the hearts of the saints. I do assure you I have heard them pray in public assemblies, that the Lord would give you meek and humble spirits, not to strive so much for uniformity as to keep the unity of the Spirit in the bond of peace. When I was in Holland, about the beginning of our wars, I remember some Christians there, that then had serious thoughts of planting in New-England, desired me to write to the Governor thereof to know if those that differ from you in opinion, yet holding the same foundation in religion, as Anabaptists, Seekers, Antinomians, and the like, might be permitted to live among you; to which I received this short answer from your then Governor, Mr. Dudley, God forbid, said he, our

OF NEW-ENGLAND.

1652]

79

love for the truth should be grown so cold that we should tolerate errors."

To this Mr. Cotton answered, and said,

"*Honoured and dear Sir,*

"My brother Wilson and self do both of us acknowledge your love, as otherwise formerly, so now in the late lines we received from you, that you grieve in spirit to hear daily complaints against us; it springeth from your companion for our afflictions therein, wherein we see just cause to desire you may never suffer like injury in yourself, but may find others to compassionate and condole with you. For when the complaints you hear of are against our tyranny and persecution in fining, whipping and imprisoning men for their consciences, be pleased to understand we look at such complaints as altogether injurious in respect of ourselves, who had no hand or tongue at all to promote either the coming of the persons you aim at into our assemblies, or their punishment for their carriage there. Righteous judgment will not take up reports, much less reproaches against the innocent. The cry of the sins of Sodom was great and loud, and reached unto heaven; yet the righteous God (giving us an example what to do in the like case) he would first go down to see whether their crimes were altogether according to the cry, before he would proceed to judgment. Gen. xviii. 20, 21. And when he did find the truth of the cry, he did not wrap up all alike promiscuously in the judgment, but spared such as he found innocent. We are amongst those (if you knew us better) you would account of (as the matron of Abel spake of herself) peaceable in Israel. 2 Sam. xx. 19. Yet neither are we so vast in our indulgence or toleration as to think the men you speak of suffered an unjust censure. For one of them, Obadiah Holmes, being an excommunicate person himself, out of a church in Plymouth patent, came into this jurisdiction, and

A CHURCH HISTORY

80

[CH. IV.

took upon him to baptize, which I think himself will not say he was compelled here to perform. And he was not ignorant that the rebaptizing of an elder person, and that by a private person out of office and under excommunication, are all of them manifest contestations against the order and government of our churches, established, we know, by God's law, and he knoweth, by the laws of the country. And we conceive we may safely appeal to the ingenuity of your own judgment, whether it would be tolerated in any civil state, for a stranger to come and practise contrary to the known principles of the church estate? As for his whipping, it was more voluntarily chosen by him than inflicted on him. His censure by the court was to have paid, as I know, thirty pounds, or else to be whipt; his fine was offered to be paid by friends for him freely; but he chose rather to be whipt; in which case, if his suffering of stripes was any worship of God at all, surely it could be accounted no better than will-worship. The other, Mr. Clarke, was wiser in that point, and his offence was less, so was his fine less, and himself, as I hear, was contented to have it paid for him, whereupon he was released. The imprisonment of either of them was no detriment. I believe they fared neither of them better at home; and I am sure Holmes had not been so well clad of many years before.

"But be pleased to consider this point a little further. You think to compel men in matter of worship is to make them sin, according to Romans xiv. 23. If the worship be lawful in itself, the magistrate compelling to come to it, compelleth him not to sin, but the sin is in his will that needs to be compelled to a Christian duty. Josiah compelled all Israel, or which is all one, made to serve the Lord their God, 2 Chron. xxxiv. 33. Yet his act herein was not blamed, but recorded among his virtuous actions.

1652.]　　　　　　　OF NEW-ENGLAND.　　　　　　　81

For a Governor to suffer any within his gates to profane the sabbath, is a sin against the fourth commandment, both in the private householder and in the magistrate; and if he requires them to present themselves before the Lord, the magistrate sinneth not, nor doth the subject sin so great a sin as if he did refrain to come.—But you say it doth but make men hypocrites, to compel men to conform the outward man for fear of punishments. If it did so, yet better be hypocrites than profane persons. Hypocrites give God part of his due, the outward man, but the profane person giveth God neither outward nor inward man.—Nevertheless, I tell you the truth, we have tolerated in our church some Anabaptists, some Antinomians, and some Seekers, and do so still at this day."*

These letters give a plain idea of the sentiments of these two great men in that day, and that of Mr. Cotton shews the absurdities of his scheme of compulsion about religion. The paying of Mr. Clarke's fine, he says, was done "contrary to my judgment."† Yet Mr. Cotton reports that he consented to it, and reflects upon Holmes for not doing the same. But I have a writing of Governor Jenks, wherein he says, "Although the paying of a fine seems to be a small thing in comparison of a man's parting with his religion, yet the paying of a fine is the acknowledging of a transgression; and for a man to acknowledge that he has transgressed, when his conscience tells him he has not, is but little if any thing short of parting with his religion; and it is likely this might be the consideration of those sufferers." And though Cotton says, "Hypocrites give God part of his due," yet in the first Christian church God struck two hypocrites dead for lying to the Holy Ghost, and said upon it, Of

* Hutchinson's Collections, p. 401–407.
† Narrative, p, 11.

82 A CHURCH HISTORY [CH. IV.

the rest durst no man join himself to them, but the people magnified them. And believers were the more added to the Lord, multitudes both of men and women. Acts v. 5—14. And how loud is this warning to all the world against lying and hypocrisy, especially in the affairs of religion! And though Mr. Cotton was exceeding confident that their churches were established by the laws of God, yet the character which he gives of his own church is more like confusion of all sentiments, than the union described in the first Christian churches.

Mr. Cotton died on December 23, 1652, soon after this letter was written. He was greatly esteemed, both in Europe and America, as a clear preacher of the gospel. And though he was so dark about Christian liberty, yet Mr. Williams says, "Since it pleased God to lay a command on my conscience to come in as his poor witness in this great cause, I rejoice that it hath pleased him to appoint so able and excellent and conscionable an instrument, to bolt out the truth to the bran. As it is my constant grief to differ from any fearing God, so much more from Mr. Cotton, whom I highly esteem and dearly respect, for so great a portion of mercy given unto him, and so many truths of Christ maintained by him."* So that his conscience obliged him to write against the errors of a man whom he highly esteemed. And in the same book he sent a letter to Governor Endicot, in which he said, "By your principles and conscience, such as you count heretics, blasphemers and seducers must be put to death. You cannot be faithful to your principles and conscience without it."† Endicot did plead conscience in putting four persons to death about eight years after; and this hath exposed New-England to reproach among the

* Preface to Williams against Cotton, 1652, p. 6.
† Tenet more bloody, p. 312.

1653.] OF NEW-ENGLAND. 83

CHURCH HISTORY OF NEW ENGLAND

nations ever since, more than any other action they ever did.

The sufferings and writings of the Baptists at this time were a cause of light to many. Mr. Henry Dunstar, President of Cambridge college, had such a turn in his mind, that he boldly preached in their pulpit, that they had no right to baptize any infant whatever. And when Mr. Mitchel, minister in the town, went to talk with him upon the subject, great scruples were raised in his own mind, about infant baptism. But he laboured hard to remove them, and at length concluded that they were from the devil, and said, "I resolved that I would have an argument able to remove a mountain, before I would recede from, or appear against a truth or practice received among the faithful."* This was in December, 1653; and Dr. Cotton Mather published it to the world in 1697, and Mr. John Cleaveland of Ipswich inserted it in a piece he published for infant baptism in 1784. Thus it has been a tradition in New-England, from the fathers of the Massachusetts to our days, that they who forsake infant baptism are deceived by the devil, though that practice is not named in the Bible! And Mr. Dunstar was turned out from being President, for rejecting it, and such a temper was discovered against him, that he removed out of their colony, and spent the remainder of his days at Scituate in Plymouth colony, where he died in 1659. Captain Johnson finished writing his history in 1652, just before this event, and then he said, "Mr. Henry Dunstar is now President of the college, fitted from the Lord for the work, and by those that have skill that way, reported to be an able proficient, both in the Hebrew, Greek and Latin languages, an orthodox preacher of the truths

* Mitchel's Life, p. 67–70.

84   A CHURCH HISTORY   [CH. IV.

of Christ, and very powerful through his blessing, to move the affections."*

At the same time he said, "Familists, Seekers, Antinomians and Anabaptists are so ill armed, that they think it best sleeping in a whole skin; fearing that if the day of battle once goes on, they shall fall among antichrist's armies; and therefore cry out like cowards, If you will let me alone, I will let you alone; but assuredly the Lord Christ hath said, He that is not with us is against us: there is no room in his army for toleratorists."† But the Baptists were so far from fear or discouragement, that they boldly persevered in their way, till they obtained deliverance. The towns of Newport and Portsmouth chose Mr Clarke, and Providence and Warwick chose Mr. Williams their agents to go to England, and plead their cause there. And that they might have a fair trial, the commissioners of the United Colonies, at their meeting in September, 1651, received a writing from Warwick, saying, "May it please this honoured committee to take knowledge, that we, the inhabitants of Shawomet, alias Warwick, having undergone divers oppressions and wrongs, amounting to great damage, since we first possessed this place; being forced thereby to seek to the honourable state of Old-England for relief, which did inevitably draw great charge upon us, to the further impairing of our estates; and finding favour for redress, were willing to wave for that time (in regard to the great troubles and employment that then lay on that state) all other lesser wrongs we then underwent, so that we might be replaced in and upon this our purchased possession, and enjoy it peaceably for time to come, without disturbance or molestation by those from whom we had formerly suffered.

    * Johnson, p. 168. His history was printed in 1654.

    † Johnson, p. 231.

1653.]   OF NEW-ENGLAND.

But since our gracious grant from the Hon. Parliament, in replacing of us in this place, we have been and are daily pressed with intolerable grievances, to the eating up of our labours, and wasting of our estates, making our lives, together with our wives and children, bitter and uncomfortable; insomuch that, groaning under our burden, we are again constrained to make our address to the Parliament." And so gave the Colonies notice to be prepared to answer their complaints there.

    This caused the commissioners of the Massachusetts, Bradstreet and Hathorne, to observe that Plymouth gave up those lands to them in 1643, to which others assented, and told of the great pains and expense they had been at about Gorton and his company, and support to the Indians, who said those men had wronged them about their lands; and desired to know if the other colonies would help them to do justice for the Indians. But the commissioners from Plymouth, Brown and Hatherly, declared that what was done in 1643, by men from their colony, was going beyond their authority, who had no right over Shawomet lands, and that the Massachusetts had no right to do all that they had done in the heart of Providence colony. And the commissioners from Connecticut and New-Haven owned that it might be so. This is all plain in their records. And Williams and Clarke sailed from Boston with these complaints in November, though Williams had hard work to get a passage from thence, notwithstanding the services he had done for them formerly.

CHURCH HISTORY OF NEW ENGLAND

When they arrived at London, each of them published the books which I have before named; and in October they obtained a vacation of Coddington's commission, and an order for their colony to unite again, under their former charter. This was brought over by William Dyre, who left it on Rhode Island, and wrote to Provi-

86   A CHURCH HISTORY   [Ch. IV.

dence and Warwick to come there and act upon it. But as these two towns had acted upon their charter all the while that the island was in confusion, they still remained two parties; and there were many against them in England. Edward Winslow, who had been Governor of Plymouth, and Edward Hopkins, who had been Governor of Connecticut, were then in England.

On April 1, 1653, Mr. Williams wrote to his constituents, and said, "The determination of our controversy is hindered by two main obstructions. The first is the mighty war with the Dutch. Our second obstruction is the opposition of our adversaries, Sir Arthur Haselrig and Colonel Fenwick, who married his daughter, Mr. Winslow, and Mr. Hopkins, both in great place; and all the friends they can make in the Parliament and Council, and all the priests, both Presbyterian and Independent; so that we stand as two armies ready to engage, observing the motions and postures each of other, and yet shy each of other." But before that month was out, Cromwell dissolved the Parliament, which altered things greatly; and the Presbyterians have never had so great power in England since, as they had before.

Mr. Williams continued there another year, and then left Mr. Clarke their agent in England, while he came over to settle affairs here. And he brought a letter from Sir Henry Vane, which contained sharp reproofs for their disorders in his colony, and wise advice about removing of them. But Williams found it very hard work to get the two parties together, and yet he did it; and they met on September 12, 1654, and elected him for their President, and then voted to have him send letters of thanks to their benefactors in England. On May 22, 1655, he was again elected President for a year. But some men had been so troublesome

1655.]   OF NEW-ENGLAND.   87

among them, that a letter was procured from the Protector in England, which said,

BY ISAAC BACKUS

"*Gentlemen,*

"Your agent here hath represented unto us some particulars concerning your government, which you judge necessary to be settled by us here; but by reason of other great and weighty affairs of this commonwealth, we have been necessitated to defer the consideration of them to a further opportunity; in the mean time we are willing to let you know, that you were to proceed in your government according to the tenour of your charter, formerly granted on that behalf, taking care of the peace and safety of those plantations, that neither, through intestine commotions or foreign invasions, there do arise any detriment or dishonour to this commonwealth or yourselves, as far as you by your care and diligence can prevent. And as for the things that are before us, they shall, as soon as other occasions will permit, receive a just and sufficient determination. And so we bid you farewell, and rest, your loving friend,

March 29, 1655.   OLIVER P.

To our trusty and well beloved, the President, Assistants, and inhabitants of Rhode Island, together with the rest of the Providence Plantations in the Narraganset Bay in New-England."

Upon receiving this, their assembly met, June 28, and enacted, "That if any person or persons be found by examination and judgment of a general court of commissioners, to be a ringleader or ringleaders of factions or divisions among us, he or they shall be sent over at his or their own charges, as prisoners, to receive his or their trial or sentence, at the pleasure of his Highness and the Lords of his council." And then all open opposition ceased in their government. And President Williams

88   A CHURCH HISTORY   [CH. IV.

wrote in November to the Massachusetts about their opposition to it; but receiving no satisfaction, he wrote again in May, 1656, and said,

"Honoured Sirs, our first request is for your favourable consideration of the long and lamentable condition of the town of Warwick, which hath been thus. They are so dangerously and so vexatiously intermingled with the barbarians, that I have long admired the wonderful power of God in restraining and preventing very great fires, of mutual slaughters breaking forth between them. Your wisdoms know the inhumane insultations of these wild creatures, and you may be pleased also to imagine, that they have not been sparing of your name as the patron of all their wickedness against our Englishmen, women, and children, and cattle, to the yearly damage of sixty,

69

eighty and an hundred pounds. The remedy, under God, is only your pleasure that Pumham shall come to an agreement with the town or colony, and that some convenient way and time be set for their removal. And that your wisdoms may see just grounds for such your willingness, be pleased to be informed of a reality of a solemn covenant between this town of Warwick and Pumham, unto which, notwithstanding he pleads his being drawn to it by the awe of his superior sachems, yet I humbly offer, that what was done was according to the law and tenour of the natives (I take it) in all New-England and America, viz. that the inferior sachems and subjects shall plant and remove at the pleasure of the highest and supreme sachems; and I humbly conceive that it pleaseth the Most High and only Wise to make use of such a bond of authority over them, without which they could not long subsist in human societies, in this wild condition wherein they are."

And he went on to remind them of the order of Parliament in 1646, that they should remove all

1656.] OF NEW-ENGLAND. 89

obstructions which they had put in the way of those who had purchased the lands in Warwick, so that they might freely enjoy their rights. He also desired them no longer to assume any power over a few persons in Pawtuxet, and to treat their colony as a distinct government.* And his request was granted.

The Massachusetts were awfully requited for their iniquity in these affairs. For when they received Pumham as their subject, they furnished him with arms and ammunition, for hunting; and in Philip's war he joined against the English, and was very active in the war, and so was his son and grandson; and Pumham was killed within twenty miles of Boston, but a few days before Philip.† How righteous are God's judgments!

The Massachusetts were fond of comparing themselves to the Israelites who conquered Canaan; and I have recited a passage in which Captain Johnson has named seven sectaries which they were to subdue, as Israel did the seven nations in the promised land; but as these are far from being parallel cases, so was the success of the two people. For the seed of Jacob were completely victorious, but the Massachusetts never subdued one of the sects which he named. And a new one now arose, who caused more disgrace to them than any others had done.

Out of the confusions in England, George Fox came forth as a zealous preacher of a new doctrine; and in 1650, he and his followers received the name of Quakers, from the trembling motions of their bodies, upon various occasions. They increased fast in England, and their sufferings animated them to travel far and near; and in the summer of 1656, some of them arrived at Boston, where

* Hutchinson's Collections, p. 279–282.
† Hubbard on said War, p. 131, 175, 176.

90   A CHURCH HISTORY   [CH. IV.

they were confined. And when the commissioners of the United Colonies met at Plymouth in September, they received a letter from the court at Boston, which said, "Having heard sometime since, that our neighbouring colony of Plymouth, our beloved brethren, in great part seem to be wanting to themselves in a due acknowledgment and encouragement of the ministry of the gospel, so as many pious ministers have (how justly we know not) *deserted their stations, callings and relations; our desire is that some such course may be taken, as that a pious orthodox ministry may be restated among them, that so the flood of errors and principles of anarchy may be prevented. Here hath arrived amongst us several persons professing themselves Quakers, fit instruments to propagate the kingdom of Satan; for the securing of ourselves and our neighbours from such pests, we have imprisoned them all till they be dispatched away to the place from whence they came." And the commissioners gave advice accordingly.†

But such measures were not taken as long as Governor Bradford lived, who died on May 9, 1657, in his 69th year. And in June following, John Brown and James Cudworth, two of their Assistants, were left out of office, and others were chosen, who were for more severe measures, though not equal to the Massachusetts; who also wrote repeatedly to the rulers of Rhode Island colony, to try to draw them into like severity, but without any success.

The Quakers held that they had a light and spirit within them, which was their highest rule of ac-

* One of these was Mr. Reyner, who went from Plymouth in 1654, and robbed them of all their church records, so that all the records they since have of former actings in their church, were collected from memory and private writings; as their late pastor told me. And how unjust was this!
† Hutchinson's Collections, p. 283–286.

1658.]   OF NEW-ENGLAND.   91

tion, and that the Scriptures were only a secondary rule; and that the external use of baptism and the Lord's supper was now out of date, and that they had those ordinances inwardly and spiritually. They also held themselves to be inspired by the Spirit of God to teach a more clear and perfect way than men had known since the days of the apostles, if they had not greater light than the apostles had. This spirit taught them to give no titles to rulers nor other men, and to use *thee* and *thou* to all. Humphrey Norton was scourged at Plymouth, in June, 1658, and then sent out of that colony; upon which he wrote to Governor Prince, and said,

"Thomas Prince, thou who hast bent thy heart to work wickedness, and with thy tongue hast thou set forth deceit; thou imaginest mischief upon thy bed, and hatchest thy hatred in thy secret chamber; the strength of darkness is over thee, and a malicious mouth hast thou opened against God and his anointed, and with thy tongue and lips hast thou uttered perverse things; thou hast slandered the innocent by railing, lying and false accusations, and with thy barbarous heart hast thou caused their blood to be shed. Thou hast through all these things broke and transgressed the laws and ways of God, and equity is not before thy eyes. The curse causeless cannot come upon thee, nor the vengeance of God unjustly cannot fetch thee up; thou makest thyself merry with thy secret malice. The day of thy wailing will be like unto that of a woman that murthers the fruit of her womb; the anguish and pain that will enter upon thy reins will be like gnawing worms lodging betwixt thy heart and liver: when these things come upon thee, and thy back bowed down with pain, in that day and hour thou shalt know to thy grief, that prophets of the Lord God we are, and the God of vengeance is our God. HUMPHREY NORTON."

92   A CHURCH HISTORY   [CH. IV.

This I copied from Plymouth records, where it was inserted, that posterity might know how their fathers were treated. And we may here also learn how secular force serves to inflame mistaken zeal; for the various punishments that were inflicted upon those people, caused their zeal to rise the higher, until the commissioners of the United Colonies met at Boston in September, 1658; and then they advised each General Court to make a law to banish Quakers on pain of death. And such a law was made at Boston the next month, by the majority of one vote only; and the other colonies would not follow their example. Many other punishments were inflicted upon the Quakers in Plymouth and New-Haven colonies, but little or none in Connecticut.

On October 20, 1659, William Robinson, Marmaduke Stevenson, and Mary Dyre, were condemned to die, for returning after they were banished on pain of death; and the two men were hanged at Boston the 27th. And though the woman was then sent away, yet she returned, and was executed June 1, 1660. And on March 14, 1661, William Leddra was hanged there for the like crime. And as Charles the second had been restored to the crown of England the year before, Governor Endicot and his court wrote to him in December, and said, "Our liberty to walk in the faith of the gospel, with all *good conscience*, was the cause of our transporting ourselves, with our wives, little ones, and our substance, from that pleasant land over the Atlantic ocean, into this vast wilderness, choosing rather the pure Scripture worship with a good conscience, in this remote wilderness among the heathen, than the pleasures of England with submission to the then so disposed and so far prevailing hierarchy, which we could not do without an evil conscience.—Concerning the Quakers, open and capital blasphemers, open seducers from the glori-

1659.] OF NEW-ENGLAND. 93

ous Trinity, the Lord Jesus Christ, our Lord Jesus Christ, the blessed gospel, and from the holy Scriptures as the rule of life, open enemies to the government itself as established in the hands of any but men of their own principles, malignant and assiduous promoters of doctrines directly tending to subvert both our church and state, after all other means for a long time used in vain, we were at last constrained for our own safety to pass a sentence of banishment against them, upon pain of death. Such was their desperate turbulence both to religion and state, civil and ecclesiastical, as that the magistrate at last, in conscience both to God and man, judged himself called for the defence of all, to keep the passage with the point of the sword held towards them; this could do no harm to him that would be warned thereby; their wittingly rushing themselves thereupon was their own act, we with humility conceive a crime bringing their blood upon their own heads."*

But William Robinson had given a paper to the court at Boston, in which he said, "The word of the Lord came expressly to me, which did fill me immediately with life and power, and heavenly love, by which he constrained me, and commanded me to pass to the town of Boston, my life to lay down in his will, for the accomplishing of his service, that he had there to perform at the day appointed." And Marmaduke Stevenson gave them another paper, in which he said, "The word of the Lord came unto me, saying. Go to Boston, with thy brother William Robinson."†

Thus it appears, that both sides pleaded a conscientious obedience to God, in their actings against each other. And from hence we may see, that the use of force in religious affairs is a *bloody practice.*

* Hutchinson's Collections, p. 326, 327.
† Bishop, p. 127–133.

94   A CHURCH HISTORY   [Ch. V.

And though king Charles put a stop to their hanging any more here, yet he said, "We cannot be understood hereby to direct or wish that any indulgence should be granted to those persons commonly called Quakers, whose principles being inconsistent with any kind of government, we have found it necessary, with the advice of our Parliament here, to make a sharp law against them, and are well content you do the like there."* And many more Dissenters died in prison in his reign, than the bloody queen Mary burnt at the stake. Open executions were now become more odious to the people, than in former days of ignorance and superstition; while private cruelty was borne with, or little regarded. But the vengeance of God will reach the most secret criminals, as well as the most open murderers.

CHAP. V.

Contention about baptism.—Two Baptist churches formed.—That at Boston is persecuted three years, and then three of them were banished.—But many are for them here, and clear letters are written in their favour from England.—After they had been confined a year, they were released from prison.—Injustice about Providence colony exposed.—And they at last prevail.—Williams disputes and writes against the Quakers.—A division in Boston church.—Clarke's faith, and his joyful end.

WE shall now return to the affairs of baptism. They who supposed that each believer stood in the same relation to his children, as Abraham did to his in the covenant of circumcision, brought none to baptism but the infants of communicants in their churches. But as those infants grew up and had

* Hutchinson's Collections, p. 379.

1662.]   OF NEW-ENGLAND.   95

children, and yet were not communicants themselves, a great trial came on to know what would become of succeeding generations. A convention of ministers met in 1657, and answered twenty-one questions upon the subject, and had them printed in London. But as this did not relieve them, another convention was called at Boston in 1659, and a synod in 1662, who introduced a half way covenant, so that they who would own it, and were regular in their lives, might have their children sprinkled, without coming to the ordinance of the supper themselves. This was pleasing to many, while others thought it to be an apostacy from the first principles of the country; and the controversy about it, in various shapes, has continued ever since.

The first Baptist church in Wales was formed near Swansea in that country in 1649. Mr. John Miles was their chief leader, and they increased to about three hundred members, by the year 1662, when he was ejected out of his place, by a cruel act of Parliament, which turned two thousand teachers out of their places in one day, for refusing fully to conform to the church of England. He then came over, with the book of church records which he had kept there, and it remains in our Swansea to this day. And at the house of John Butterworth in Rehoboth, in 1663, John Miles, elder, James Brown, Nicholas Tanner, Joseph Carpenter, John Butterworth, Eldad Kingsley, and Benjamin Alby, solemnly covenanted together as a church of Christ, to obey him in all his ordinances and commandments. They were in Plymouth colony, where they had ever enjoyed much more liberty than any had in the Massachusetts. Mr. Brown was son to John Brown, who had long been a magistrate in that colony, and his son served them afterwards in that office for eleven years, in a time when his brethren in the Massachusetts were fined, imprison-

96   A CHURCH HTSTORY   [CH. V.

ed and banished. Indeed Mr. Miles and his church were complained of to court, for holding their meetings in Rehoboth, where was a Congregational church, and a small fine was imposed upon them for it. But in 1667, the Court granted them the town of Swansea, where the church has continued by succession ever since, and is the fourth Baptist church in America.

The fifth was formed in the Massachusetts. The light that was gained in 1653, when President Dunstar preached against infant baptism in Cambridge, caused Thomas Gould, who lived near him in Charlestown, to examine the matter so much, that when he had a child born in 1655, he could not bring it to be sprinkled. For this he was called before the church in Charlestown, and he told them that he could see no light for infant baptism, and therefore could not in conscience bring his child to it. Upon this,

CHURCH HISTORY OF NEW ENGLAND

ministers, rulers and brethren laboured with him, but could not convince him. He was still willing to commune with that church, if they would let him do it without carrying his child to an ordinance, which he had no faith in; and he read that whatsoever is not of faith is sin. And because of this, and also his going out of meeting when they sprinkled infants, they censured him in their church, and punished him in their courts for more than seven years. At length three Baptist brethren came over from England, recommended from churches there, and met with him and others in private houses. And on May 28, 1665, Thomas Gould, Thomas Osborne, Edward Drinker, John George, Richard Goodale, William Turner, Robert Lambert, Mary Goodale, and Mary Newell, "joined in a solemn covenant, in the name of the Lord Jesus Christ, to walk in fellowship and communion together in the practice of all the holy appointments of Christ, which he had, or should further make known unto them."

1665.]   OF NEW-ENGLAND.   97

Goodale came from London, and Turner and Lambert from Dartmouth; the others were of our country, though none of them were church members before, but Gould and Osburne, both of Charlestown; from whence they were excommunicated, after they were baptized. These facts I gathered from their records and writings. They were of such a peaceable disposition, and so far from disturbing others, as the Quakers did, that their rulers hardly knew where to find them. But on August 20, 1665, Richard Russel, one of their magistrates, issued a warrant to the constable of Charlestown, requiring him in his Majesty's name, to labour to discover where these people were, and to require them to attend on the established worship, or if they would not, to return their names and places of abode to the next magistrate. This was done, and some of them were brought before their court of Assistants in September, to whom they presented a confession of their faith, in which they said, "Christ's commission to his disciples is to teach and baptize, and those who gladly receive the word and are baptized, are fit matter for a visible church." But this was loudly complained of, as implying that none were visible saints, who were not baptized by immersion; though they held that they ought to be visible saints before they were baptized. Thus men turn things upside down. And the court of Assistants charged them to desist from their practice; and because they did not, Gould, Turner, Osburne, Drinker and George, were brought before their General Court in October, to whom they presented their confession of faith, and closed with saying, "If any take this to be heresy, then do we with the apostle confess, that after the way which they call heresy, we worship God, the Father of our Lord Jesus Christ, believing all things that are written in the law and the prophets and apostles."

98   A CHURCH HISTORY   [CH. V.

But the Court called this a contemning of their authority and laws, and declared them to be no lawful church assembly, and said, "Such of them as are freemen are to be disfranchised, and all cf them, upon conviction before any one Magistrate or Court, of their further proceeding herein, to be committed to prison until the General Court shall take further order with them." Dr. Mather tries to vindicate the Court herein, because the Baptists acted against the law of the government; but a noted Presbyterian minister says, "This condemns all the dissenting congregations that have been gathered in England, since the act of uniformity in the year 1662." And says he, "Let the reader judge, who had most reason to complain; the New-England churches, who would neither suffer the Baptists to live quietly in their communion, nor separate peaceably from it; or these unhappy persons, who were treated so unkindly for following the light of their consciences."*

Yet for following that light, they pursued them with fines and imprisonment, for three years; and then the court of Assistants appointed a meeting at Boston, April 14, 1668, and called six ministers to manage a dispute whether those persons ought not to be banished, for holding a separate meeting from their churches. And they sent a warrant to Thomas Gould, which said, "You are required in his majesty's name to give notice to John Farnum, Thomas Osburne, and the company, and you and they are alike required to give your attendance, at the time and place above mentioned, for the end therein expressed." And as this was heard of at Newport, Mr. Clarke and his church sent William Hiscox, Joseph Tory, and Samuel Hubbard, to assist their brethren, and they got to Boston three days before the dispute. And it was carried on

* Magnalia, B. 7. p. 27. Neal on New-England, vol. 1 p. 304, 305.

1668.]   OF NEW-ENGLAND.   99

two days by those ministers, with allowing the Baptists but little liberty to speak for themselves; and it was closed by Mr. Mitchel, with the words of Moses, who said to Israel, If there arise a matter too hard for thee in judgment, between blood and blood, between plea and plea, and between stroke and

CHURCH HISTORY OF NEW ENGLAND

stroke, being matters of controversy within thy gates; then shalt thou arise, and get thee up into the place which the Lord thy God shall choose; and thou shalt come unto the priests the Levites, and unto the judge that shall be in those days, and inquire; and they shall shew thee the sentence of judgment: and thou shalt do according to the sentence, which they of that place, which the Lord shall choose, shall shew thee; and thou shalt observe to do according to all that they inform thee; according to the sentence of the law which they shall teach thee, and according to the judgment which they shall tell thee, thou shalt do; thou shalt not decline from the sentence which they shall shew thee, to the right hand nor the left. And the man that will do presumptuously, and will not hearken unto the priest (that standeth there before the Lord thy God) or unto the judge, even that man shall die; and thou shalt put away the evil from Israel. Deut. xvii. 8—12.

Thus the sentence that was given from the law of God, in the place he chose, under the direction of the Urim and Thummim, was applied to the sentence of rulers and ministers at Boston, according to the laws of men. That they then applied this scripture in this manner, appears from their colony records, compared with the writings of Samuel Hubbard and Mr. Gould. And thirty years after, Mr. Stoddard brought the same scripture to prove, that all men ought to submit to a national synod, as I shall prove hereafter.

Their General Court in May called those Baptists before them, to know whether they were convinc-

100   A CHURCH HISTORY   [Ch.V.

ed of their evil in withdrawing from their churches, by what said ministers had laid before them; but they declared that they were not at all convinced of any evil in so doing. The Court then called them obstinate Anabaptists, whom they were bound in conscience to proceed against; and gave sentence that Thomas Gould, William Turner and John Farnum, should be gone out of their jurisdiction by the 20th of July, not to return again without their leave. And as Gould was then a prisoner, by the sentence of a former Court, he was liberated from thence, in order that he might obey this sentence. Mr. Mitchel, who read off said scripture against them, died suddenly, eleven days before the time set in their sentence of banishment; but this gave no relief to these sufferers. And because they did not obey their sentence, these three men were imprisoned in Boston for near or quite a year.

How any who feared God, could go on to act against others, as these rulers and ministers did, may seem very strange in our days; but a careful search into their history will open the cause of it. Mr. Wilson, the first minister of Boston, was in great esteem with other ministers, who came round him in May past, and desired him to give his dying testimony of what he conceived to be the cause of the displeasure of God against this country. He told them that he had long feared the following sins as chief among others, which provoked God greatly. "1. Separation. 2. Anabaptism. 3. Corahism, when people rise up as Corah, against their ministers or elders, as if they took too much upon them, when indeed they do but rule for Christ, and according to Christ. 4. Another sin I take to be, the making light of, and not subjecting to the authority of synods."* These things he delivered as his dying

* Morton, p. 195, 196.

1668.] OF NEW-ENGLAND. 101

testimony; and he died August 7, 1668, just after those Baptists were put in prison there. No one can easily tell how great impression such things had upon their minds. Indeed some were of a different opinion, and when their General Court met in the fall, they presented a petition in favour of those sufferers, and said, "We humbly beseech this honoured Court, in their Christian mercy and bowels of compassion, to pity and relieve these poor prisoners; whose sufferings are doubtful to many, and some of great worth among ourselves, and grievous to the hearts of God's people at home and abroad. Your wisdoms may be pleased to think of some better expedient, and seriously to consider whether an indulgence, justifiable by the word of God, pleaded for and practised by Congregational churches, may not, in this day of suffering to the people of God, be more effectual, safe and inoffensive than other ways, which are always grievous, and seldom find success." And they spoke highly of the good lives of those Baptists, as another plea in their favour. Captain Hutchinson, Captain Oliver, and many others signed this petition; but some were fined for it, and others were compelled to confess their fault, for reflecting upon the court. But Deputy-Governor Willoughby was against these proceedings.* An account of these things was sent to England, and a letter from thence to Captain Oliver said,

"*My dear Brother*,

"The ardent affection and great honours that I have for New-England transport me, and I hope your churches shall ever be to me as the gates of heaven. I have ever been warmed with the apprehension of the grace of God towards me in carrying me thither. But now it is otherwise; with joy to ourselves and grief to you be it spoken.

* Hutchinson, vol, i. p. 227, 269.

102   A CHURCH HISTORY   [CH. V.

Now the greater my love is to New-England, the more am I grieved at their failings. It is frequently said here, that they are swerved aside towards Presbytery; if so, the Lord restore them all. But another sad thing that much affects us is, to hear that you even in New-England persecute your brethren; men sound in the faith; of holy life; agreeing in worship and discipline with you; only differing in the point of baptism. Dear brother, we here do love and honour them, hold familiarity with them, and take sweet counsel together; they lie in the bosom of Christ, and therefore they ought to be laid in our bosoms. In a word, we freely admit them into churches; few of our churches, but many of our members are Anabaptists; I mean baptized again. This is love in England; this is moderation; this is a right New Testament spirit. But do you now bear with, yea more than bear with the Presbyterians? Yea, and that the worst sort of them, those who are the corrupted, rigidest; whose principles tend to corrupt the churches; turning the world into the church, and the church into the world; and which doth no less than to bring a people under mere slavery. It is an iron yoke, which neither we nor our Congregational brethren in Scotland were ever able to bear. I have heard them utter these words in the pulpit, that it is no wrong to make the Independents sell all they have, and depart the land; and many more things I might mention of that kind; but this I hint only, to shew what cause there is to withstand that wicked tyranny which was once set up in poor miserable Scotland, which I verily believe was a great wrong and injury to the reformation. The generality of them here, even to this day, will not freely consent to our enjoyment of our liberty; though through mercy the best and most reformed of them do otherwise. How much therefore would it concern dear New

1669]   OF NEW-ENGLAND.   103

England to turn the edge against those who, if not prevented, will certainly corrupt and enslave, not only their own, but also your churches? Whereas Anabaptists are neither spirited nor principled to injure nor hurt your government nor your liberties; but rather these be the means to preserve your churches from apostacy, and to provoke them to their primitive purity, as they were in the first planting; in admission of members to receive none into your churches but visible saints, and in restoring the entire jurisdiction of every congregation complete and undisturbed. We are hearty and full for our Presbyterian brethren's equal liberty with ourselves; oh that they had the same spirit towards us! But oh how it grieves and affects us, that New-England should persecute! Will you not give what you take? Is liberty of conscience your due? And is it not as due unto others who are sound in the faith? Amongst many scriptures, that in the fourteenth of Romans much confirms me in liberty of conscience thus stated. To him that esteemeth any thing unclean, to him it is unclean. Therefore though we approve of the baptism of the immediate children of church members, and of their admission into the church when they evidence a real work of grace; yet to those who in conscience believe the said baptism to be unclean, it is unclean. Both that and mere ruling elders, though we approve of them, yet our grounds are mere interpretations of, and not any express scripture. I cannot say so clearly of anything else in our religion, neither as to faith or practice. Now must we force our interpretations upon others, pope like? How do you cast a reproach upon us who are congregational in England, and furnish our adversaries with weapons against us! We blush and are filled with shame and confusion of face, when we hear of these things. Dear brother, we pray that God would open your eyes,

104   A CHURCH HISTORY   [Ch. V.

and persuade the hearts of your magistrates, that they may no more smite their fellow servants, nor thus greatly injure us their brethren, and that they may not thus dishonour the name of God. My dear brother, pardon me, for I am affected; I speak for God, to whose grace I commend you all in New-England; and humbly craving your prayers for us here, and remain your affectionate brother,
ROBERT MASCALL."

Finsbury, near Morefield,
        March 25, 1669.

        This was copied by Mr. Samuel Hubbard, from whence I took it. Dr. Goodwin, Dr. Owen, and ten other ministers wrote to the Massachusetts rulers the same day, in a moving manner, and said, "We are sure you would be unwilling to put an advantage into the hands of some, who seek pretences and occasions against our liberty, and to reinforce the former rigour. Now we cannot deny but this hath already in some measure been done, in that it hath been vogued, that persons of your way, principles and spirit, cannot bear with dissenters from them. And as this greatly reflects upon us, so some of us have observed how already it has turned to your own disadvantage." Yet Dr. Mather says, "I cannot say that this excellent letter had immediately all the effect it should have had."* So that they were imprisoned about a year, because they would not voluntarily go out of that jurisdiction. And the year after, six magistrates gave a warrant to take up Gould and Turner again, and Turner was actually put in prison upon the old sentence, and lay there a long time; but Gould went and lived and preached upon Noddle's island in the harbour, where they did not

* Magnalia, B. 7. p 27, 28.

1669]   OF NEW-ENGLAND.   105

pursue him. For a great many rulers and others abhorred such conduct. But we must now take a review of other things.

When the rulers of the Massachusetts yielded to the order of Parliament about Warwick, they were far from giving up their designs upon the lands in Providence colony. They claimed much of the west part of it, because of the Pequot conquest; and in 1657 and 1658, they sent men and got deeds of much land in the heart of the Narraganset country. The Narraganset Indians were also so uneasy about the death of their great sachem Miantenimo, that they often attempted to revenge his death, but were overpowered by forces sent, once and again, from the Massachusetts; and in 1660, they compelled those Indians to mortgage all their lands to them, for what they said was due to the Massachusetts. And because two Baptist brethren, Tobias Sanders and Robert Burdick, went to work upon lands which they had procured from their government in Westerly, they were imprisoned by the Massachusetts in 1662, who then wrote to the rulers of Providence colony about it, as appears by the records of both colonies. In the mean time, Mr. Winthrop went over to England, and obtained a charter, dated April 23, 1662, which united Connecticut and New-Haven in one colony. Their eastern boundary was described to be "By the Narraganset river, commonly called Narraganset Bay, where said river falleth into the sea." And by this general description they claimed the Narraganset country. For when the commissioners of the United colonies met at Boston in September, they wrote to the rulers of Providence colony, and mentioned this charter to Connecticut, which they said, "Granted the lands at Pawcatuck and Narraganset, which we hope will prevail with you to require and cause your people to withdraw themselves, and desist from further disturbance."

106   A CHURCH HISTORY   [CH. V.

Now they should have remembered, that in 1643, they interpreted the Narraganset river, the western boundary of Plymouth colony, so as to include the lands where Gorton was settled; and all that the Massachusetts did to him was founded upon that interpretation, which supposed Pawcatuck to be the western boundary of Plymouth colony. Yet now they would claim all the Narraganset country by Connecticut charter. What great blindness was here! And it was soon discovered by the chapter which Mr. Clark procured for his colony, dated July 8, 1663, which said, "Pawcatuck river shall be also called, alias, Narraganset river; and to prevent future disputes that otherwise might arise thereby forever hereafter, shall be construed, deemed and taken to be the Narraganset river, in the late grant to Connecticut colony, mentioned as the eastwardly bounds of that colony." Yet they were so resolute that it should not be so, that they proposed to send an agent over to England, to get that line altered. Upon which Mr. Williams wrote to Connecticut rulers, and said,

"It looks like a prodigy or monster, that countrymen among savages in a wilderness; that professors of God and one Mediator, of an eternal life, and that this is like a dream, should not be content with those vast large tracts which all the other colonies have (like platters and tables full of dainties) but pull and snatch away their poor neighbour's bit or crust; and a crust it is, and a dry hard one too, because of the natives continual troubles, trials and vexations." And as to claims from the Pequot conquest, he said, "Having ocular knowledge of persons, places, and transactions, I did honestly and conscientiously, as in the holy presence of God, draw up from Pawcatuck river, which I then believed and still do is free from all English claims and conquests. For although there were some Pequots on this side the river, who by reason of some

1670.]   OF NEW-ENGLAND.   107

sachem's marriages with some on this side, lived in a kind of neutrality with both sides; yet upon the breaking out of the war, they relinquished their land to the possession of their enemies the Narragansets and Nyanticks, and their land never came into the condition of the lands on the other side, which the English by conquest challenged: so that I must affirm, as in God's holy presence, I tenderly waved to touch a foot of land in which I knew the Pequot wars were maintained, and were properly Pequot, being a gallant country. And from Pawcatuck river hitherward, being but a patch of ground, full of troublesome inhabitants, I did, as I judged inoffensively, draw our poor and inconsiderable line." And he says of their second charter, "Mr. Winthrop, upon some mistake, had intrenched upon our line, and it is said upon the lines of other charters also; but upon Mr. Clarke's complaint, your grant was called in again, and it had never been returned, but upon a report that the agents, Mr. Winthrop and Mr. Clarke, were agreed by mediation of friends; and it is true they came to a solemn agreement under hands and seals, which agreement was never violated on our part."*

This letter was dated June 22, 1670. And though the case was not then carried again to England, yet this fine was not settled in fifty years after. But in 1720, Governor Jenks was sent over as agent upon this controversy, and it was settled in 1729, the line to be Pawcatuck river. And in 1741, their easterly line was settled, which gave their colony Littlecompton, Tiverton, Bristol, Warren, Barrington, and Cumberland, which they had not enjoyed before. Thus all the lands, and all the liberties that were asked for by Mr. Williams and Mr. Clarke, were finally obtained in that colony, though others exerted all their powers against

* Historical Society, vol. 1. p. 278–280.

108   A CHURCH HISTORY   [Ch. V.

it. And these things give great encouragement to all who may come after us, to perseverance in right ways, and a warning against all injustice and oppression.

Mr. Williams had also another difficulty now to encounter, in which he was successful. Though Mr. Coddington, and other men of note, submitted to his government in 1656, yet as they soon joined with the Quakers, they refused to be active in that government. Their plea was, that they were obliged in conscience to refrain from taking any oath. Therefore the form of an engagement to the government was enacted for them in 1665, which it was hoped they would take; but in March, 1666, they objected against it, and prevailed with their Assembly to make a law to allow them to make their submission in their own words, either before the court or before two magistrates. And then they were as fond of being rulers as any men, and Mr. Nicholas Easton was Governor in 1672 and '73, and Mr. Coddington in 1674 and '75, who were then Quakers. And as Williams believed that their principles were hurtful to government, as well as dangerous to the souls of men, and George Fox and other teachers of theirs were come over, he wrote fourteen propositions upon the subject, and sent them to Newport, proposing to Fox or his friends, to hold a dispute upon seven of them at Newport, and upon the other seven at Providence, upon any days that they should appoint.

Fox then sailed for England, but John Stubs, John Burnyeat, and William Edmondson undertook it; and Williams held, a dispute with them in August, 1672, three days at Newport, and one at Providence. And he wrote a large account of it, which was printed at Cambridge, 1676; and soon after it came out, several of the Quakers were left out of office. Upon this, Mr. Coddington sent the book over to Fox, with a bitter letter against

1672.] OF NEW-ENGLAND. 109

Williams, and he with Burnyeat wrote a reply, which they called, "A New-England firebrand quenched." And it was printed in England, in 1678.

Mr. Williams dedicated his book to them, wherein he said, "From my childhood, now above threescore years, the Father of lights and mercies touched my soul with the love of himself, to his only Begotten Son, the true Lord Jesus, to his holy Scriptures, &c. His infinite wisdom hath given me to see the city, court and country, the schools and universities of my native country, to converse with some Turks, Jews, Papists, and all sorts of Protestants; and by books to know the affairs and religions of all countries. My conclusion is, that *Be of good cheer, thy sins are forgiven thee*, Mat. ix. 2, is one of the joyfullest sounds that ever came to poor sinful ears. How to obtain this sound from the mouth of the Mediator who spoke it, is the greatest dispute between the Protestants and the bloody whore of Rome; and this is also the greatest point between the Protestants and yourselves, as also, in order to this, about what the true Lord Jesus Christ is."

They were so much upon what Christ did within them, that he says George Fox, in a former book, "cannot endure to hear the word *human*, as being a new name and never heard of in Scripture. Fox knows, that if Christ Jesus be granted to have had such a soul and body as is human or common to man, down falls their Dagon before the ark of God, viz. their idol of a Christ called light within them."* To which it was answered, "There is no such word that calleth Christ's body and soul *human*; and whether is Christ's body celestial or terrestrial."†

And this opinion prevailed so much at Newport, that Mr. Clarke and his church, after much labour,

* Williams, p. 51. † Fox, p. 43.

110 A CHURCH HISTORY [CH. V.

excluded three men and two women from their communion, October 16, 1673, for holding "That the man Christ Jesus was not now in heaven nor earth, nor any where else, but that his body was entirely lost." This Mr. Comer says he took from their records. Such was their language then, let it be altered ever so much since. And as to government, Fox published a book in 1659, in which he said, "that the magistrate of Christ, the help government for him, he is in the light and power of Christ; and he is to subject all under the power of Christ, into his light, else he is not a faithful magistrate; and his laws are agreeable, and answerable according to that of God in every man."* Williams brought this to prove that their spirit was arbitrary and persecuting; but Fox said, "Is there one word of persecution here? or can Roger Williams think himself a Christian, and look upon it to be persecution, for Christ's magistrates by Christ's light and power, to subjected all under the power of Christ, and to bring all into this light of Christ? or can he think such an one an unfaithful magistrate? or are those laws, and the execution of them persecution, that are agreeable and answerable to that of God in every man? These are George Fox's words. Such magistrates, such laws, such power and light and subjection, is George Fox for, and no other."†

And as two women had appeared as naked as they were born, before many people, the one at Salem and the other at Newbury, and had been whipt for it, which George Bishop called persecution, Williams mentioned it, and that he thought persons must be bewitched to call this persecution. But Fox said, "We do believe thee, in that dark, persecuting, bloody spirit, that thou and the New-England priests are bewitched in, you cannot be-

* Williams, p. 207, 208.　　　　† Fox, p. 229, 230.

1673.]　　　　　　OF NEW-ENGLAND.　　　　　111

lieve that you are naked from God and his clothing, and blind; and therefore hath the Lord in his power moved some of his sons and daughters to go naked; yea, they did tell them in OLIVER'S days, and the long Parliament's, that God would strip them of their church profession and of their power, as naked as they were. And so they were true prophets and prophetesses to the nation, as many sober men have confessed since; though thou and the old persecuting priests in New-England remain in your blindness and nakedness."*

And through their book they called him a cruel persecutor for disputing against their principles and behaviour, while he abhorred the use of any force against them on that account. And having obtained his end in the dispute, he never troubled them or himself any more about it.

But the dispute about baptism was again brought up in the Massachusetts. Mr. John Devenport had published his testimony against the result of the synod of 1662, which allowed persons to bring their children to baptism, who were not fit to come to the Lord's supper themselves; and as a majority of the first church in Boston were of his mind, they obtained him for their pastor, soon after Mr. Wilson died. But a minor part of the church were for the new scheme, and they separated from the majority, pleading that Mr. Devenport had no right to leave his people at New-Haven, in order to be a minister in Boston. And in May, 1669, a number of ministers assisted in forming the minor party into another church; and in July Governor Bellingham called his council together, fearing, he said, "A sudden tumult, some persons attempting to set up an edifice for public worship, which he apprehended to be detrimental to the public peace." But the majority of his council voted to let them

* Fox, p. 9.

112   A CHURCH HISTORY   [CH. V.

go on; though a hot contention about it continued through the year. And in May, 1670, the house of Representatives chose a committee to inquire into the causes of God's displeasure against this land; and they reported that they were, "declension from the primitive foundation work, innovations in doctrine and worship, opinion and practice; an invasion of the rights, liberties and privileges of churches, an usurpation of a lordly and prelatical power over God's heritage, subversion of gospel order, &c." And the acting of the ministers who formed said new church they called, "irregular, illegal, and disorderly." But of fifty members who were in their next house, there were but twenty of these; and they declared against what the others had done.* Such was the influence of ministers in that day. And in May, 1682, Edward Randolph, who was trying to get away their charter, wrote to England, and said, "there was a great difference betwixt the old church and the members of the new church, about baptism and their members joining in full communion with either church: This was so high that there was imprisoning of parties and great disturbances; but now, hearing of my proposals for ministers to be sent over, they are now joined together, about a fortnight ago, and pray to God to confound the devices of all who disturb their peace and liberties."† That new church is since called the Old South.

Whilst Mr. Clarke was in England, a new Baptist church was formed out of the first church in Newport, holding to the laying on of hands upon every member after baptism, about the year 1656, which was the third Baptist church in America, and is still continued by succession. And as other colonies were then trying to draw his colony into vi-

* Hutchinson, vol. 1. p. 272–274.
† His Collections, p. 532.

1673.]   OF NEW-ENGLAND.   113

olent measures against the Quakers, the Legislature of Rhode Island colony wrote to Mr. Clarke and said, "We have found, not only your ability and diligence, but also your love and care to be such concerning the welfare and prosperity of this colony, since you have been entrusted with the more public affairs thereof, surpassing the no small benefit which we had of your presence here at home, that we in all straits and incumbrances, are emboldened to repair to you for further and continued care, counsel and help; finding that your solid and Christian demeanor hath gotten no small interest in the hearts of our superiors, those noble and worthy senators, with whom you had to do in our behalf, as it hath constantly appeared in our addresses to them, we have by good and comfortable proof found, having had plentiful experience thereof." And so they went on to entreat him to use all his influence in their favour, that they might not be compelled to persecute the Quakers, and he succeeded therein. This was dated, November 5, 1658, the month after the law was made at Boston to banish them on pain of death.

Mr. Clarke continued their agent in England, until he obtained the charter from the king which I mentioned before, to procure which he mortgaged his farm in Newport, willing to venture his estate in so good a cause. He came over to Newport in 1664, and their assembly voted to pay him for all his expenses, in obtaining their charter and other ways, and to give him a considerable reward for his services; but it was a long time before they paid him only for his expenses in their service.

From that time he continued the pastor of the first church in Newport, until he died in peace. A small church was formed out of that, in December, 1671, holding to the seventh day sabbath, which yet continues. This made the sixth Baptist church

114   A CHURCH HISTORY   [CH. V.

in America. Mr. Clarke left a confession of his faith in writing, in which he said,

"The decree of God is that whereby he hath from eternity set down with himself what shalt come to pass in time, Eph. i. 11. All things, with their causes, effects, circumstances, and manner of being, are decreed by God. Acts ii. 23. Him being delivered by the determinate counsel and foreknowledge of God, &c. Acts iv. 28. This decree is most wise. Rom. xi. 33. Most just. Rom. ix. 13, 14. Eternal. Ep. i. 4, 5. 2 Thess. ii. 13. Necessary. Psalm xxxiii. 11. Prov. xix. 21. Unchangeable. Heb. vi. 17. Most free. Rom. ix. 18. And the cause of all good. James i. 17. But not of any sin. 1 John i. 5. The special decree of God concerning angels and men is called predestination. Rom. viii. 30. Of the former, viz. angels, little is spoken in the holy Scriptures; of the latter more is revealed, not unprofitable to be known. It may be defined the wise, free, just, eternal and unchangeable sentence or decree of God, determining to create and govern men for his special glory, viz. the praise of his glorious mercy and justice. Rom. ix. 17, 18. and xi. 36. Election is the decree of God, of his free love, grace and mercy, choosing some men to faith, holiness, and eternal life, for the praise of his glorious mercy. 1 Thess. i. 4. 2 Thess. ii. 13. Rom. viii. 29, 30. The cause which moved the Lord to elect them who are chosen was none other but his mere good will and pleasure. Luke xii. 32. The end is the manifestation of the riches of his grace and mercy. Rom. ix. 23. Eph. i. 6. The sending of Christ, faith, holiness and eternal life, are the effects of his love, by which he manifesteth the infinite riches of his grace. In the same order God doth execute this decree in time, he did decree it in his eternal counsel. 1. Thess. v. 9. 2 Thess. ii. 13. Sin is the effect of man's free will, and condemnation is an effect of justice inflicted

1673.]   OF NEW-ENGLAND.   115

upon man for sin and disobedience. A man in this life may be sure of his election. 2 Peter i. 10. 1 Thess. i. 4. Yea, of his eternal happiness, but not of his eternal reprobation; for he that is now profane, may be called hereafter."

This faith, which was also held by Mr. Williams, moved them to spend their lives for the welfare of mankind, and to establish the first government upon earth, since the rise of antichrist, which gave equal liberty, civil and religious, to all men therein. Though many have imagined, that because the leaders of the Massachusetts professed this faith, that it was inconsistent with the allowance of equal privileges to all mankind. Therefore I thought it best here to save a view of the faith of these men, who were persecuted by the Massachusetts, because they thought that good men ought

CHURCH HISTORY OF NEW ENGLAND

to enforce their faith with the sword. But this last opinion should ever bear the blame of all the injuries which they did to others, and not the faith above described.

Mr. Clarke was influenced so much by faith and love, that through many changes, and doing of public business, both in Europe and America, I have never found one blemish upon his character, noticed in any record or writing that I ever saw. In the laff day of his life, he said,

"Whereas I John Clarke of Newport, in the colony of Rhode Island and Providence Plantations, in New-England, physician, am at this present, through the abundant goodness and mercy of my God, though weak in body, yet sound in my memory and understanding, and being sensible of the inconveniences that may ensue in case I should not set my house in order, before this spirit of mine be called by the Lord to remove out of this tabernacle, do therefore make and declare this my last will and testament, in manner following: willingly and readily resigning up my soul unto my merciful Redeemer, through faith in whose death I firmly hope

116   A CHURCH HISTORY   [CH. V.

and believe to escape from that second hurting death, and through his resurrection and life, to be glorified with him in life eternal. And my spirit being returned out of this frail body, in which it hath conversed for about sixty-six years, my will is that it be decently interred, without any vain ostentation, between my loving wives, Elizabeth and Jane, already deceased, in hopeful expectation, that the same Redeemer who hath laid down a price both for my soul and body, will raise it up at the last day a spiritual one, that they may together be singing hallelujah unto him to all eternity."* O how glorious is such an end!

* Taken from his original will, dated April 20, 1676; and he left our world the same day. His first wife was Elizabeth Harges, who had an annual income of twenty pounds sterling, from lands left her in Bedfordshire. In a power of attorney to recover it, given May 12, 1656, he styled himself John Clarke, physician of London. She died at Newport, without issue; and he married Jane Fletcher in February, 1671, by whom he had a daughter; but they both died in 1672. His third wife was the widow Sarah Davis, who survived him, and he gave her the use of his farm in Newport, during her natural life, and then the income of it was to go to the poor, and to support civil and religious teaching. It has produced 200 dollars a year, and it has thus been a public benefit ever since. His brother Joseph Clarke was sometimes a

magistrate in their government, and he was a member of the first church in Newport, above forty years; and his posterity are numerous and respectable unto this day.

1676.]   OF NEW-ENGLAND.   117

CHAP. VI.

A terrible Indian war.—It prevailed most in the Massachusetts.—Some whom they had employed against Providence colony, revenge themselves on their employers.—But the Baptist sufferers now overcame evil with good, and the war was closed.—Many Christian Indians never joined in it.—Two Baptist churches formed among them, and others in our days.—More severities against the Baptists.—Their house for worship nailed up in Boston, and writings against them, which they answered.—Death of some of their ministers.—The Massachusetts charter vacated.—Then same of their eyes were opened to see their errors.

WE are now come to the time when they had the most terrible war with the Indians, that ever was known in this part of the country. And in it there appeared a vast difference between the Indians who had been well treated before, and those who had been treated injuriously. The execution of the great sachem of the Narragansets, after he had been taken captive, and then delivered up to the English, raised such a spirit of resentment among them, that they often attempted to revenge his death. And such danger of their doing it appeared in 1645, that the colony raised an army against them, when an instruction to their General said, "You are to use your best endeavours to gain the enemies' canoes, or utterly to destroy them; and herein you may make good use of the Indians our confederates, as you may do upon other occasions, having due regard to the honour of God, who is both our sword and shield, and to the *distance* which is to be observed betwixt Christians and barbarians, as well in wars as in other negotiations."*

* Hutchinson's Collections, p. 151.

118   A CHURCH HISTORY   [CH.VI.

And though fear of gunpowder, want of union among themselves, and the want of an able leader, suspended the war for many years, yet it now came on terribly.

Philip, a son and successor to old Massassoit, had been preparing for it for several years; and because it was discovered to the English, by one of his friends, that friend was murdered in Middleborough, and the murderers were taken and executed at Plymouth. Upon this the war broke out immediately, and nine men were killed in Swansea, June 24, 1675, and the alarm was given; and an army both from Boston and Plymouth met there in four days, and made their head-quarters at the house of Mr. Miles, the Baptist minister of Swansea. Philip soon fled from his station at Mount Hope, now Bristol, over to the east side of the great river. And upon this the Massachusetts army marched into the Narraganset country, and brought the Indians there to promise not to join with Philip, and then they returned, and joined with Plymouth forces to fight against him. But he soon came back over the river, and made his way up into Worcester county, where some English were killed in July, as Captain Hutchinson and others were on August 2, near Brookfield. Major Willard then marched up and relieved that town, upon which the Indians went further westward, and burnt most of the houses in Deerfield, September 1, and Northfield a few days after, when one Captain and about twenty men were slain. And on September 18, as Captain Lothrop went with his company to guard some teams, in bringing off grain from Deerfield, they were surprised by the Indians, who slew him and more than seventy of his men. Deerfield was then deserted, and thirty houses were burnt in Springfield, and some men slain there. On October 19, Hatfield was assaulted by

1676.]   OF NEW-ENGLAND.   119

many Indians, but they were bravely repulsed, and many of them retired into Narraganset.

Upon a small tract of upland, within a large swamp in that country, they had built and stored the strongest fort that they ever had in these parts. Therefore the colonies raised an army of a thousand men, under General Winslow, and destroyed it on December 19, with great stores of provision, and many hundreds of the enemy; but with the loss of six English Captains, and 170, some said 210 men killed or wounded. A terrible storm of snow made the case much more distressing. And as much provision was destroyed in that fort, the Indians were greatly distressed, and many perished; but a great thaw in January, 1676, enabled them to get some food out of the ground, and they again went up northward, and burnt the deserted houses in Mendon, and made an onset upon Lancaster, February 10, burning their houses, and killed or captivated forty persons, of whom Mrs. Rowlandson, wife to the minister, was one, who published an account of her captivity. Similar mischiefs were done at Groton, Malborough, Sudbury, and Chelmsford; and on February 21, they came down upon Medfield, but twenty miles from Boston, and burnt many houses, and killed eighteen men. On the 25th they did damage at Weymouth, still nearer to Boston. On March 12, they took Clarke's garrison in Plymouth, killing several persons; and on the next day they burnt all Groton to the ground, so that the place was deserted for some time. In the same month they burnt many houses in Warwick, Providence and Rehoboth. And on March 26, near Patucket river, Captain Pierce engaged with a body of Indians, who proved to be more than he expected, when he and near sixty of his men were cut off, though it was said they slew 140 Indians. And the western part of the Massachusetts was now in great dis-

120   A CHURCH HISTORY   [CH. VI.

tress, so that new forces were raised to help them.

William Turner, and other Baptists, who had suffered from the rulers of the government, were as ready to lend a helping hand against the common enemy, as any among them. He had offered his service in the beginning of the war, but it was not then accepted; but now he was called forth, and made Captain of a company, and his brother Drinker Lieutenant, and the company were mainly Baptists, who marched up in the beginning of this month, with others, and drove off the enemy from Northampton, March 14. Many of the enemy then came down the country again, and did much mischief as before described, and they also killed Captain Wadsworth and about thirty of his men at Sudbury, April 18. Most of the western forces were now come down the country, and Captain Turner was left the chief commander above.

Upon this the enemy felt more secure, and seven or eight hundred of them resorted to the great falls above Deerfield upon the fishing design. Two captive lads made their escape, and informed how secure the Indians were, upon which Captain Turner and Captain Holyoke collected about an hundred and seventy men, and went up silently in the night, and tied their horses at some distance, and a little before break of day, May 18, came upon them unawares, "fired into their very wigwams, killing many upon the place, and frighting others with the sudden alarm of their guns, made them run into the river, where the swiftness of the stream carried them down a steep fall, and they perished in the waters; some getting into canoes were sunk or overset by the shooting of our men; others creeping under the bank of the river, were

CHURCH HISTORY OF NEW ENGLAND

espied by our men and killed with their swords. Some of their prisoners owned afterwards that

1676.] OF NEW-ENGLAND. 121

they lost above three hundred men, some of them their best fighting men that were left. Nor did they seem ever to recover themselves after this defeat, but their ruin followed directly upon it." When they were first fired upon, they cried out Mohawks! but when they discovered their mistake in the morning, they rallied their forces, and Captain Turner being unwell, and not able to guide their retreat so agreeably, 38 men fell, of whom he was one, who was afterwards found and buried.* All the rest of the Baptists were spared and returned.

Captain Benjamin Church of Duxborough, in Plymouth colony, carried his family on to Rhode Island in the beginning of the war, and he was very serviceable therein. And as he knew that the Sokonet Indians were forced into the war by Philip, he ventured over among them in June, 1676, and gained them over to the English, to fight against Philip, and they were very successful from day to day, until they killed him at Mount Hope, August 12, 1676, after which peace was soon restored in these parts.†

This summary of that cruel war is collected from a variety of histories and accounts. Connecticut forces were very helpful in the war, and they lost three captains at the Narraganset fort; namely, Gallop, Seily and Marshal, and a number of their men; but they had scarce any damage done in any of their towns, while they and the Mohegan Indians did great exploits in the war. It began in Plymouth colony, where a few men were killed, and Captain Pierce was of their colony. But the Massachusetts lost eight captains, viz. Hutchinson, Beers, Lothrop, Devenport, Gardner, Johnson,

* Hubbard's History, p. 157–161.
† Pumham, before spoken of, was killed a few days before Philip.

122 A CHURCH HISTORY [CH. VI.

Wadsworth and Turner, and a great many men. And the towns of Northfield, Deerfield, Brookfield, Mendon, Lancaster and Groton, were all broken up for some years; and they lost a vast deal of property.

Mr. John Eliot, of Roxbury, had begun to teach Christianity to some Indians about 1646, and Mr. Winslow, their agent in England, obtained a charter from the Parliament in 1649, to incorporate a society to promote that work; and Eliot learned the Indian language, and translated the Bible into it, which passed one edition in 1664, and another in 1684, with some other books. Mr. Daniel Gookin, a magistrate and a Major General in their government, was also his helper in the affair; and they had formed twelve praying societies among the Indians before this war, some of them as high up the country as Dudley and Woodstock; but they were all scattered in the war, and many of their praying Indians became bloody enemies, and were slain in the war, or hanged after it at Boston. Those that remained were afterwards collected by Mr. Eliot into four societies; but they are all dissolved since.

But the Indians on Cape Cod, and on the islands south of it, scarce any of them ever joined in the war against the English. They had not only been treated in a friendly manner, but much pains had also been taken to teach them Christianity. Mr. Richard Bourn engaged in that work as early as 1658, and in 1670 he was ordained the pastor of a church among them, by the assistance of Mr. Eliot and others. And in 1674, he wrote to Major Gookin, that upon and near the Cape there were seven praying societies among the Indians, of whom an hundred and forty could read, and some of them could write. Marshpee, between Sandwich and Barnstable, was the greatest feat of them; and a religious society has continued there ever since, and a Baptist church was formed and organized among them in 1797.

1676.] OF NEW-ENGLAND. 123

Mr. Thomas Mayhew obtained a grant of Martha's Vineyard, and went to live there in 16423 where he was the chief ruler of the English inhabitants, and his son Thomas was their minister. And about 1646 he began to preach to the Indians on the island; and to promote the cause, his father informed them, that by an order from the crown of England he was to govern the English who should inhabit there; that his royal master had power far above the Indian monarchs, but that as he was great and powerful, so he was a lover of justice, and would not invade their jurisdiction, but would assist them if need required; that religion and government were two distinct things, and their sachems might retain their just authority, though their subjects became Christians. And he practised accordingly, and would not suffer any to injure them, either in goods or lands. They always found a father and protector in him; and he was so far from introducing any form of government among them against their wills, that he first convinced them of the advantage of it, and even brought them to desire him to introduce and settle it. And a Christian church was formed among them in 1659, in which four officers were ordained in 1670, by Mr. Eliot and others. And they had soon two churches on the Vineyard, and one on Nantucket. Old Mr. Mayhew said in 1674, "There are ten Indian preachers, of good knowledge and holy conversation; seven jurisdictions, and six meetings every Lord's day." So many were on the Vineyard, beside a church at Nantucket.

And when the war came on the next year, the Christian Indians were furnished with arms and ammunition to defend the islands against the enemy; and they were so faithful therein, that when any landed to solicit them to join in the war, though some were related by blood and others by marriage, yet the islanders directly brought them

124   A CHURCH HISTORY   [CH. VI.

before the Governor to attend his pleasure. And by a divine blessing on these means, though the Indians on the island were twenty to one of the English, yet they lived in peace and security through all that dreadful war on the main land. Young Mr. Mayhew had sailed for England, in 1657, and was lost at sea, but he left Peter Folger a school-master among the Indians; and he removed to Nantucket about four years after, and taught them there. He became a Baptist, and there was a Baptist church formed among the Indians on the Vineyard, and another at Nantucket, by 1693.* That on the Vineyard continues to this day, but the Indians are nearly all dead on Nantucket. Peter Folger was grandfather to the famous Dr. Benjamin Franklin.

Ninagret, sachem of the south part of the Narragansets, did not join in that war, and their successors have continued there in Charlestown; and in and after 1741, many of them were hopefully converted, and a Baptist church was formed among them, which still remains, though many of them have removed up to the Oneida country. Also in 1741, many of the Mohegans were happily changed, of whom Samsom Occum was one; but many of them have removed also to said Oneida country.

As ministers and rulers were still earnest to keep up the power of the church over the world, so they could not do it without oppressing the Baptists, who increased considerably. Hence their law to banish them was reprinted in 1672; and they were often fined or imprisoned. Mr. William Hubbard, who preached their election sermon at Boston, May 3, 1676, said, "It is made, by learned and judicious writers, one of the undoubted rights of sovereignty to determine what religion shall be

* Magnalia, B. 6. p. 56. Appendix to Mayhew's Indian converts, p. 291–296. Historical Society, vol. 1. p. 168–207. vol. 3. p. 189, 190.

1677.] OF NEW-ENGLAND. 125

publicly professed and exercised within their dominions. Why else do we in New-England, that profess the doctrine of Calvin yet practise the discipline of them called Independent or Congregational churches, but because the authority of the country is persuaded that is most agreeable to the mind of God?"* But why did they and their fathers dissent from the church of England? In a dedication of his sermon to their rulers, he said, "If he was not mistaken who said, it is morally impossible to rivet the Christian religion into the body of a nation without infant baptism, by proportion it will necessarily follow, that the neglect or disuse thereof will directly tend to root it out." But this was spoken with a view that good men should ever have the government in their hands.

Hence when Dr. Increase Mather preached their election sermon, May 23, 1677, he referred to Mr. Cotton, who said, "The Lord keep us from being bewitched with the whore's cup, lest whilst we seem to detest and reject her with open face of profession, we do not bring her in by the back door of toleration."† And Mather said, "I believe that antichrist hath not at this day a more probable way to advance his kingdom of darkness, than by a toleration of all religions and persuasions."‡ This he reprinted with other sermons, in 1685, after their charter was taken away. But he suffered so much directly after, that he and others got such a toleration established in Boston in 1693, though they could not get it extended through the country. For fifty years before they lost their charter, no man had a vote for their ministers or rulers, but communicants in their churches; but under their second charter, the wicked had as much power in their government as the righteous, which discovered the

* Said Sermon, p. 35.
† Tenet washed, p. 192.
‡ His Sermons, p. 106.

126 A CHURCH HISTORY [CH. VI.

necessity of a toleration; though their present views were such, as prevented their seeing it.

In September, 1679, Mather was scribe of a synod that was called to give their opinion about what were the causes of the judgments of God upon the land; and in their result they said, "Men have set up their thresholds by

CHURCH HISTORY OF NEW ENGLAND

God's thresholds, and their polls by his polls. Quakers are false worshippers, and such Anabaptists as have risen up among us, in opposition to the churches of the Lord Jesus, receiving into their society those who have been for scandal delivered unto Satan; yea, and improving those as administrators of holy things, who have been (as doth appear) justly under censure, do no better than set up altars against the Lord's altar." And their result was approved by their General Court.*

Upon the coming out of this, from the highest authority in the country, the Baptists carefully reviewed their past conduct, and they found but four men who were censured by Congregational churches, before they received them into their church, and one of them was of Dr. Mather's church, which served to raise his resentment. They therefore sent and obtained copies of their dealings with him, which discovered that the member got angry when the church was dealing with him, and spake and acted in a wrong manner. Upon which the Baptists obliged him to offer satisfaction to that church, which he did both by word and by writing; but as his principles were inconsistent with a returning into their communion, they would not revoke their censure.†

This Baptist church had increased so much, that in February, 1677, they concluded to divide into two churches; but in January, 1678, they agreed to build them a meeting-house in Boston, and not

* Magnalia, B. 5. p. 87–89.
† Russel's Narrative, p. 8.   Willard's Answer, p. 21.

1679.]   OF NEW-ENGLAND.   127

to divide till they could get a minister settled there. Mr. Miles of Swansea had often preached to them, and they requested him to become their pastor, and for Mr. John Russell to supply his place in Swansea. But he returned home, and Mr. Russell was ordained in Boston, July 28, 1679. They built their house for worship so cautiously, as not to let others know what it was designed for, until they met in it, February 15, 1679. But in May following, a law was made to take it from them, if they continued to meet in it; therefore they refrained from it for a while. News of that law was sent to England, from whence the king wrote to the rulers here, July 24, 1679, and said, "We shall henceforth expect that there shall be suitable obedience in respect of freedom and liberty of conscience, so as those that desire to serve God in the way of the church of England, be not thereby made obnoxious or discountenanced from sharing in the government, much less that any other of our good subjects (not being papists) who do not agree in the Congregational way, be by law subjected to fines or forfeitures, or other incapacities, for the same; which is a severity the more to be wondered at, whereas liberty of conscience was made one principal motive for your first transportation into those parts."*

Some friends in London informed the Baptists of this, upon which they met in their house again, but their chief leaders were brought before the court of Assistants for it, in March, 1680; and because they would not promise not to meet there again, the court sent an officer, who nailed up the doors of their house, and forbid their meeting there any more upon their peril, without leave from court. Not long after the house was opened by an unknown hand, and they met there till May, when

* Hutchinson's Collections, p. 520.

128   A CHURCH HISTORY   [Ch. VI.

The Baptists were convented before the General Court at Boston, and pleaded that their house was built when there was no law against it, and the king had now written in their favour. But the Court only forgave what was past, and forbid their meeting there any more. In the March before, Dr. Increase Mather published a pamphlet against the Baptists in general, and against those in Boston in particular. And in May Mr. Russell wrote an answer to what he had said against their character, and it was printed in London the same year, with a preface signed by William Kiffen, Hansard Knollys, Daniel Dyke, William Collins, John Harris and Nehemiah Coxe, noted Baptist ministers. And they said therein, "It seems most strange that our Congregational brethren in New-England, who with liberal estates, chose rather to depart from their native soil into a wilderness, than to be under the lash of those who upon religious pretences took delight to smite their fellow-servants; should exercise towards others the like severity that themselves with so great hazard and hardship sought to avoid; especially considering that it is against their brethren, who profess and appeal to the same rule with themselves for their guidance in the worship of God, and the ordering their whole conversation." And they observed that persecutors in England then tried to justify themselves by these severities in America.

In 1681, Mr. Willard of Boston wrote an answer to Russell, and Dr. Mather wrote a preface to it, in which he said, "I would entreat the brethren who have subscribed the epistle to consider that the place may sometimes make a great alteration as to indulgence to be expected. It is evident that such toleration is not only lawful in one place, but a necessary duty, which would be destructive in another place. That which is needful to ballast a great ship, will sink a small boat." From whence

1682.] OF NEW-ENGLAND. 129

we may learn, that it was their weakness and not their strength, which caused them to be so hard with their Baptist brethren. For the extending of baptism to infants in a state of nature, and supporting their worship by force, in the name of their king, who forbid it, was indeed weak business.

Mr. John Russell, pastor of the Baptist church in Boston, died there December 21, 1680, much lamented, and his posterity are respectable among us to this day. Elder Isaac Hull was still living, but he was aged and infirm. Therefore the church wrote to London, June 27, 1681, and said, "We conceive that there is a prospect of good encouragement for an able minister to come over; in that there seems to be an apparent and general apostacy among the churches who have professed themselves Congregational in this land; whereby many have their eyes opened, by seeing the declensions and confusion that is among them." To this they received a kind answer, dated October 13, 1681, signed by William Kiffen, Hansard Knollys, Daniel Dyke, William Collins, Nehemiah Coxe, Edward Williams, William Dix, Robert Snelling, Tobias Russell, Maurice King, and John Skinner. And on July 20, 1684, they received John Emblen from England, who became their pastor for about fifteen years, until his death.

Elder Thomas Olney was pastor of the Baptist church in Providence, for above forty years, till he died in 1682, leaving a good character, and his posterity are numerous to this day. Obadiah Holmes was pastor of the first church in Newport, from soon after Mr. Clarke's death, until he died, October 15, 1682, aged 76, and his posterity are now large, in New-England and New-Jersey.

By assistance from Boston, a Baptist church was formed at Kittery, in the Province of Maine, in September, 1682, when William Scraven was

130 A CHURCH HISTORY [CH. VI.

ordained their pastor; but cruel persecution soon scattered them, some to South-Carolina, some to New-Jersey, and some to Boston again, where they were useful afterwards. Mr. Miles of Swansea died there in a good old age, February 3, 1683; and Mr. Samuel Luther succeeded him in his office for more than thirty years. In April, the same year, Mr. Roger Williams was taken to rest, and he hath a large posterity among us to this day. He was honoured of God to be instrumental of founding the first civil government upon earth, since the rise of antichrist, that allowed equal religious liberty, and he was serviceable therein unto the age of 84. And for godly sincerity in public actings, and overcoming evil with good, it is believed no man on earth exceeded him in that age.

A dreadful storm came upon this country the year after; for the charter of the Massachusetts was vacated in 1684, and amazing confusions followed it. Their government of the church over the world, which had been upheld for fifty years, with a vast deal of labour to themselves, and oppression upon others, was now dissolved; and the measures which they had meted to others, were meted to them with a vengeance. Sir Edmond Andros, with his council in 1686, made laws and imposed taxes upon all without any house of representatives; and they declared that as their charter was forfeited, their lands belonged to the king, and each man must come and buy new titles from them, or be turned off from their lands, which should be disposed of to others. And as the officers of the town of Ipswich refused to assess a tax, which was imposed without a house of representatives, and Mr. Wise their minister justified them in it, he and those officers were brought before the court at Boston, where they pleaded Magna Charta, and the laws of England, in their justification. But

1687.]   OF NEW-ENGLAND.   131

one of the judges said, "You must not think that the laws of England will follow you to the ends of the earth. Mr. Wise, you have no more privilege left you, than not to be sold for slaves; and no man of the council contradicted it." And one of them also said, "It is a fundamental point, consented to by all Christian nations, that the first discoverer of a country inhabited by infidels, gives right and dominion of that country to the prince in whose service the discoverers were sent." But the Massachusetts replied and said, "This is not a Christian, but an unchristian principle."* Yes; and it was as much so when Mr. Williams was banished for testifying against this and other evils.

Mr. Bradstreet was active in banishing Mr. Williams, and he now felt much of these calamities, when the government was dissolved of which he was at the head. Dr. Mather, also, who had done much against the Baptists, was now cruelly persecuted by evil men; one of whom forged a letter in his name, which was shown to the king and council in England, and exposed him to reproach and sufferings there. And because he wrote to a friend that he thought one of their oppressors here forged said letter, he was prosecuted for

CHURCH HISTORY OF NEW ENGLAND

defamation on that account, and though he was acquitted upon trial, yet they attempted to take him up again for it. The supporting of ministers in the country was interrupted, and Episcopal worship was forcibly carried into one of the meeting-houses in Boston. These things were so distressing, that when they heard that king James had published a declaration for liberty of conscience, in 1687, the ministers of Boston proposed with their people to keep a day of thanksgiving for it; but Andros said if they did, he would clap a guard of soldiers at the doors of their meeting-houses, and so prevented it.

* The Revolution in New-England vindicated, p. 16, 44.

132   A CHURCH HISTORY   [CH. VI.

Upon these multiplied troubles, they concluded to send Dr. Mather their agent to England; but their enemies tried to hinder it, and he privately got away, and sailed to England, in the spring of 1688, and thanked the popish king James, for his declaration for liberty of conscience to all.

  So great a turn was given to his mind, that he then concluded that the parable of the tares of the field required a general toleration about religion; and he said, "For an uppermost party of Christians to punish men in their temporal enjoyments, because in some religious opinions they dissent from them, or with an exclusion from the temporal enjoyments which would justly belong unto them, is a ROBBERY."* All his life afterwards was agreeable to this belief, though many ministers in our country have been guilty of such robbery ever since. One religious sect have held a power to take away the property of the people for ministers, to the constant injury of dissenters from them.

  Dr. Mather had several interviews with King James, till he found him to be so deceitful, that he refrained from any more concern with him, and waited for William to come to the throne. But Andros was so much afraid of it, that he imprisoned the man who first brought his proclamation to Boston; though this alarmed the country so much, that the people flocked in by thousands, April 18, 1689, and confined Andros and his party, until they were sent to England by an order from thence; and the former rulers here were restored to their places, and managed the government till the new charter arrived.

* His Life, p. 59

1692.]   OF NEW-ENGLAND.   133

CHAP. VII.

The world governs the church.—But Boston is exempted from it.—Plymouth colony was so at first.—Great declensions are lamented.—But they increase.—Episcopal society constituted.—They try for an establishment here.—Ministers try for a lordly power.—They obtain it in Connecticut.—Hooker was against it.—Norwich and Windsor reject it; and Wise, Moody and Mather also.—But Stoddard was not so.—The Baptists are favoured at Boston.—Hollis is liberal to Cambridge college.

THE new charter for the Massachusetts contained many privileges, though it took away some which they had before. It was dated October 7, 1691, and reserved a power in the crown always to appoint the two chief officers of government; and no law could be made without the consent of the Governor, and when that was obtained, the King in council could disannul any law, within three years after it was made. William intended by this to prevent their making any more persecuting laws, and it had that effect fifty years after, when Connecticut imprisoned men for preaching the gospel, but the Massachusetts could not do so. Yet other evils were not prevented; and taxing of our trade, and being under kingly governors, finally separated these colonies from Britain. Plymouth colony, on the one hand, and the Province of Maine on the other, were now united with the Massachusetts.

When the new charter arrived, May 14, 1692, the country was so involved in confusion about witchcraft, that twenty persons were executed on that account, in about four months. And when their General Court met, on October 12, they made laws to compel every town to have and

134   A CHURCH HISTORY   [CH. VII.

support an orthodox minister, and to empower their county courts to punish every town who neglected it. The whole power of choosing, and of supporting religious ministers was put into the hands of the voters in each town, who acted therein without any religious qualification in themselves. Formerly the church had governed the world, but now the world was to govern the church, about religious ministers. Our Lord says, "Except a man be born again, he cannot see the kingdom of God." John iii. 3. And his kingdom evidently here means his church; yet no regard is paid to his authority, as far as the world governs in religious affairs.

CHURCH HISTORY OF NEW ENGLAND

Therefore Dr. Mather, and other fathers in Boston, obtained an exemption from these laws, in February, 1693, which Boston has enjoyed ever since. But the country in general is governed by the world, about religious ministers, to this day. When that first law was made, they did not remember that any town had more than one church in it. But now an act was passed to allow each church to elect her own minister, and then to present him to the voters in the society who met with them for worship; and if they received him, all that society must be compelled to support him. If the Selectmen of any town neglected to assess the salary that was ordered for their minister, their county courts were to fine them forty shillings for the first offence, and four pounds for the second. And they attempted to force the town of Swansea to receive a Congregational minister, where there never had been any but Baptist churches, nor ever have to this day. The second church was now formed there.

When they were under the government of Plymouth colony, their ministers were treated as regular ministers, and one of the brethren of the. first church in Swansea was elected a magistrate

1693.]   OF NEW-ENGLAND.   135

in their government for eleven years together. Neither was a college education held to be essential for a Congregational minister there, as it was in the Massachusetts; for Mr. Jonathan Dunham was ordained the pastor of the church at Edgarton in 1694; and Mr. Samuel Fuller, after preaching sixteen years in Middleborough, was ordained pastor of a church that was constituted there in 1694. He was much esteemed as a gospel minister, until he died there, August 24, 1695, aged 66. Mr. Isaac Cushman was invited to succeed him, but he chose to settle at Plymton, where he before had a call; and he was ordained there in 1698, where he was a great blessing for about forty years. Mr. Samuel Arnold was also the first minister in Rochester, where he was long useful; and neither of these were educated at any college. And though Mr. John Cooke was censured by Mr. Reyner at Plymouth, a little before he left that church, and robbed them of their records, yet Cooke was a Baptist minister in Dartmouth for many years, from whence spring the Baptist church in the east borders of Tiverton.

The Massachusetts were three years in finding out what to do when a congregation did not concur with their church, in the choice of a pastor; but in May, 1695, they enacted, that in such a case, the church should call a council, of three or five churches, and if they approved of the choice of the church, the congregation must submit and support him; if not, then the church must give up her choice, and call another minister; and so they have acted ever since. And it may be serviceable to know what eminent fathers then thought about the state of religion among them.

Mr. Samuel Torry of Weymouth delivered the election sermon at Boston, May 16, 1683, when he said, "There is already a great death upon religion, little more left than a name to live; the

136   A CHURCH HISTORY   [CH. VII.

things which remain are ready to die, and we are in great danger of dying together with it; this is one of the most awakening and humbling considerations of our present date and condition. Oh the many deadly symptoms, symptoms of death that are upon our religion! Consider we then how much it is dying respecting the very being of it, by the general failure of the work of CONVERSION; whereby only it is that religion is propagated, continued, and upheld in being among any people. As conversion work doth cease, so religion doth die away; though more insensibly, yet most irrecoverably."* And in 1697, Dr. Increase Mather wrote a dedication of Mitchel's life, in which he said, "Dr. Owen has evinced, that the letting go this principle, that particular churches ought to consist of *regenerate persons*, brought in the great apostacy of the Christian church. The way to prevent the like apostacy in these churches, is to require an account of those who offer themselves to communion therein, concerning the work of God on their souls, as well as concerning their knowledge and belief."† Three years after he published another book, which he dedicated to the churches of New-England, to whom he said, "If the begun apostacy should proceed as fast, the next thirty years, as it has done these last, surely it will come to that in New-England (except the gospel itself depart with the order of it) that the most conscientious people therein will think themselves concerned to gather churches out of churches." And having clearly proved that Christ has given to his churches the sole right, each of electing her own pastors, he declares it to be "Simonical to affirm that this sacred privilege may be purchased with money."‡ And the next year after this book

* Said Sermon, p. 11.   † Said dedication, p. 16.
‡ Mather on gospel order, 1700, p. 12, 67, 68.

1700.]   OF NEW-ENGLAND.   137

was published, it was highly recommended by Mr. John Higginson, and Mr. William Hubbard, the two oldest ministers in the government, as may be seen

CHURCH HISTORY OF NEW ENGLAND

in Wise's works, printed in 1773. Mr. Willard published a book in 1700, in which he says, "It hath been a frequent observation, that if one generation begins to decline, the next that follows usually grows worse, and so on, until God pours out his Spirit again upon them. The decays which we already languish under are sad; and what tokens are on our children, that it is like to be better hereafter? God be thanked that there are so many among them who promise well; but alas, how doth vanity, and a fondness after new things abound among them? How do young professors grow weary of the strict profession of their fathers, and become strong disputants for those things which their progenitors forsook a pleasant land for the avoidance of!"*

A new church was formed in Brattle Street, Boston, in 1699, with a professed design to receive communicants upon lower terms than their fathers did; and in 1700, Mr. Solomon Stoddard of Northampton published a book in London, wherein he expressly held, that the Christian church is national; and that all baptized persons, who are not openly scandalous, ought to come to the Lord's supper, "though they know themselves to be in a natural condition." And by confounding the work of Jewish and Christian officers together, he asserted that the power of receiving, censuring and restoring members is wholly in officers, and says, "The brethren of the church are not to intermeddle with it." Again he says, "A national synod is the highest ecclesiastical authority upon earth." Finally he says, "Synods have power to admonish,

* Christian History, vol. i. p. 101.

138   A CHURCH HISTORY   [CH. VII.

to excommunicate, and deliver from those censures, and every man must stand to the judgment of the national synod. Deut. xvii. 12."* These indeed were the same principles, which our fathers fled into America to avoid; and this last text is the same which was brought in 1668, to justify their banishing the Baptists.

Episcopalians were also then striving for power over this country. On June 16, 1701, a society was incorporated in England for that purpose, even to propagate what they called the gospel in America. They sent over missionaries, and got so far in about 12 years, as to obtain an order from the crown to bring a bill into Parliament, to establish Episcopacy here, and they expected it would speedily be done, when the queen was suddenly taken away by death; and they could not get the two succeeding kings to revive the scheme.†

When the General Court met at Boston, October 15, 1702, they made another law to empower each county court, after fining such Assessors of towns as did not obey their orders, to appoint others to do it, and then to procure warrants from two justices of the quorum, requiring the constables of delinquent towns and districts to collect such taxes, upon the same penalties as for other taxes; and the fines imposed upon delinquent officers were to go to pay said new Assessors for their service. At the same time the ministers through the government were trying for a classical power above all the churches. A number of ministers signed proposals for such a scheme, November 5, 1705, just an hundred years after the gunpowder plot. But Mr. John Wise wrote a sharp answer to these proposals, which prevented their taking place here; though they were soon received in Connecticut;

* Stoddard on instituted churches, p. 12, 21, 29, 33.
† Chandler's Appeal in 1767, p. 50–54.

1708.]   OF NEW-ENGLAND.   139

for the third Governor Winthrop died there, Nov. 27. 1707, upon which a special meeting of their General Court was called, December 17, to choose a new Governor. By a law then in force, he was to be chosen out of a certain number of men in previous nomination; but they broke over this law, and elected an ordained minister for their Governor; and he readily quitted the solemn charge of souls, for worldly promotion, and was sworn into his new office, January 1, 1708, after which they repealed the law which they had before broken. Mr. Gurdon Saltonstall was the Governor so chosen; and he took the proposals of 1705, and presented them to their Legislature, where it was observed that there was not one text of scripture in them. And as this would not do, the proposals were silently withdrawn; and when they met at Hartford, May 13, 1708, an act was passed which said, "This Assembly, from their own observation, and from the complaint of others, being made sensible of the defects of the discipline of the churches of this government, arising from the want of a more explicit asserting of the rules given for that end in the Holy Scriptures, from which would arise a firm establishment amongst ourselves, a good and regular issue in cases subjected to ecclesiastical discipline, glory to Christ our Head* and edification to his members, hath seen fit to ordain and require, and it is by authority of the same ordained and required, that the ministers of the churches, in the several counties of this

CHURCH HISTORY OF NEW ENGLAND

government, shall meet together at their respective county towns, with such messengers as the churches to which they belong shall see cause to send with them, on the last Monday in June next, there to consider and agree upon those methods and rules for the management of ecclesiastical discipline,

* Can Christ be the head of a worldly government?

140   A CHURCH HISTORY   [CH. VII.

which by them shall be judged agreeable and conformable to the word of God; and shall at the same meeting appoint two or more of their number to be their delegates, who shall all meet together at Saybrook at the next commencement to be held there,* where they shall compare the results of the ministers of the several counties, and out of and from them to draw a form of ecclesiastical discipline," which should be presented to the Assembly for their acceptance, and the expense of those meetings was to be paid out of their treasury. This order was obeyed, and a scheme of discipline was drawn up, which was established by law the next month. Their second article says,

"That the churches, which are neighbouring each to other, shall consociate for mutually affording to each other such assistance as may be requisite, upon all occasions ecclesiastical;" and they formed two kinds of judicatures for that purpose. The first are consociations, consisting of ministers meeting in their own persons, and the churches by their messengers, of whom each church might send one or two, though the want of them should not invalidate the acts of the council; but none of their acts were valid without the concurrence of the majority of the pastors present. They were to be the standing council in each circuit; though in cases of special difficulty they may call the next consociation to sit and act with them. They are to have one or more consociation in each county. They are to have a new choice of messengers and moderators once a year, or oftener; and the last moderator is to call a new meeting when it is judged proper. Their sentence is to be final and decisive. Their other judicatures are called associations, which are meetings of ministers by themselves in

* Then the college was there, which is since at New-Haven.

1708.]   OF NEW-ENGLAND.   141

each circuit, as often as they think proper, to hear and answer questions of importance, to examine and license candidates for the ministry, to receive complaints from individuals or societies, and to direct to the calling of the council to try the same, if they think proper; to direct destitute churches in calling and settling pastors, and to make complaint to their Legislature against any whom they think negligent of their duty in these things. And each association is to choose one or two delegates, to meet once a year from all parts of their government in a general association.

Their fourth article says, "that according to the common practice of our churches, nothing shall be deemed an act or judgment of any council, which hath not a major part of the Elders present concurring, and such a number of the messengers present, as to make the majority of the council." Which is a naked falsehood; for this was so far from being common, that such a practice was never known before in New-England. If the major vote of the ministers is necessary in all their acts, to what end are any delegates sent from their churches? Are they not mere cyphers?

Mr. Hooker of Hartford, one of the best ministers who ever came to America, says, "A particular congregation is the highest tribunal, unto which the grieved party may appeal in the third place, if private council, or the witness of two have seemed to proceed too sharply, and with too much rigour against him; before the tribunal of the church, the cause may easily be scanned and sentence executed according to Christ. If difficulties arise in the proceeding, the council of other churches should be sought to clear the truth; but the power of censure rests still in the congregation where Christ placed it." And, speaking of the acts of councils, he says, "They set down their determinations, assure truths in their judgments, and so

142   A CHURCH HISTORY   [CH. VII.

return them to the particular churches from whence they came; and their determinations take place, not because they concluded so, but because the churches approved of what they have determined; for the churches sent them, and therefore are above them."*

Thus Congregational principles are, that ministers have no right in councils, but as they are sent by each church, and that their judgments are not binding until the church approves of them; but in this new scheme, the ministers attend councils without being sent by their churches, and their judgments are above all their churches. And yet they have the face to call this the common practice of their churches in former times.

Mr. John Woodward was then minister of Norwich, and he got the act of their Legislature, which approved of that scheme, and read off the first part of it to his congregation, without the clause which allowed of a dissent

CHURCH HISTORY OF NEW ENGLAND

from it: but Richard Bushnel and Joseph Backus, Esquires, their representatives, gave them that clause; but he got a major vote to adopt it, upon which said representatives, and other fathers of the town, withdrew from that tyranny, and held worship by themselves for three months. For this the minister and his party censured them, and then sent a letter to their Legislature, that Norwich had sent scandalous men for their representatives, who were under church censure, and they were expelled the house. But it was not long before the minister consented to call a council; and they had council after council for about six years. Mr. Stoddard was moderator of one of them, and the Governor also came there to try what his influence would do. The last council met there, August 31, 1716, and by their advice he was dismissed, and he quitted the ministry, and

* Survey of church discipline, part 4. p. 19, 47.

1715.]   OF NEW-ENGLAND.   143

went to farming, for which it is likely he was better qualified. The church in Norwich determined to abide by their old principles, and it was well known, that when their church was constituted at Saybrook in 1660, with the approbation of other ministers, Mr. James Fitch was ordained their pastor, by the laying on of the hands of their two deacons, as a token that the power of ordination is in each church. They came and planted Norwich the same year, and Mr. Fitch was greatly esteemed as a minister of the gospel for near fifty years. Mr. Timothy Edwards, father of the President, with his church at Windsor, also refused to receive this new scheme. But many ministers in the Massachusetts were so fond of it, that they presented a petition to their Legislature, in 1715, that they would call a synod to introduce it; and the council voted to grant it, but other branches did not concur. Yet a law was then made, to require each county court to charge the grand jury to prosecute every town or district who neglected to settle or support such ministers as they called orthodox; and if they could not bring them to do it, the court was to make complaint to the Legislature, and they were to order such sums to be assessed on delinquent towns as they judged proper, and the ministers were to draw their salaries out of the state treasury. But some others were of a very different mind; for two ministers wrote to Mr. Wise, and desired him to print a second edition of his piece against the said proposals, which they said, "will be a testimony that all our watchmen were not asleep, nor the camp of Christ surprised and taken before they had warning." This was the language of Mr. Samuel Moody of York, and Mr. John White of Gloucester, men of eminent piety and usefulness. Mr. Wise complied with their request. Mr. Backus of Norwich had requested the same, when he went as far as Boston and Ipswich to consult about their

144   A CHURCH HISTORY   [CH. VII.

affairs, before Norwich minister was dismissed. Dr. Increase Mather also now published a book, in which he said, "For ministers to pretend to a negative voice in synods, or for councils to take upon them to determine what elders or messengers a church shall submit unto, without the choice of the church concerned; or for ministers to pretend to; be members of a council without any mission from their churches, nay, although the church declares that they will not send them; is *prelectical*, and essentially differing not only from Congregational, but from Presbyterian principles. And now that I am going out of the world, I could not die in peace, if I did not discharge my conscience in bearing witness against such innovations, and invasions on the rights and liberties belonging to particular congregations of Christ.''*

This was the testimony of the oldest minister then in this province, who had been twice to England, and had been President of Harvard college sixteen years, so that his knowledge must have been very extensive; and yet his testimony was little regarded by many. And the declension of the churches kept pace with the corruption of their ministers; for Mr. Stoddard published a sermon from the twelfth of Exodus, in 1707, wherein he held forth, "that as all persons in Israel who were circumcised were required to eat the passover, so all baptized persons, if they were not scandalous, ought to come to the Lord's Supper." And he went so far as to say, "That a minister who knows himself unregenerate may nevertheless lawfully administer baptism and the Lord's Supper. Men who are destitute of saving grace, may preach the gospel, and therefore administer and so partake of the Lord's Supper. For, (says he) the children of God's people should be baptized, who are gen-

* Disquisition concerning councils, 1716, p. 13.

1716.]   OF NEW-ENGLAND.   145

erally at that time in a natural condition. And the sacrament is a converting ordinance for church members only, and not for other men."* Against this doctrine, Dr. Mather published a dissertation in 1708, wherein he brings the awful case of the man who came in without a wedding garment, and of them who eat and drink the Supper unworthily; to avoid which, all are called to

CHURCH HISTORY OF NEW ENGLAND

examine themselves whether they be in the faith; also that all the churches to whom the apostles wrote, were called saints, and faithful brethren in Christ Jesus, and the Lord added to the church such as should be saved; and much more to the same purpose. But as long as he held to infant baptism, Mr. Stoddard was so far from yielding to him, that he published a reply in 1709, wherein all his arguments turn upon these points, "That if unsanctified persons might lawfully come to the Passover, then such may lawfully come to the Lord's Supper; and they who convey to their children a right to baptism, have a right themselves to the Lord's Supper, provided they carry inoffensively."† He could plainly see that there was no half way in the Jewish church; and his opponent could see as plainly that fruits meet for repentance were required in order for baptism, even of those who were in Abraham's covenant. But as tradition had taught them both that the Christian church was built upon that covenant, neither of them could convince the other, though they were two of the most able ministers in the land.

By these things Dr. Mather was brought to treat the Baptists in quite another manner than formerly. Mr. Ellis Callender joined to their church in Boston in 1669, and was a leading member of it in 168[0], when their house was nailed up; and he

* Said Sermon, p. 13, 27, 28.
† Appeal to the learned, p. 50, 89.

146   A CHURCH HISTORY   [CH. VII.

became the pastor of it in 1708. On August 10, 1713, his son Elisha became a member of it, after which he went through Harvard College in Cambridge. Dr. Mather had appeared so friendly to the Baptists, that he and his son, and Mr. John Webb, were called, and assisted in ordaining Mr. Elisha Callender, as pastor of the Baptist church in Boston, May 21, 1718. Dr. Increase Mather wrote a preface to the ordination sermon, in which he said, "It was a grateful surprise to me, when several brethren of the Antipædobaptist persuasion came to me, desiring that I would give them the right hand of fellowship in ordaining one whom they had chosen to be their pastor." Dr. Cotton Mather preached the ordination sermon, in which he spake much against cruelties which had often been exercised against dissenters from the ruling powers, both in this and other countries, and then said, "If the brethren in whose house we are now convened, met with any thing too unbrotherly, they with satisfaction hear us expressing our dislike of every thing that looked like persecution in the days that have passed over us."*

112

Mr. Ellis Callender was a good man in 1680, when the house was nailed up, in which his son was now ordained by the help of a minister, who then had influence in said event. He was then very zealous against those whom he now gave fellowship to; and this may afford a teaching lesson to after ages. Many are earnest in our days to compel all to support Congregational worship, who are far from acting with the sincerity that their fathers did.

From this time the Baptist principles were in more esteem; and Samuel Jennings, Esq. a representative for Sandwich, was baptized by Mr. Elisha Callender, June 9, 1718, and joined to his church,

* Said Sermon, p. 38, 39.

of which he continued a member until he died in 1764. This did not hinder his being elected a representative again, nor of his serving in other offices for his town. And such a revival came on in Swansea, in 1718, as caused the addition of fifty members to the first church there in five years, of which an account was sent to Mr. Thomas Hollis of London, one of the most liberal men upon earth. Dr. Mather had some acquaintance with him, when he was in England thirty years before; and now, hearing of these transactions, his heart was wonderfully enlarged towards our country. Soon after Mr. Callender was ordained, he and his church wrote to friends in London, and an hundred and thirty-five pounds were sent from thence, to enable them to repair their meeting-house. And in 1720, Mr. Hollis sent over so much money as to found a professorship of theology in Harvard College, with a salary of eighty pounds a year to the professor, and ten pounds per annum to ten scholars of good character, four of whom should be Baptists, if any such were there. Also ten pounds a year to the college treasurer, for his trouble, and ten pounds more to supply accidental losses, or to increase the number of students. And in 1726, he founded in that college a professorship of the mathematics and experimental philosophy, with a salary of eighty pounds a year to the professor; and he sent over an apparatus for the purpose, which cost about an hundred and fifty pounds sterling, beside large additions to the college library. No man had ever been so liberal to it before as was this Baptist gentleman.

CHURCH HISTORY OF NEW ENGLAND

CHAP. VIII.

Freetown oppressed.—Also Tiverton and Dartmouth.—They got relief from England.—Increase Mather died.—His son tries for more power; but is checked from England.—He dies.—Pharaoh imitated.—Many are imprisoned.—Religion revived.—Comer converted.—He is serviceable in many places.—He and others die.—Congregational churches at Newport and Providence.—A great work at Northampton. Several Baptist churches formed.

EQUAL liberty was then enjoyed in Boston, while other towns were oppressed. In 1718, a law was made to compel all the country to assist in building or repairing Congregational meeting-houses; and in 1719, another attempt was made to force Swansea to receive and support one of their ministers, when they had two Baptist churches and three ministers then in the town, and no other religious society therein. Freetown, on the east side of Swansea, called Mr. Thomas Craghead, a minister from Ireland, to be their pastor, September 9, 1717, and he accepted of their call; but instead of an amicable agreement with them about his support, he went to the court at Bristol in January, 1718, and procured an order from thence to compel Freetown to pay him a salary of sixty-five pounds a year, to begin from the day he was chosen their minister. And for refusing to pay it, about fourteen of the inhabitants were imprisoned at Bristol, one of whom was a member of a Baptist church in Newport. These things produced much trouble in courts for two or three years, till the minister was forced to leave the town, and the broils therein lasted for several generations.

Tiverton and Dartmouth were the only remaining towns in the province which had not received

1723.]   OF NEW-ENGLAND.   149

any Congregational ministers. Therefore a complaint against them was made to their Legislature in May, 1722, and they voted a salary for such ministers, to be assessed upon all the inhabitants of said towns, which the ministers were to draw out of the State treasury. But their Assessors sent and obtained an account of how much was added to their tax on that account, and then left it out of their assessment. For this, two Assessors of each town were seized in May, 1723, and were imprisoned at Bristol, until they sent to England, and got that act disannulled by the king and Council. One of those sufferers was Philip Tabor, pastor of the Baptist church on the borders of Tiverton and

Dartmouth. But before the order for their release arrived, two more Assessors of Dartmouth were put in prison, for not assessing a like tax imposed for 1723; though upon the arrival of that order, they were released by an act of the Legislature here. Yet the ministers were so far from yielding to these things, that they presented a petition to their Legislators, in May, 1725, that they would call a synod, to give their advice about what were the evils which caused the judgments of Heaven upon the country, and what were the evangelical means which should be used to remove the same, signed by Cotton Mather, in the name of the ministers assembled in their general convention.* But the consideration of this petition was put off to the next meeting of their Legislature.

Episcopalians sent an account of it to England, and a sharp reprimand was sent from the British court to Lieutenant Governor Dummer, for giving any countenance thereto, as being an invasion of the king's prerogative, who only could lawfully call synods; and a command to him to cause such a meeting to cease, if it was convened, and to cause

* Hutchinson, vol. 2. p. 322.

150   A CHURCH HISTORY   [CH. VIII.

the chief actors therein to be punished if they did not immediately disperse. Before this, Dr. Increase Mather died, August 23, 1723, in the eighty-fifth year of his age, having been a preacher of the gospel sixty-five years. We have before seen how he testified against the power which ministers had assumed over the churches; but his son was so fond of it, that when Governor Saltonstall died in 1724, he preached a funeral sermon for him at Boston, and got it printed at New-London. And he published a book in 1726, in which he expressed his resentment against Mr. Wise for writing against the proposals of 1705. Having mentioned that four synods had been called by authority in the Massachusetts, he says, "The synods of New-England know no weapons, but what are *purely spiritual*. They have no secular arm to enforce any canons; they ask none; they want none. And they cannot believe, that any protestant secular arm would, upon due information, any more forbid their meetings, than they would any of the religious assemblies upheld in the country."* Yet many were banished upon the result of the synod of 1637, and the Baptist meeting-house in Boston was nailed up, after the synod of 1679. Yea, and he was now earnest to have Congregational ministers supported by taxes imposed "in the king's name." He approved of the practice of some towns, who involved the salary for ministers in a general town tax;† and there never was any law made here to exempt the Baptists from taxes to Congregational ministers, until after Dr. Mather died, February 13, 1728, aged 65.

But in May following, an act was made to exempt the persons of Baptists and Quakers from such taxes, if they lived within five miles of their

* An account of the discipline in the churches of New-England p. 172, 173, 184.
† Ibid, p. 21, 22.

1724.]   OF NEW-ENGLAND.   151

respective meetings, and usually attended worship there on Lord's days; of which they must give an account to their county courts in June annually, upon oath or affirmation, after which the clerk of each court was to give a list of their names to the Assessors of each town or precinct. In this, arbitrary power was carried beyond what it was in Egypt; for Pharaoh said, "Go ye, serve the Lord; only let your flocks and herds be stayed." Let their polls be exempted, but their estates and faculties taxed, said the Massachusetts. Herein they imitated him; but they went beyond him in two other points; for Pharaoh said, "Go not very far away but these allowed only five miles, though many of their parishioners must go much further than that to meeting, even to this day; neither did Pharaoh require a list of the people upon oath, as these did.

Yet this small favour was denied to dissenters in Rehoboth for this year; and for refusing to pay a tax to Congregational ministers there, twenty-eight Baptists, two Quakers, and two Episcopalians were seized and imprisoned at Bristol, in March, 1729. Though Governor Burnet and his council gave their opinion in favour of these people, yet they were confined in prison till they or their friends paid the money. In the fall after, an act was passed to exempt their estates as well as persons, yet still under a five mile limitation.

But we will gladly turn to more agreeable things; for although the majority of Congregational ministers were very corrupt, yet some of them were faithful and successful. In the beginning of 1705, such a revival of religion was granted at Taunton, in the county of Bristol, under the ministry of Mr. Samuel Danforth, as turned the minds of most of the inhabitants, from vain company and many immoralities, to an earnest attention to religion, and the great cencerns [sic.] of the soul and eternity; and they had something of the same nature at this time

152   A CHURCH HISTORY   [CH. VIII.

in Boston.* In 1721, the Spirit of God was so remarkably poured out upon the inhabitants of Windham in Connecticut, under the ministry of Mr. Samuel Whiting, and such a great change was made, that fourscore persons were added to their communion in about half a year, for which they kept a day of public thanksgiving.† One curious event happened there, which I will mention. The word preached was such a looking-glass to one man, that he seriously went to Mr. Whiting, and told him he was very sorry that so good a minister as he was should so grossly transgress the divine rule, as to tell him his faults before all the congregation, instead of coming to deal with him privately. The minister smiled, and said he was glad that truth had found him out, for he had no particular thought of him in his sermon.

Norwich, ten miles from Windham, enjoyed much of the like blessing the same year, from whence my pious mother dated her conversion. Boston shared something of the same, when God in judgment remembered mercy for many; for the small-pox came into the town in April, 1721, and prevailed through the year. It appeared to have happy effects upon many minds, while it carried a large number into eternity. One instance of conversion there I shall mention. John Comer was born in Boston, August 1, 1704, and sat under the ministry of the Dr. Mathers. He was put out to learn a trade; but he had such a desire for learning, that by the influence of Dr. Increase Mather, he was taken from it, and put to school in December, 1720. He had serious concern about his soul from time to time, until he had caught that distemper; and he says, "Nothing but the ghostly countenance of death, unprepared for, was before me, and no sight of a reconciled God, nor

* Christian History, vol. i. p. 108–112. † p. 130–134.

1724.]   OF NEW-ENGLAND.   153

any sense of the application of the soul cleansing blood of Christ to my distressed soul. I remained in extreme terror, until November 22, 1721. All the interval of time I spent in looking over the affairs of my soul; and on that day I was taken sick. As soon as it was told me that the distemper appeared, all my fears entirely vanished, and a beam of comfort darted into my soul, and with it satisfaction from those words, 'Thou shalt not die, but live, and declare the works of the Lord.' Yea, so great was my satisfaction, that immediately I replied, to my aunt who told me, then I know I shall not die now; but gave no reason why I said so."

CHURCH HISTORY OF NEW ENGLAND

He recovered, and pursued his learning at Cambridge, where he joined to a Congregational church in February, 1723. Ephraim Crafts, his intimate friend, had joined to the Baptist church in Boston just before. This Comer thought to be a very wrong action, and took the first opportunity he had to try to convince him of it; but after considerable debate, Comer was prevailed with to take Steennett upon baptism, the reading of which gave a great turn to his mind. However, he concluded to be silent about it; and as education was cheapest at New-Haven, he went and entered the College there in September, 1723, and continued a member of it until October, 1724; when infirmity of body caused his return to Boston by water; and a terrible storm at sea, with the death of a dear friend just as he arrived, brought eternity so directly before him, as to spoil his plausible excuses for the neglect of baptism. He informs us, that those words of Christ, "Whosoever shall be ashamed of me, and of my words, in this adulterous and sinful generation, of him also shall the Son of Man be ashamed, when he cometh in the glory of his Father, with the holy angels," had such influence upon him, that, after proper labours with those

154   A CHURCH HISTORY   [CH. VIII.

he was previously connected with, he was baptized, and joined to the Baptist church in Boston, January 31, 1725, and concluded to pursue his studies in a private way. In May following, he went to keep school in Swansea, and was soon called to preach the gospel in the first church there; and on May 19, 1726, he was ordained a pastor of the first church in Newport, colleague with elder Peckum.

Mr. Peckum had been pastor of that church sixteen years, but his gifts were small, and he had but seventeen members in his church; though such a blessing was granted on the ministry of Mr. Comer, that thirty-four were added to them in three years. They had no public singing, until he, with a blessing, introduced it; neither had they any church records, before he got a book, and collected into it the best accounts that he could get of their former affairs.

As it has been a common thing in all ages, when men have declined from the power of religion, to fix upon some external practice to supply the want of it; so this was now evident among the Baptists in these parts, and upon a very disputable point too. For in the law of Moses, a great variety of washings or bathings were required, and also the laying on of hands upon the head of their sacrifices, as a token of their sins being laid thereon; and this evidently pointed to laying our sins upon Christ, who bare our sins in his own body on the tree. And those washings were a clear type of the washing of regeneration, and renewing of the Holy Ghost, which God sheds on us abundantly through Christ Jesus our Saviour. All must allow these to be foundation points. And the same word that is rendered baptisms in the sixth chapter to the Hebrews, is rendered washings in the ninth; and divers washings, and carnal ordinances there, refer most certainly to Jewish ceremonies. But the doctrine which was held forth in those washings,

1728.]　　　　　　　OF NEW-ENGLAND.　　　　　　　155

and laying on of hands, was evidently the doctrine of the renewing of the Holy Ghost, and of our acceptance with God by having our sins laid upon Christ, who made atonement for them.

But receiving it as a foundation principle in Christianity, that every believer must pass under laying on of hands after baptism, in order to be received into church communion, caused a reparation among the Baptists in Newport and Providence in 1652, which still continued in Newport. And as Mr. Comer thought that Reparation to be wrong, and yet that laying on of hands after baptism was warrantable, he preached it up in that way, on November 17, 1728, without first acquainting his church with his being of this mind. Therefore two of the most powerful members, who disliked his searching preaching, took this as a handle to crowd him out of their church. This was a sore trial to him, but they prevailed to have him dismissed in January, 1729, and he then passed under hands, and was received into the second church in Newport, where he preached one half of the Lord's days with elder Daniel Wightman for two years. A revival of religion began in that church a little before, and forty members were added to it in those two years, at the close of which they had 150 members, being the largest church in the colony. Governor Jenks then lived in Newport, and communed with that church, who supported Comer liberally. In March, 1731, he went a journey into New-Jersey, and as far as Philadelphia, and was greatly pleased with the faith and order of the Baptist churches in those parts.

Upon his return, receiving an invitation from Rehoboth, he was dismissed from Newport, and removed to Rehoboth in August, where a church was formed, and he was installed their pastor, January 26, 1732. In the mean time, Mr. John Callender from Boston was ordained in the first

156　　　　　　　A CHURCH HISTORY　　　　　　　[CH. VIII.

CHURCH HISTORY OF NEW ENGLAND

church in Newport, a colleague with elder Peckum, October 13, 1731. Also Mr. Nicholas Eyres, who came from England to New-York, was called to Newport, and was settled as a colleague with elder Wightman the same month.

Mr. Elisha Callender of Boston had been sent for to Springfield, where he baptized seven persons in July, 1727, and Mr. Comer visited them in October following, and was there when the great earthquake came on in the evening of the 29th of that month. After he was settled in Rehoboth, he visited the people in Sutton and Leicester, in June, 1732, and baptized eight persons in those two towns, one of whom was Daniel Denny, Esq. who came from England. The next month he preached in Middleborough, and baptized one man there. In November following, he baptized fifteen at home, in one day; and before the close of 1733, his church had increased to 95 members, beside many seals of his ministry who joined to other churches. He was a small man, but of sprightly powers both of body and mind, and did much towards the revival of doctrinal and practical religion among the Baptists; and collected many papers, and wrote many things that have been very serviceable in our history. But his constant labours and exertions in this noble cause, wasted his vital strength, and he fell into a consumption, of which he died in Rehoboth, May 23, 1734, before he was thirty years old. Elder Ephraim Wheaton, pastor of the first church in Swansea, died the 26th of April before, aged 75, having two hundred members in his church. These things I have carefully collected from various records and writings.

On September 16, 1735, a Baptist church was formed in Sutton, and September 28, 1737, Benjamin Marsh and Thomas Green were ordained their joint pastors. But on September 28, 1738, by mutual agreement, the brethren at Leicester became

1738.]   OF NEW-ENGLAND.   157

a church by themselves, and Green their pastor. On November 4, 1736, a Baptist church was gathered in Brimfield; and on November 4, 1741, Ebenezer Moulton was ordained their pastor. March, 24, 1738, a century after the deed of Rhode Island was obtained of the Narraganset Indians, Mr. John Callender delivered a sermon at Newport, which he published with enlargements, containing the best history of that colony then extant. But his uncle at Boston was taken away by death the last day of that month; and he finished his course in the happy manner following: March 21, he said, "When I look on one hand, I see nothing but sin, guilt and discouragement; but when I look on the other, I see my glorious Saviour, and the merits of his precious blood, which cleanseth from all sin. I cannot say I have such transports of joy as some have had, but through grace I can say I have gotten the victory over death and the grave." Being asked what word of advice he had for his church, he earnestly replied, "Away with lukewarmness! Away with such remissness in attending the house of prayer, which has been a discouragement to me, and I have been faulty myself." The Boston Evening Post of April 3, says, "Friday morning last, after a lingering sickness, deceased the Reverend Mr. Elisha Callender, minister of the Baptist church in this town; a gentleman universally beloved by people of all persuasions, for his charitable and catholic way of thinking. His life was unspotted, and his conversation always affable, religious, and truly manly. During his long illness he was remarkably patient, and in his last hours (like the blessed above) pacific and entirely serene; his senses good to the last. *I shall*, said he, *sleep in Jesus*, and that moment expired."

Mr. Comer gives us an account of the first planting of the Congregational churches in Rhode Island colony. Mr. Nathanael Clap from Dorches-

158   A CHURCH HISTORY   [CH. VIII.

ter began to preach in Newport in 1695, and continued his labours there, under many discouragements, until a church was formed, and he was ordained their pastor, November 3, 1720. But in 1727, one Mr. John Adams, a young minister, came and preached there; and because Mr. Clap would not consent to have him settled as his colleague, a party council from the Massachusetts divided the church, and Adams was ordained over a majority of the church, April 11, 1728; and Mr. Clap was shut out of his meeting-house, and his people built another for him. But in about two years, Adams's people dismissed him without a recommendation. Congregational ministers also took much pains to introduce their worship into Providence; to promote which, an association of ministers in and near Boston, wrote to Governor Jenks, and other men of note in that town, October 27, 1721, and said, "With what peace and love societies of different modes of worship have generally entertained one another in your government, we cannot think of it without admiration; and we suppose, under God, it is owing to the choice liberty granted to Protestants of all persuasions, in the royal charter graciously given you; and to the wise and prudent conduct of the gentlemen that have been Governors and Justices in your colony." And so went on to desire them to countenance and encourage the preaching of their ministers among them. The town of Providence wrote an answer to them, February 23, 1722, signed by Jonathan

Sprague, wherein they say, "This happiness principally consists in their not allowing societies any superiority one over another; but each society supports their own ministry, of their own free-will, and not by constraint or force, upon any man's person or estate; and this greatly adds to our peace and tranquility. But the contrary, that takes any man's estate by force, to maintain their own or any other

1738.]   OF NEW-ENGLAND.   159

ministry, it serves for nothing but to provoke to wrath, envy and strife." And they went on to mention how such things were continued in their government.

An anonymous reply to this was published the fall after, which contained a mean reflection against Sprague's character, without any thing that could vindicate their own conduct. In January, 1723, Sprague wrote a brief vindication of his character, and then said, "Why do you strive to persuade the rising generation, that you never persecuted nor hurt the Baptists? Did you not barbarously scourge Mr. Obadiah Holmes, and imprison John Hazel of Rehoboth, who died and came not home? And did you not barbarously scourge Mr. Baker, in Cambridge, the chief mate of a London ship? Where also you imprisoned Mr. Thomas Gould, John Russell, Benjamin Sweetser, and many others, and fined them fifty pounds a man. And did you not take away a part of said Sweetser's land, to pay his fine, and conveyed it to Solomon Phips, the Deputy-Governor Danforth's son in law, who after by the hand of God ran distracted, dying suddenly, saying he was bewitched? And did you not nail up the Baptist meeting-house doors, and fine Mr. John Miles, Mr. James Brown, and Mr. Nicholas Tanner? Surely I can fill sheets of paper with the sufferings of the Baptists, as well as others, within your precincts; but what I have mentioned shall suffice for the present." Mr. Sprague was a minister for many years to a Baptist society, in the east part of Smithfield, then a part of Providence, where he died in January, 1741, aged 93. Mr. Comer knew him, and speaks of him as a very judicious and pious man.

A Congregational church was constituted in Providence, and Mr. Josiah Cotton was ordained their pastor, October 23, 1728. The year before, on October 29, 1729, about ten in the evening,

160   A CHURCH HISTORY   [Ch. VIII.

came on the greatest earthquake that had then been known in this country, and great numbers were awakened thereby, in all parts of the land, many of whom appeared to be truly turned to God, though others soon forgot their danger. But greater things are before us, as to real reformation, and one instrument of it deserves particular notice; namely, Mr. Jonathan Edwards, who was born at Windsor in Connecticut, October 5, 1703; was educated at Yale College, and began to preach the gospel in 1722, and was ordained at Northampton, colleague with his grandfather Stoddard, February 15, 1727. Mr. Stoddard died February 11, 1729, after having preached there about sixty years. He preached the clear doctrines of grace, and had great success in his ministry, notwithstanding his opinion about terms of communion and church government, before described.

It was a low time among them for several years, until a revival of religion began in Northampton, in 1733, and it arose so high in the spring of 1735, that Mr. Edwards entertained hopes that about thirty were converted in a week, for six weeks together; so that scarce a grown person in the place remained unaffected, and many children were effectually called. The same work was powerful in about twelve adjacent towns in the county of Hampshire, and they had something of it in various parts of Connecticut. Mr. Edwards wrote a narrative of this great work, in 1736, which was printed in England as well as America, and caused great joy to many; though it was but as dropping, before a plentiful shower, as will appear in the next chapter.

1740.] OF NEW-ENGLAND. 161

CHAP. IX.

The low state of religion in our land.—But a glorious revival was now granted; and it spread far.—Yet laws were made against it in Connecticut, and writings against it in the Massachusetts, though inconsistent.— Ministers are punished by the General Court of Connecticut.—Some make retractions.—But President Edwards condemns opposers.

THE first fathers of New-England held, that each believer stands in the same relation to his children as Abraham did to his, in the covenant of circumcision; and therefore that each believer had a right to bring his children to baptism, which no others had. But forty years after, a door was opened for those who had been baptized in infancy, and were not scandalous, to bring their infants to baptism, though none were to come to the ordinance of the supper without a profession of saving grace. Yet in forty years more, an open plea was published, before described, for all baptized persons, who were not openly scandalous, to come to the Lord's Supper, as well as to bring their children to

CHURCH HISTORY OF NEW ENGLAND

baptism. And in a third forty years, these things had turned the world into the church, and the church into the world in such a manner, as to leave very little difference between them. But as it is said of false teachers, "They are of the world, therefore speak they of the world, and the world heareth them," so it was generally in our land. 1 John, iv. 5. And in England the declension had gone so far, that in 1736, bishop Butler said, "It is come, I know not how, to be taken for granted, by many persons, that Christianity is not so much as a subject of inquiry; but that it is now at length discovered to be fictitious; and accordingly they

162   A CHURCH HISTORY   [CH. IX.

treat it as if in the present age this were an agreed point among all people of discernment, and nothing remained but to set it up as a principal subject of mirth and ridicule, as it were by way of reprisals, for its having so long interrupted the pleasures of the world."*

But when the enemy was thus coming in like a flood, the Spirit of the Lord lifted up a standard against him. Mr. George Whitefield, who was born in the city of Gloucester, December 16, 1714, converted while in the university of Oxford in 1733, and ordained in 1736, was wonderfully furnished with grace and gifts, to proclaim doctrinal and practical Christianity through the British empire. He sailed from England in December, 1737, to Georgia, and returned through Ireland to England in December, 1738. He embarked again for America in August, 1739, and travelled and laboured with great success, as far northward as New-York. He returned back to Georgia, from whence he went to South Carolina, and sailed from thence to New-England, where he had been earnestly invited, and landed at Newport, September 14, 1740, and preached there three days, from whence he came to Boston the 18th. After preaching there and near it many days, he went as far eastward as Old York, to see our excellent Moody; and then he returned and preached at Boston till October 12, after which he went up westward to Northampton, to see Mr. Edwards, and roused the people there; he then turned down by Hartford and New-Haven, and away to New-York, through New-Jersey and Philadelphia, and embarked from Delaware Bay, December 1, 1740. And he then said, "O my soul, look back with gratitude on what the Lord hath done for thee in this excursion. I think it is the seventy-

* Preface to his Analogy.

1640.]   OF NEW-ENGLAND.   163

fifth day since I arrived at Rhode Island. My body was then weak, but the Lord has much renewed its strength. I have been enabled to preach, I think, one hundred and seventy-five times in public, besides exhorting frequently in private. I have travelled upwards of eight hundred miles, and gotten upwards of seven hundred pounds sterling, in goods, provisions and money, for the Georgia orphans. Never did God vouchsafe me greater comforts. Never did I see such a continuance of the divine presence in the congregations to whom I have preached."*

When he went through New-Jersey, he prevailed with Mr. Gilbert Tennant to take a tour into this field, which was white already unto the harvest; and he came to Boston in December, and laboured in these parts till March, when he came round by Plymouth, Middleborough, Bridgwater, Taunton, Newport and Providence, and so returned home through Connecticut. Both of them, in their preaching, laid open the dreadful danger of hypocrisy, as well as profaneness, and spake as plainly against unconverted ministers and professors, as any other sort of sinners, and the effects were exceeding great and happy.

Some indeed tried to persuade the world, that the great change then made in the land, was chiefly owing to the mechanical influence of their terrible words, gestures, and moving ways of address. But Mr. Prince says, "As to Mr. Whitefield's preaching, it was, in the manner, moving, winning and melting; but the mechanical influence of this, according to the usual operation of mechanical powers, in two or three days expired, with many in two or three hours; and I believe with the most as soon as the sound was over, or they got out of the house, or in the first conversation they fell into. But with

* Collection of his Journals, p. 437.

164 A CHURCH HISTORY [CH. IX.

the *manner* of his preaching, wherein he appeared to be *in earnest*, he delivered those *vital truths* which animated all our martyrs, made them triumph in flames, and led his hearers into the view of that vital, inward, active piety, which is the mere effect of the mighty and supernatural operation of a DIVINE POWER on the souls of men; which only will support and carry through the sharpest trials, and make meet for the inheritance of the saints in light." As to Mr. Tennant, he says, "In private converse with him I found him to be a man of considerable parts and learning; free, gentle, condescending; and from his own various experience, reading the most noted writers on

CHURCH HISTORY OF NEW ENGLAND

experimental divinity, as well as the Scriptures, and converting with many who had been awakened by his ministry in New-Jersey, where he then lived; he seemed to have as deep an acquaintance with the experimental part of religion as any I have conversed with, and his preaching was as searching and rousing as ever I heard. He seemed to have no regard to please the eyes of his hearers with agreeable gestures, nor their ears with delivery, nor their fancy with language; but to aim directly at their hearts and consciences, to lay open their ruinous delusions, shew them their numerous, secret, hypocritical shifts in religion, and drive them out of every deceitful refuge, wherein they made themselves easy with a form of godliness without the power."*

Religion was much revived at Boston, Northampton, and other places in the fall and winter; and in the two years following, the work spread through most parts of New-England, New-York, New-Jersey, and Pennsylvania, beyond all that was ever known before in America. Several ministers, who were converted before, were now greatly quickened, and spent much of their time in travel-

* Christian History, vol. ii. p. 384–387.

1741.]   OF NEW-ENGLAND.   165

ling and preaching in various parts of the land. Others, who had been blind guides before, were now spiritually enlightened, and heartily joined in this great work; three of them were Mr. William Hobby of Reading, Mr. John Porter of Bridgwater, and Mr. Daniel Rogers, a tutor in Harvard College, who all acknowledged Mr Whitefield to be the instrument of their conversion. A number of young scholars also met with a change in these times, and came into the ministry, in which they did much for the good of souls. Religious meetings, and religious conversation, engaged the attention of a great part of the people in most parts of the land. A reformation of life, confessing their former faults, and making restitution for injuries done; were evident in many places; and a vast number of all ages, made a profession of religion, and joined to the several churches where they lived.

But a great majority of the ministers and rulers through the land disliked this work, and exerted all their powers against it; and as many imperfections appeared therein, this gave them many plausible excuses for so doing. But Mr. Edwards delivered a sermon at New-Haven, in September, 1741, in which he well distinguished between the marks of a true work of God, and all false appearances of it, which was printed and spread through the nation, and was much esteemed. An anonymous answer to it was soon published at Boston, and many appeared against the work in the Massachusetts; but they could not get any law made against it, as they did in Connecticut.

Governor Talcot died there in October, 1741, while their Legislature was sitting, who then elected another Governor, who was greatly in favour of ministerial power; and they called a consociation of ministers to meet at Guilford in November, and they drew up a number of resolves, in

166   A CHURCH HISTORY   [CH. IX.

one of which they said, "That for a minister to enter into another minister's parish, and preach or administer the seals of the covenant, without the consent of, or in opposition to the settled minister of the parish, is *disorderly*." Mr. Robbins of Branford had done something like it before at New-Haven, for which others had reproved him, and he had made some concession to them. In December he received a letter from a Baptist minister in Wallingford, informing him that Dr. Bellamy had preached to their society to mutual satisfaction, and desiring that he would do the like. This request appeared agreeable, and he appointed a meeting for the purpose, January 6, 1742. But two days before that time, a deacon from Wallingford brought him a letter, signed by 42 men in their town, and another signed by two ministers who lived by the way, desiring him not to go to preach to those Baptists, without giving any reason against it, but their desire. And as this did not appear to him a sufficient reason to violate his promise, and to disappoint a people who were desirous to hear the gospel, he went and preached two sermons to them. Yet for this he was complained of as a *disorderly* person, to the consociation of New-Haven county, February 9. He asked how it could be disorderly, since he preached to a particular religious society, at the request of their pastor. They answered, that it was not a lawful society, but a disorderly company. He replied, that Governor Talcot had advised Wallingford collectors not to distrain ministerial taxes from them; and the authority sent them annual proclamations for Fasts and Thanksgivings, as to other societies.* But they disregarded these reasons, and expelled him out of their consociation!

* That Baptist church in Wallingford was formed, and Mr. John Merriman was ordained their pastor, in 1739.

1742.]   OF NEW-ENGLAND.   167

CHURCH HISTORY OF NEW ENGLAND

This was about the time that Mr. David Brainard was expelled out of Yale College, who did the most afterwards towards spreading Christianity among the Indians of any man in our day. How far were the above actions from a catholic behaviour towards the Baptists, pretended to by many!

Those ministers procured a law to be made in May, 1742, wherein it was enacted, that if any settled minister in their government should preach in the parish of another without his consent, he should lose all the benefit of their laws for his support; and that if any man who was not a settled minister, should go into any parish and preach without such consent, he should be imprisoned until he gave an hundred pound bond not to do so again; and if any minister came out of any other government, and preached without such consent, he should be taken up by authority, and carried as a vagrant person out of Connecticut. At the same time they had an old law, by which every person was to be fined ten shillings, who drew off from parish ministers, and met for worship in a place separate from them. What tyranny was this! And though the Massachusetts had no power to make such laws about preachers, yet said Connecticut law was printed in a Boston newspaper, and many did all they could against travelling ministers, and against the work in general.

But Mr. Edwards published a book on the other side, in 1742; shewing that the work then going on in the land was a glorious work of God; the duty of all to acknowledge and promote it, and the great danger of the contrary; wherein its friends had been injuriously blamed; what ought to be corrected among them, and what ought positively to be done to promote the work. This book was much esteemed in Europe as well as America. Yet Dr. Charles Chauncy of Boston was so much

168   A CHURCH HISTORY   [CH. IX.

displeased with it, that he set off and travelled through the country, as far as Philadelphia, picking up all the evils that he could find, and some reports that were not true, concerning the work, and published them in 1743, as an answer to Edwards. In an introduction of above thirty pages, he tries to prove that this work was carried on by the same spirit and errors that were condemned by the synod of 1637. But what has been before recited, and much more that might be produced, plainly shews the contrary. He then spends about three hundred pages upon what he calls, "things of a bad and dangerous tendency, in the late religious appearances in New-England." And the first thing which he so calls, is itinerant preaching, which he says had its rise in these parts from Mr. Whitefield, who was followed by Mr. Tennant, and others. And before he cited any Scripture against it, he mentioned their law against it in Connecticut, which he observed had been printed in one of the Boston papers. After which he produced what is said in the Scriptures concerning idle, disorderly walkers, who eat the bread of others for nought. 2 Thess. iii. 6—11. And then he mentioned the caution against being busybodies in other men's matters. 1 Peter, iv. 15. But this could not answer his turn, without mending the translation, and observing that the word busybody, is *episcopos*, which is often translated bishop; and the evil here warned against, he says, is "One that plays the bishop in another's diocess."* But it is well known, that the word means an overseer, and is so rendered in Acts xx. 28. A busybody then is an overseer in the affairs of others, and in the two Scriptures which he produced, it is applied to Christians in general, and is not confined to ministers. All should take heed that they do not intermeddle with the affairs of

* Chauncy's Thoughts, p. 36–42.

1743.]   OF NEW-ENGLAND.   169

others, which do not belong to them. Two other Scriptures he brings which belong to ministers, that condemn the commending of themselves, and entering into the line of others, and the building upon another man's foundation. 2 Cor. x. 12—17. Rom. xv. 20. And these are his Scriptures to prove, that a minister ought not to preach in any parish where another was settled by the laws of men, without his consent.* But all ought to know, that the line of conduct which God has drawn in his word, and the foundation which he has laid for his church, is as high above all establishments for worship by human laws, as heaven is above the earth. And the reader will judge whether the above application of those Scriptures to worldly establishments, is not corrupting the word of God. For travelling preachers of the gospel through the world, were the great means that God made use of, to lay the foundation of the Christian church, in the apostolic age. And travelling preaching hath often been blessed for the good of souls in every age, and in every country where the gospel has come.

Another thing which Dr. Chauncy complains of, as of a dangerous tendency, is a spirit of rash and censorious judging; this he says first appeared in Mr. Whitefield, who seldom preached, but he had something or other in his sermon against unconverted ministers. Chauncy says, "I freely confess, had the ministers of New-England lost their character as men of religion, by a deportment of themselves contradictory to the gospel, I should have found no fault with any representations of them as bad men; nay, dangerous enemies to

CHURCH HISTORY OF NEW ENGLAND

the kingdom of Christ: for I am clearly of the mind, that a visibly wicked minister is the

* P. 43–45.

170 A CHURCH HISTORY [CH. IX.

greatest scandal to religion, and plague to the church of God; nor is it a hurt, but a real service to the cause of Christ, to expose the characters of such, and lessen their power to do mischief."* But to prove that their character was good, he recites the words of Dr. Cotton Mather, who said, "No man becomes a minister in our churches, till he first be a communicant; and no man becomes a communicant, until he hath been severely examined about his *regeneration*, as well as his conversation."†

But when was it so? This testimony was published in 1696; but four years after Mr. Stoddard published his opinion, that if men were not openly scandalous, they ought to come to communion in the church, though they knew themselves to be unregenerate; and this opinion had spread over the whole country before Mr. Whitefield came into it. Nay, Dr. Chauncy himself said afterwards,

An uncharitable and censorious spirit is ever to be watched against, much of which appeared in that day among all orders of men. And Dr. Chauncy discovered a large share of it, and he published many censures of others, and of some in high authority. Governor Law of Connecticut, in a proclamation for their annual fast, February 16, 1743, called all his subjects to confess and be humbled for their sins, which he said were, "The great neglect and contempt of the gospel and the ministry thereof, and the prevailing of a spirit of error,

* Page 140, 141.
† Page 142.   ‡ Sermons on breaking of bread, p. 106.

1743.] OF NEW-ENGLAND. 171

disorder, unpeaceableness, pride, bitterness, uncharitableness, censoriousness, disobedience, calumniating and reviling of authority; divisions, contentions, reparations and confusions in churches; injustice, idleness, evil speaking, lasciviousness, and all other vices and impieties which abound among us." This Chauncy has inserted in his book.* This proclamation was published so early as to have influence in their election of rulers; and Deacon Hezekiah Huntington of Norwich, who had been one of their council three years, was then left out of it, and a man was elected in his room, who had sent men to prison for preaching and exhorting the year before. Huntington had been greatly engaged in the reformation then going on in the land, and he continued stedfast therein all his days.

A new church had been formed in New-Haven, and another at Milford, which had been tolerated by their county court, and they had put themselves under the care of a presbytery in New-Jersey. But the Legislature that met at Hartford in May, 1743, enacted, "That those commonly callest presbyterians or congregationalists shall not take benefit of the act of toleration." And they also declared that no other dissenters from the established way of worship, but such as should "Before the Assembly take the oaths and subscribe the declaration provided in the act of Parliament, in cases of like nature, should be tolerated." Mr. John Owen of Groton, was complained of for preaching against their laws in April before; therefore he was ordered to be brought before the Legislature at their next session.

In the mean time a Presbyterian minister was sent from the Jerseys, to preach to said societies in Milford and New-Haven; and for preaching at

* His Thoughts, p. 295, 296.

172   A CHURCH HISTORY   [CH. IX.

Milford, he was taken up by authority, and carried as a vagrant person out of their government. But when he was let go, he came back and preached at New-Haven. And as the people concealed him on week days, an officer came on a Lord's day morning and seized him at their meeting-house door, and carried him away. Yet he returned again and preached to the people; an account of which was laid before their Legislature in October following, when it was enacted, that any minister who should do so again, should be imprisoned until he should give an hundred pound bond not to do so any more. Such was their treatment of a minister of Christ, whose name and title since was Samuel Finley, D. D. President of New-Jersey College.

As Mr. Owen avoided being taken, and like complaints were exhibited against Mr. Pomroy, both were ordered to be brought before the Assembly the next May. Accordingly, at their meeting at Hartford, May 10, 1744, Owen came with an humble confession, and they forgave him, he paying costs. Pomroy was brought, and stood trial for some hours; but he was condemned, and ordered to be committed, till he would pay costs, and bind himself for one year, in a recognizance of fifty pounds, not to offend again in like manner. He then yielded to their requirements. And Mr. James Devenport, who had gone as far in condemning the settled ministers, and in promoting separations from them, as any minister in these parts, wrote a retraction of those things, and sent it to Boston, where Mr. Prince published it, in September, 1744.* After which, scarce any settled minister in New-England ventured to preach in any parish, without the consent of the settled minister.

* Christian History, vol. 2. p. 237–240.

1744.]   OF NEW-ENGLAND.   173

Yet Mr. Edwards had before said, "If ministers preach never so good doctrine, and are never so painful and laborious in their work, yet if at such a day as this, they shew to the people, that they are not well affected to this work, but are very doubtful and suspicious of it, they will be very likely to do their people a great deal more hurt than good: for the very same of such a great and extraordinary work of God, if their people were suffered to believe it to be his, and the example of other towns, together with what preaching they might hear occasionally, would be likely to have a much greater influence upon the minds of the people, to awaken and animate them in religion, than all their labours with them. And we that are ministers, by looking on this work from year to year, with a displeased countenance, shall effectually keep the sheep from their pasture, instead of doing the part of shepherds to them, by feeding them; and our people had a great deal better be without any settled minister at all, at such a day as this.—The times of Christ's remarkably appearing in behalf of his church, and to revive religion, and advance his kingdom in the world, are often spoken of in the prophecies of Scripture, as times wherein he will remarkably execute judgment on such ministers or shepherds, as do not feed the flock, but hinder their being fed, and so deliver his flock from them, as Jeremiah xxiii. Ezekiel xxxiv. Zech. x. Isaiah xlvi. &c."* How   And we have before seen, that Dr. Increase Mather in the year 1700, said, "If the began apostacy should proceed as fast, the next thirty years, as it has done these last, surely it will come to that in New-England, that the most conscientious people therein will think themselves concerned to gather churches out

* Edwards' Thoughts, 1742, p. 133–136.

A CHURCH HISTORY [CH. X

of churches." And though he knew not the exact time, yet this came to pass in forty-five years, in the following manner.

CHAP. X

Of Canterbury separation.—Association letter against it.—But separations multiply, though persecuted.—The work at Middleborough.—Of President Edwards.—Of Mr. Whitefield.—Robbins persecuted, but delivered.— Sufferings at Norwich and Canterbury.

MR. Elisha Paine was born in Eastham, on Cape Cod, and was well instructed in the principles of the first church in Plymouth, and was well established therein. His father removed his family to Canterbury, in Connecticut, and was one of the men who formed a church there in 1711. He had four sons, whom he brought up in the nurture and admonition of the Lord; and they appeared to be acquainted with experimental religion. His son Elisha was become one of the greatest lawyers in Connecticut, and was much prospered in the world, before the law was made in 1742, to imprison men for preaching the gospel; but he then quitted their courts, and went forth preaching the gospel through the land. The church in Canterbury was then without a pastor; and on January 27, 1743, they voted to adhere to the Cambridge platform instead of that of Saybrook. Soon after, Mr. Elisha Paine set off in preaching the gospel to the northward; but for preaching in Woodstock, which then belonged to the Massachusetts, he was taken up, in February, and was sent to Worcester jail, under pretence of his breaking a law against mocking or mimicking of preaching. But four ministers in Connecticut, being in-

OF NEW-ENGLAND.

formed of it, gave a certificate, that they esteemed him to be qualified to preach the gospel. In May the court at Worcester were forced to release him, as having been imprisoned without law; and he went round preaching the gospel for about a fortnight, and then returned home. On July 8, he set off again, and travelled to Providence, Bristol, Boston, Cambridge, and as far northward as Dunstable and Lancaster, preaching with great power. He returned home December 3, having preached 244 sermons, as appears by his journal. In June, 1744, he went and preached at Eastham and Harwich, which caused a separation, and then a Baptist church in Harwich. Upon his return to Canterbury, a division took place there in the following manner: The parish had called a young minister to preach to them, by whom most of the church were not edified. The parish therefore called a committee of their association in August to give advice in the case. Mr. Paine was requested to give them his objections against said candidate; but he would not, because they were not called by the church. Another member gave them a copy of the vote of the church against him, which they called the act of the aggrieved *part* of the church; and they advised the parish to go on and settle said candidate. For this, Mr. Paine wrote to one of those ministers in September a sharp reproof for wronging the truth in calling that a part of the church, which was the church itself. Upon this he was seized and imprisoned at Windham before the month was out, for preaching in Windham the spring before, without the consent of parish ministers. Mr. Paine gave bonds to the jail-keeper, so as to have liberty to preach in the yard; and he soon had so large a congregation to hear him, that his persecutors found they weakened their own cause by confining him there. They therefore released him about October 19.

176 A CHURCH HISTORY [Ch. X.

In the mean time, as the church in Canterbury had no other way to avoid hearing a man who did not edify them, they withdrew from their meeting-house, and met at another house. And John and Ebenezer Cleaveland, members of it, as they also were of Yale College; being at home in vacation time, met for worship with their own church; but for nothing but so doing they were expelled from the college. And Mr. Paine was repeatedly cited to appear before the ministers of that county, to answer to complaints they had received against him; but he knew them too well to submit himself to their power. Twelve of them met in November, and published a testimony against him in a newspaper. And near all the ministers in Windham county met and published a letter to their people, dated December 11, 1744, signed by Joseph Coite, Ebenezer Williams, Joseph Meacham, Samuel Dorrance, Solomon Williams, Jacob Eliot, Marston Cabot, Samuel Mosely, Ephraim Avery, Ebenezer Devotions Eleazer Wheelock, Abel Stiles, Stephen White, John Bass, Richard Salter, William Throope. They brought Deut. xiii. 1—3. as a warning to their people against hearing Mr. Paine and his brethren, and then said, "The case here supposed is an attempt to draw the people to idolatry, and this, you will say, is not your case. These prophets and dreamers endeavour to draw you to Christ, and not from him; but then they endeavour to draw you from his institutions, to a way of worship which he has not instituted. Though the case is not so strong, yet the argument against your compliance is the same; for whatsoever worship God has not instituted and directed in his word, is false worship, and therefore if there seem to be never so many appearances of God's power attending it, you may not go after it, any more than after a false god."*

* Association letter, p. 43.

1745.]   OF NEW-ENGLAND.   177

Upon which we may observe, that Christ calls the field the world, and says of the wheat and tares, "Let both grow together until the harvest." But he says to his church, "Put away from among yourselves that wicked person." Yet these ministers held the field to be the church, and that Christ would not let his servants root up the tares, "even, when they *appeared*."* But how far is such worship from the instituted church of Christ! Yea, while they were for having the tares grow in the church, they would not let the children of God grow peaceably in the world, but took up and imprisoned many of them.

On November 27, 1744, the church of Canterbury met, and sixteen members against twenty-three, voted to send for their consociation to come and ordain the candidate whom the parish had chosen; and they met there for that purpose on December 26; but not having the majority of the church for him, they could not proceed according to their own laws. At length they called the parish together, and got them to vote, that they were willing their Legislature should set off those who did not choose their candidate, as a distinct religious society; and so went on and ordained him as the minister of that parish. But as the church did not desire any new incorporation by the laws of men, but only petitioned to be exempted from taxes to a minister they never chose, their petition was disregarded, their goods were torn away, or their persons imprisoned for his support for fifteen years, without the least compassion from the ministers who acted in that ordination. These, and many other things, moved a number of teachers and brethren to meet at Mansfield, October 9, 1745, and form a new church; and they elected Mr.

* Page 21.

178.]   A CHURCH HISTORY   [CH. X.

CHURCH HISTORY OF NEW ENGLAND

Thomas Marsh of Windham to be their pastor, and appointed his ordination to be on January 6, 1746. But he was seized the day before, and was imprisoned at Windham, for preaching without leave from parish ministers. On the day he was to have been ordained, a large assembly met, to whom Mr. Elisha Paine preached a good sermon, at the close of which about thirteen parish ministers came up, and tried all their influence to scatter that flock, whose shepherd had been smitten; though, instead of it, they elected and ordained Mr. John Hovey as their pastor the next month. Mr. Marsh was confined in prison till June, and then their court released him, and in July he was ordained as a colleague with Mr. Hovey; and many such churches were soon after formed and organized.*

What our Lord says about putting a piece of new cloth into an old garment, and new wine into

* Mr. Solomon Paine was ordained at Canterbury, September 10; Thomas Stevens at Plainfield, September 11; Thomas Dennison at Norwich farms, October 29; Jedidiah Hide at Norwich town, October 30; *Matthew Smith* at Stonington, December 10; John Fuller at Lyme, December 25; Joseph Snow at Providence, February 12, 1747; Samuel Wadsworth at Killingly, June 3; Paul Park at Preston, July 15; *Elihu Marsh* at Windham, October 7; Ebenezer Frothingham at Weatherfield, October 28; Nathanael Shepard in Attleborough, January 20, 1748; *Isaac Backus* at Bridgwater, April 13; John Paine at Rehoboth, August 3; *William Carpenter* at Norton, September 7; *John Blunt* at Sturbridge, September 28; *Ebenezer Mack* at Lyme, January 12, 1749; Joshua Nickerson at Harwich, February 23; Samuel Hide at Bridgwater, May 11; John Palmer at Windham, May 17; *Samuel Hovey* at Mendon, May 31: Samuel Drown at Coventry, October 11; Stephen Babcock at Westerly, April 4, 1770; *Joseph Hastings* at Suffield, April 17; Nathanael Ewer at Barnstable, May 10; Joshua Morse at New-London, May 17; Jonathan Hide at Brookline, January 17, 1751; Ezekiel Cole at Sutton, January 31; Ebenezer Wadsworth at Grafton, March 20; Shubael Stearns at Tolland, March 20; Nathanael Draper at Cambridge, April 24; Peter Werden at Warwick, May 17, &c.

Those in *Italic* became Baptists afterwards; Drown, Babcock, Morse, Stearns, Draper and Werden were so before.

1747.]   OF NEW-ENGLAND.   179

old bottles, was remarkably verified at this time. Great numbers of young converts had joined to their old churches; but a regard to the pure laws of

Christ, from the new wine of love to God and love to men, could not be contained in churches which were governed by the laws and inventions of men, obeyed from the love of worldly honour and gain, or a desire to get life by their own doings, any more than a piece of new cloth could agree with an old garment, or new wine could be contained in old bottles. Instead of it, the rent was made worse, or the bottles were broken.

The consociation of Windham county met in January, 1747, and received accounts of these transactions, and then adjourned a month, and sent citations to Mr. Paine, and others of those ministers, to appear before the lawful ministers of their parishes, or a committee of their council, to offer what they had to say in vindication of themselves. But they were far from an inclination to submit themselves to such judges. When said consociation met again, they published a copy of the confession of faith and covenant of the new church in Mansfield, and their objections against the same, and their judgment against all those new churches, and got these things printed at Boston, in a pamphlet of 22 octavo pages. To these means were added the imprisonment of Mr. Frothingham five months, Mr. John Paine eleven months, and Mr. Palmer four months, all at Hartford, for preaching without the consent of parish ministers. Mr. Solomon Paine suffered imprisonment also at Windham for a fortnight, on the same account, and many others suffered the like. And three gentlemen, only for being members and deacons in these separate churches, were, at different times, expelled out of their Legislature, namely, Captain Obadiah Johnson, of Canterbury, Captain Thomas Stevens, of Plainfield, and Cap-

180   A CHURCH HISTORY   [CH. X.

tain Nathan Jewet, of Lyme. But overstraining their power weakened it, and it began to decline; for Deacon Hezekiah Huntington was again elected into their council at Hartford in May, 1748; and he continued in that office, and was also Judge of Probate, and Chief Judge of their County Court, until he died in 1773. These things were done in Connecticut; but we must now return to the affairs of the Massachusetts.

Mr. Peter Thatcher was the third minister of Middleborough, where he began to preach in 1707, and he was much engaged in that work, especially in and after the glorious year 1741; and his success was so great, that there were above three hundred and forty communicants in his church when he died, April 22, 1744.* But the parish committee, directly after his death, exerted all their influence against the church, about calling another minister. And when the church had voted to hear Mr. Sylvanus Conant four Sabbaths upon probation, the parish committee went and got another man to preach there the same days; so that the church withdrew, and met at another place till his probation time was out, and then elected him for their pastor, and presented their choice to the parish. Upon this, said committee made a new regulation of voters, wherein they excluded seven or eight old voters, and made about nineteen new ones; and they negatived the choice of the church. But the church sent for a council of five other churches to settle the matter; and by their help Mr. Conant was ordained their pastor, March 28, 1745. Yet less than a quarter of the church called themselves the standing part of it, and went on and ordained another minister the next October, and held the old house and ministerial land, and taxed all the parish for his support. The church built another

* Christian History, vol. ii. p. 77–79, 99.

meeting-house, and went on to support their minister; but such a party spirit prevailed, even in their Legislature, that they could get no relief from thence in about four years. Though such a turn was then made, that the parish was divided into two promiscuously, and each man had liberty to choose which he would be of, and each was to support his own minister. When this liberty was obtained, the opposing party were soon sick of the minister they had ordained, and used violence against him until they got him away, and obtained a dissolution of their society. Does not this, as well as the experience of Canterbury, shew the great evil of allowing the world to govern the church about religious ministers?

　　　　And where church and world are one, it is no better, as now appeared at Northampton. The excellent Mr. Edwards was settled there, with his grandfather Stoddard, upon the opinion that the Lord's Supper was a converting ordinance, and he had gone on fifteen years in that way, until he was fully convinced that it was contrary to the word of God; and he also found that gospel discipline could not be practised in such a way. No sooner was his change of mind discovered, in 1744, than most of his people were inflamed against him, and never would give him a hearing upon the reasons of his change of sentiments; but they were resolute to have him dismissed. As he could not get them to hear him preach upon the subject, he printed his thoughts upon it, in 1749, though most of them would not read his book. In it he says, "that baptism, by which the primitive converts were admitted into the church, was used as an exhibition and token of their being visibly *regenerated*, dead to sin, and alive to God. The saintship, godliness and holiness of which, according to Scripture, professing Christians and visible saints do make a profession and have a visibility, is

182   A CHURCH HISTORY   [Ch. X.

not any religion and virtue that is the result of common grace, or moral sincerity (as it is called) but *saving grace.*" And to prove this, he referred to Rom. ii. 29. vi. 1—4. Phil. iii. 3. Col. ii. 11, 12.* Though he did not design it, yet many others have been made Baptists by the same Scriptures, and the same ideas from them. But Mr. Stoddard's doctrine had prevailed so far in that part of the country, that in all the county of Hampshire, which then included all our state west of Worcester county, not less than sixty miles wide and seventy miles long, there were but three ministers who did not hold that doctrine; and the church at Northampton denied Mr. Edwards the liberty of going out of that county, for any of those whom he was to choose to settle their controversy. At last they yielded that he might go out of that county for two, as each party was to choose five. But when the council met, in June, 1750, one of the churches whom Mr. Edwards sent to, had sent no delegate to the council, though their minister came and acted in the council, so that by the majority of one vote, Mr. Edwards was *separated* from the flock he dearly loved. Thus one of the best men in our land was rejected from his place and employment, only for coming into the belief that a profession of saving faith was necessary in all who came into communion in the church of Christ. But as this was evidently a good cause, so God was with him in it, so that he afterwards wrote a book which opened the true nature of the liberty of the will of moral agents, beyond any thing that ever was published in latter ages; and that and many other works of his are still greatly esteemed in Europe, as well as America. He was very useful in the ministry, until he died President of New-Jersey College, March 22, 1758, in his 56th year.

* On a right to Sacraments, p. 20–23.

1748.]   OF NEW-ENGLAND.   183

Mr. Whitefield came a second time into New-England, in the fall of 1744; when such opposition appeared against him, as never was seen before against any minister of the gospel in our land. The Corporation of Harvard College soon published a testimony against him, which was followed with one from an association of ministers at Weymouth, and another at Marlborough, with a third in the county of Barnstable, besides many

CHURCH HISTORY OF NEW ENGLAND

individuals; and in February, 1745, Yale College did the like, and represented that he intended to root out all the standing ministers in our land, and to introduce foreigners in their stead. This was so opposite to truth, that all his life was evidently spent in labouring for the conversion and edification of precious souls, while he left the building and government of churches to others; though when persons were brought to a saving knowledge of Christ, they could not be easy under teachers who were strangers to him, for he says, "A stranger will they not follow, but will flee from him; for they know not the voice of strangers." And if many ministers in our land had not been strangers to Christ, how could they have acted as they did?

Those who had cast Mr. Robbins out of their consociation, for preaching to the Baptists without their consent, could not let him alone; because while he continued a pastor of the first church in Branford, and yet was not with them, it weakened their power. Therefore in May, 1743, they received a complaint against him, signed by six of his people; and they appointed a committee to go to him upon it, before he knew who the complainants were, or what they complained of. But when he found who they were, he went and gave them satisfaction, and they wrote an account of it to said committee, but they would come, and insisted upon it, that Mr. Robbins must go and be reconciled to their association. This he tried for without suc-

184   A CHURCH HISTORY   [CH. X.

cess. Yet, seeing what a storm was gathering, he drew three confessions, and went to another of their meetings, and offered them, wherein he went as far as he could towards giving them satisfaction, short of confessing that he broke the law of God in preaching to those Baptists as he did. But as he could not in conscience confess that, they rejected all his confessions. And in May, 1745, they received a larger complaint against him, without his having any previous notice of it, and another committee was sent to him, who prevailed with him to go and offer a fourth confession to their association, wherein he pleaded that his ignorance of its being a crime to preach to the Baptists as he did, might apologize for him, so that a reconciliation might be effected with them, and among his people. But they refused to be satisfied with any thing short of his confessing that he broke the law of God in preaching to the Baptists against their consent. He then went home and laid this confession before his society, who voted that it was sufficient, and they desired him to continue in the ministry with them, and also that no councils or committees might be sent there again without their request. And his church met November 4, 1745, and renounced the Saybrook platform, and said, "We receive the Scriptures of the

Old and New Testament, as the only perfect rule and platform of church government and discipline;" though they did not renounce fellowship with the consociated churches.

This was worse in their view than all he had done before; and a much larger complaint was received against him than before, and a consociation was appointed to try it at Branford, September 30, 1746; and Mr. Robbins was required "in the name of Christ" to appear before them. But he drew an answer to each article of their complaint, and laid them before his church, who chose a committee to

1748.] OF NEW-ENGLAND. 185

lay a copy of their former votes before the consociation, and earnestly to deny their jurisdiction over them. This was accordingly done; yet they resolved that Mr. Robbins was under their jurisdiction, and went on to hear accusations against him in his absence, and to condemn him in ten articles of his public teaching, without naming any witnesses, or any time or place when or where either of them were delivered. And concerning his conduct, they say, "He hath led off a party with him, to rise up against and separate from the ecclesiastical constitution of this colony, under which this church was peaceably established; reproachfully insinuating in a church meeting, that under the Saybrook platform it is king association in opposition to Jesus Christ the only King of the church. In which articles, upon mature deliberation, we judge the said Mr. Robbins is criminally guilty of the breach of the third, fifth and ninth commands, and of many gospel rules, for which he ought to give Christian satisfaction, by making a confession to the acceptance of this consociation."* This he was so far from doing, that he published a narrative of the whole affair at Boston, in which the reader may find all the above particulars.

The consociation waited a year, and then met on September 29, 1747, and after telling much of their lenity and his obstinacy, they say, "This consociation do now upon the whole judge and determine the said Mr. Robbins unworthy the ministerial character and Christian communion; and accordingly do, *in the name of the Lord Jesus Christ*, according to the word of God, and the powers invested in this consociation by the ecclesiastical constitution of this government, depose the said Mr. Philemon Robbins from his ministerial office, and

* Robbins' Narrative, p. 28, 29.

186 A CHURCH HISTORY [CH. X.

CHURCH HISTORY OF NEW ENGLAND

ministerial and pastoral relation to the first church in said Branford, and debar and suspend him from communion in any of the churches of our Lord Jesus Christ."* This is in an answer to Mr. Robbins, which they published in 1748; in which they say of his voting with his church to renounce the Saybrook platform, "There was no more validity in such a vote, than there would have been in that, if the major part of the first society in Branford had voted to renounce the civil government of Connecticut.†" And a petition was sent to their General Court, that they would turn Mr. Robbins out of his meeting-house, that a regular minister might be settled therein. But such glaring conduct opened their eyes, and they ordered a council to be called out of other counties, who prevailed with New-Haven consociation to restore Mr. Robbins to a seat with them, which he held to his death in 1781; but his church sent no messenger with him. And their General Court revived their former acts of toleration to dissenters, and ordered a new edition of their laws to be printed, which was done in 1750, out of which their late persecuting laws were left, without any express repeal of them. Governor Wolcot published a pamphlet against the Saybrook scheme; and Governor Fitch endeavoured to explain away their power, which has since much declined.

An end was thus put to their imprisoning men for preaching; but still they were resolute for compelling all to support those parish ministers. Let it be observed, that the fathers of Plymouth colony held, that the ministers of Christ are to be supported only by his laws and influence, and not at all by the laws of men enforced by the sword of the magistrate; and many who now came out in a separation from these churches, descended from

* Answer to Robbins, p. 117.   † Page 86.

1752.]   OF NEW-ENGLAND.   187

those Plymouth fathers, and meant conscientiously to follow their good principles, in which others joined them; but for so doing, they suffered much, for several years, until their oppressors found their own cause was weakened thereby, and so desisted. A short view of two places may give a general view of the whole.

The minister of the first church in Norwich was settled in 1717, upon the old principles of New-England; but in 1744, he procured a vote of the major part of the church, to admit communicants into it without so much as a written account of any inward change of heart at all. At the same time he openly declared his attachment to the Saybrook platform, which the church renounced when they settled him. Therefore a large number of the church drew off, and formed another church, and settled another minister; yet they were still taxed to the old minister, and many were imprisoned therefor. Of this, and their temper under their sufferings, a private letter from a widow of fifty-four years old may give some idea.

NORWICH, NOV. 4, 1752.
> *"Dear Son,*
>
> "I have heard something of the trials among you of late, and I was grieved till I had strength to give up the case to God, and leave my burthen there. And now I would tell you something of our trials. Your brother Samuel lay in prison twenty days. October 15, the collector came to our house, and took me away to prison about nine o'clock, in a dark rainy night. Brothers Hill and Sabin were brought there next night. We lay in prison thirteen days, and then were set at liberty, by what means I know not. Whilst I was there, a great many people came to see me; and some said one thing and some another. O the innumerable snares and temptations that beset me,

more than I ever thought of before! But, O the condescension of Heaven! Though I was bound when I was cast into this furnace, yet was I loosed, and found Jesus in the midst of the furnace with me. O, then I could give up my name, estate, family, life and breath, freely to God. Now the prison looked like a palace to me. I could bless God for all the laughs and scoffs made at me. O the love that flowed out to all mankind! Then I could forgive, as I would desire to be forgiven, and love my neighbour as myself. Deacon Griswold was put in prison the 8th of October, and yesterday old brother Grover, and are in pursuit of others; all which calls for humiliation. This church hath appointed the 13th of November to be spent in prayer and fasting on that account. I do remember my love to you and your wife, and the dear children of God with you, begging your prayers for us in such a day of trial. We are all in tolerable health, expecting to see you. These from your loving mother,

ELIZABETH BACKUS."

They afterwards imprisoned her brother for such taxes, while he was a member of their Legislature; and they went on in such ways for about eight years, until the spiritual weapons of truth and love, vanquished those carnal weapons, which have not been so used in Norwich since. And the same may be observed of Canterbury. Mr. Elisha Paine was ordained pastor of a church on Long Island in May, 1752; but as he came over to Canterbury the fall after, he was seized and imprisoned at Windham, November 21, 1752, for a tax to the minister whom the church rejected. Upon which he said, "I cannot but marvel to see how soon the children will forget the sword that drove their fathers into this land, and take hold of it as a jewel, and kill their grandchildren therewith. O that men could see how far this is from Christ's rule! that all things,

1752.]	OF NEW-ENGLAND.	189

which we would have others do unto us, that we should do even so unto them. I believe the same people, who put this authority into the hands of Mr. Cogswell, their minister, to put me into prison for not paying him for preaching, would think it very hard for the church I belong to, and am pastor of, if they should get the upper hand, and tax and imprison him, for what he should be so unjustly taxed at; and yet I can see no other difference, only because the power is in his hands; for I suppose he has heard me as often as I ever have him, and yet he hath taken from me by force two cows and one steer, and now my body held in prison, only because the power is in his hands." And on December 11, he wrote to the Assessors of Canterbury, and reminded them of the cruelty of the two beasts at Rome, and then said, "What your prisoner requests of you is, a clear distinction between the ecclesiastical constitution of Connecticut, by which I am now held in prison, and those thrones or beasts, in the foundation, constitution and support thereof. For if you can shew, by Scripture and reason, that they do not all stand on the throne mentioned in Psalm xciv. 20, but that the latter is founded on the rock Christ Jesus, I will confess my fault, and soon clear myself of the prison. But if this constitution hath its rise from that throne, then come forth to the help of the Lord against the mighty; for it is better to die for Christ, than to live against him. From an old friend to this civil constitution, and long your prisoner.
ELISHA PAINE."*
Five days after he was released; but the extremity of a severe winter kept him long from his family, who suffered much in an unfinished house for want of his help. Mr. Solomon Paine

* Mr. Paine continued the pastor of his church on Long Island, till he died, in 1775, aged 84.

190	A CHURCH HISTORY	[CH. XI.

published a book this year, to shew "the difference between the church of Christ, and the churches established by law in Connecticut." And though they continued this oppression until 1771, yet their minister was then dismissed; and many confessed their faults in those oppressions, and equal liberty has been enjoyed in Canterbury ever since.

CHAP. XI.

The cause why Baptist churches increased in several places, though opposed by many.—Two who were against them die.—The corruption of many exposed.—Episcopalians try for power here.—The great Earthquake awakens many.—More Baptist churches formed.—A new revival of religion among them and others.—Providence College constituted.—Light given about baptism by Pædobaptists; and by writings concerning religious establishments.—The evil of them opened.—Particularly at Boston.— Universalism exposed.—New revivals.—Whitefield dies.—Certificate laws exposed.—The war comes on.—The Baptists unite with their country in it.— The Quakers did not.

WHEN religion was revived in 1741, there were but nine Baptist churches in all the Massachusetts government, and none in New-Hampshire or Vermont. As Pædobaptist instruments were chiefly used in that work, and the most of the old Baptists were not clear in the doctrines of grace, they were generally prejudiced against it. Yet the great change, that was then wrought in many minds, was the evident cause of the spread of the Baptist principles in our land, which have increased ever since. The subjects of that work of grace embraced two ideas which produced this effect. The

1752.]   OF NEW-ENGLAND.   191

first is, that saving faith is necessary to give any soul a true right to communion in the church of Christ. The second is, that there is no warrant for a half way covenant therein. And as infants are generally in the state of nature when they are said to be brought into covenant, infant baptism expires before these principles. Yet, natural affection, education, honour, gain and self-righteousness, all conspire together to prejudice people against becoming Baptists. It is not strange, therefore, that but few became such for many years.

The pastor of the Baptist church in Boston was dark in doctrine, and opposed the revival of religion that began there in 1740; therefore a few of the church drew off, and formed another church in 1742, and ordained a pastor

CHURCH HISTORY OF NEW ENGLAND

in 1743, who was a clear preacher of the gospel, and many joined with them from adjacent towns. A second Baptist church was also formed and organized in Rehoboth, in 1743. The like was done at Stonington in Connecticut the same year. And they increased so much in New-Jersey, that Mr. Dickinson, the first President of their college, wrote a pamphlet against them, which was printed both in New-York and Boston, in 1746. But it was sent over to London, and Dr. Gill published an answer to it in 1749; to which Mr. Peter Clark replied in 1752; and this examination of the subject caused light to be spread in our land.

More than threescore members of the separate church in Sturbridge, including all their officers, were baptized in 1749. Elder Ebenezer Moulton, of Brimfield, baptized the first part of them, and many others about the same time. In September that year, he baptized ten persons in Bridgwater, and three in Raynham. The month before, a controversy was brought into the separate church in the joining borders of Bridgwater and Middleborough, which was managed in an unhappy manner,

192   A CHURCH HISTORY   [CH. XI.

and served to prejudice many against the Baptist principles; yet they gradually prevailed, until their pastor and others were baptized in 1751, and others afterwards, who yet held communion with their old brethren for a number of years. Several lively preachers were received among the old Baptists in Narraganset, who had much success there; and Baptist elders went from thence, and baptized many in the separate churches in Connecticut, and it seemed as though all those churches would become Baptists; but for fear of it, fierce opposition was raised against what was called *rebaptizing*, which was declared to be a very wicked action, and some retracted it. This caused much unhappiness, and councils were called upon it, and a general meeting of churches at Exeter in May, 1753, and a larger one at Stonington in May, 1754; but they could not settle the controversy. Though the communing of all real saints together, appeared to be of great importance, yet many found by degrees that it could not be done in that way; for they saw that if they came to the Lord's Supper with any who were only sprinkled in their infancy, it practically said they were baptized, when they believed in their consciences that they were not. And practical lying is a great sin. We ought to use all the freedom towards all men, and towards Christians especially, that we can with a good conscience; but neither Scripture nor reason can require us to violate our own consciences for any cause whatever. An upon these principles the first Baptist church in Middleborough was constituted, January 16, 1756, and their former pastor was installed in his office, June 23 following. This was the first Baptist church which was formed in an extent of country of more than an hundred miles long, from Bellingham to the end of Cape Cod, and near fifty miles wide, between Boston

1758.]　　　　　　　　OF NEW-ENGLAND　　　　　　　　193

and Rehoboth, in which are now above twenty churches.

In two years before, gospel preachers from New-York and New-Jersey, had travelled several times to Newport and Swansea, and laboured among our old Baptist churches with success; and a reformation in doctrine and conduct followed, and also a friendly intercourse with our new churches. Mr. Solomon Paine, who had opposed the Baptists much, died October 25, 1754, and Mr. Thomas Stevenson, November 13, 1755, after which that opposition abated. But a cruel war now came on, which turned the minds of people off from the great concerns of the soul and eternity, to the confusions of this world. The ministers who had been against the late glorious work, were now using all their art to render the doctrines of sovereign grace odious; and the doctrine of Jesus Christ being truly the Son of God, and justification by faith in his righteousness, was treated with scorn and contempt, in a publication at Boston in 1755. And the same spirit appeared in Connecticut. The Baptist minister and Church of Wallingford removed from thence in 1750; but when the Congregational minister, who had persecuted Mr. Robbins, died there in 1756, his people had great difficulties about settling another. Among twenty candidates, they could not agree about any one of them. Therefore in the spring of 1758, they were advised to send to Cambridge, and they did so, and a man came highly recommended from thence, and the majority elected him for their pastor; and appointed his ordination to be on October 11. But instead of acting by Saybrook platform, they sent for such ministers as suited them, in their own county, and in other places, who were of their party. God says, "Mark them which cause divisions and offences, contrary to the doctrine which ye have learn-

194　　　　　　　　A CHURCH HISTORY　　　　　　　　[CH. XI.

ed, and avoid them; for they that are such, serve not our Lord Jesus Christ, but their own belly; and by good words and fair speeches deceive the hearts of the simple." Rom. xvi. 17, 18. This word has been abundantly cast upon all men who have separated from ministers who were supported by force; though they have paid no regard to two characters, described in the text. The first is, them who *cause divisions*; the second is, their acting *contrary to the doctrine* which the Christian church have learned; for Christ himself caused divisions between his church and the world. And because the ministers of Windham county ordained a candidate in Canterbury, in 1744, contrary to the minds of the majority of the church, divisions and offences were caused thereby through the land. Another division was now coming on about *doctrines*; for some members of the church in Wallingford, had visited their candidate, and desired to know his thoughts, "about original sin, and the saints' perseverance, the power of free-will, and falling from grace," but he refused to tell them. As they were not willing to sit under such a teacher of souls, their consociation was convened at Wallingford the day before the ordination was to be, to hear and act upon a complaint exhibited against their candidate; but he and his party protested against their meeting at that time, and refused to be tried by them. The ministers whom they had called, formed themselves into a council, and went into the meeting-house, and heard the candidate vindicate himself, before judges that his accusers refused to be tried by. Though while they were there, they received a paper, signed by ninety-five inhabitants of that parish, who possessed about half the freehold estate therein, desiring them not to proceed in the ordination; and also a message from their consociation, warning and beseeching them not then to proceed; yet in the face of all this,

1759.]   OF NEW-ENGLAND.   195

they went on and ordained him as the pastor of that parish.

Such an instance was never before known in our land; therefore the consociation adjourned, and called the southern consociation of Hartford county to meet with them; but they could not bring said party to be tried by them; therefore at their meeting of April 3, 1759, they gave the sentence of noncommunion against the minister so ordained in Wallingford, and against the members of the church who should continue with him. They declared the ministers of their county who acted in that ordination to be *disorderly persons*, until they gave satisfaction for that offence; and they were Joseph Noyes, Isaac Stiles, and Chauncy Whittlesey of New-Haven, Samuel Whittlesey of Milford, Theophilus Hall of Meriden, and Jonathan Todd of East-Guildford. Two of these were sons of the old minister of Wallingford, and one of them was the tutor for whom David Brainard was expelled from college.

Mr. Todd and William Hart wrote in favour of these men, and Mr. Edward Eelles and Noah Hobart wrote against them; and all the above things appear in their publications. Mr. Robbins was one of their judges, in an affair which affords useful lessons. Here we may see how SELF can blind the children of men. The scene of these actions was in the same town from whence all their actings against him originated. He only preached there occasionally; they settled a minister in the parish. He acted against the desire of two ministers and forty two inhabitants; they against their consociation, and ninety-five inhabitants. In the first case the Saybrook scheme was fairly renounced, and the word of God taken in its room; in the other they only protested against the meeting of the consociation at that time, but intended to be

of it afterwards. These things caused a division in the town, and another church and minister were settled there; two Baptist churches also are since formed in Wallingford. And their conduct produced like effects in other places.

The preaching of Mr. Ebenezer White of Danbury, was not liked by a minor part of his hearers, and they went and complained of him to their association, and advised to the calling of the consociation of that district to hear and act upon it. But when Mr. White heard of it, he called his church together, June 28, 1763, and they renounced the Saybrook platform, which many of them never liked, though they did not renounce communion with the churches who were under it. When the consociation of the eastern district of Fairfield county met at Danbury in August, Mr. White and his church informed them of what they had done, and refused to be tried by them. Yet they would hear the case, and finding it to be very difficult, they adjourned, and called in the consociation of the western district of that county to act with them. After other adjournments, and much labour, they at their meeting of March 27, 1764, rejected Mr. White and a large majority of his church, and held the minority as the church and society in Danbury, and refused to recommend Mr. White as a preacher to any people, until he gave them satisfaction. But five ministers entered their protest against this last article, the first of whom was Mr. David Judson of Newtown, who, with his church, afterwards renounced the Saybrook platform. Thus those ministers caused divisions and offences, from place to place, by acting upon that arbitrary scheme. And there are now two Baptist churches in Danbury, and one in Newtown, with 125 members in the three churches, and 104 in the two in Wallingford. These were their numbers in 1802.

What Dr. Chauncy and others had published about Bishops in each parish, encouraged the ministers who were ordained by Bishops in England, to deny that any who were not so ordained could have any just right to administer gospel ordinances. And they erected an episcopal church in Cambridge, near the college; at the opening of which a discourse was delivered, which contained bitter reflections upon the Fathers of this country, for their separation from the church of England. To this Dr. Jonathan Mayhew of Boston, published a smart answer, but a reply was returned, said to be written by the Archbishop of Canterbury. This controversy was warmly carried on, until the American war came on, which issued in our independence of Britain.

The great earthquake, on the morning of November 18, 1755, served to awaken a number of people, and that and other means were blessed for the conversion of several in the time of the war that then came on. The second Baptist church in Middleborough was formed Nov. 16, 1757, and the third on Aug. 4, 1761, and pastors were ordained in each of them. Baptist churches were likewise formed and organized in 1761, in Norton and in Ashfield.

A revival of religion came on in the third Baptist church in Middleborough in May, 1762, and prevailed so through all the summer, that people held frequent meetings on week days as well as the Sabbaths, and great numbers were hopefully converted and added to the church; and it spread among other denominations. Although many said they would all come to want, because they neglected their worldly business so much, yet a few seasonable showers, in a great drought, caused a double crop of corn, so that they had enough for themselves, and much to spare for others at a distance, where their crops were much cut short, which was very convincing to many. This

198   A CHURCH HISTORY   [CH. XI.

work was much more pure, and people acted more understandingly, than in our former revivals; and if all would learn to seek first the kingdom of God, and his righteousness, they would find an addition of all needful good unto them.

This work was very extensive afterwards in many parts of this land. It came on in Ipswich, under the ministry of Mr. John Cleaveland, near the close of 1763, and caused the addition of ninety communicants to his church in less than a year. And the work was great at Providence, Norwich, and many other places in 1764; and in March that year it was greater at Easthampton on Long-Island, where one Jew was converted. And as a Baptist minister went through Woodstock in Connecticut, in December 1763, he preached a sermon to a few people, one of whom was a young man, who had been a leader in vanity; but he was then seized with conviction, and was converted in March after, upon which four of his old companions came to try if they could not draw him back to his old ways; which they were so far from doing, that his labours with them produced a change in their minds; a great work was wrought in the town, a Baptist church was formed there, and he was ordained their pastor in 1768. And other things concurred to open a wide door for the spread of Baptist principles in our land.

Until now they had never had the government of any college, for the education of youth in human learning. Their churches in Pennsylvania and New-Jersey, had held an annual meeting to promote their welfare, ever since 1707; and it now appeared expedient to them, to endeavour to erect a college in Rhode Island government, for the above purpose. Mr. James Manning, who was born in Elizabethtown, October 22, 1738, graduated at Princeton college in 1762, and ordained a minister of the gospel, appeared to them a suitable

1769.]   OF NEW-ENGLAND.   199

man to lead in this work. Therefore, on a voyage to Halifax, he called at Newport, and proposed the affair to a number of Baptist gentlemen, and they liked it well; and though they met with some opposition, yet they obtained a charter for a college, in February, 1764, from their Legislature, in which the President was always to be a Baptist, and so were the majority of the corporation, though some of the Episcopal, Quaker and Congregational denominations were to be of it. No religious test was ever to be imposed upon the scholars, though great care was to be taken about their morals.

Mr. Manning removed his family to Warren in July, where a Baptist church was then formed, and he ministered to them. In September, 1765, he was chosen President of the college, and diligently attended to the duties of it, until seven young gentlemen took their first degrees there, September 7, 1769. In the spring after the college was removed to Providence, where a large brick edifice was erected for it, and a house for the President, all by personal generosity; and no government upon earth ever gave any thing towards said buildings, or for the college funds; though vast sums had been given by the governments of the Massachusetts and Connecticut to their colleges. But the buildings, library, and funds of this college, were all produced voluntarily, and chiefly from the inhabitants of Providence, many of whom sprung from the planters of the first Baptist church in America. O how far was this from the thoughts of the Massachusetts, when they banished Roger Williams for opposing the use of force in religious affairs!

Mr. Hezekiah Smith was a classmate with Manning, and was ordained a minister of the gospel. Having travelled and preached it to the southward as far as Georgia, he came into New-England

200   A CHURCH HISTORY   [CH. XI.

in the spring of 1764, and preached much, among various denominations, with an expectation of going back in the fall; but a destitute parish in Haverhill prevailed with him to stay and preach to them, which he did with success; and a Baptist church was formed in the heart of the town, May 9, 1765. Upon which many raised opposition against him, and things were published against the Baptists in general; to which answers were returned; and the more their principles were examined, the more they were embraced. Controversies among their opponents had a like effect; for in 1768, Dr. Joseph Bellamy began a dispute against the halfway covenant, which was pursued for several years. Dr. Moses Mather was one who wrote against him, and he held up the covenant with Abraham, as a covenant that all ought to be in, in order to use the means of grace for their conversion. But Dr. Bellamy replied, and said, "the unbaptized have as good a right to read and hear the word of God, as the baptized have; and as good a right to believe and embrace the gospel. For by Christ's last commission, the gospel is to be preached to all nations; yea, to every creature; and that previous to, and in order to prepare men for baptism. Mark xvi. 15, 16. So that there is not the least need of being in his external covenant, in order to have as good a right to hear and believe, and to be justified by the gospel, as any men on earth have; for there is no difference. Rom. iii. 22."* And how strong is this reasoning for the baptism of believers only! But greater things were then before them.

When the British court had determined to tax America, their bishops had great hopes of establishing their worship upon it; and one of them then said, "We may assure ourselves that this benefit will flow to the church from our present most gracious

* Reply to Mather, p. 75.

1769.]   OF NEW-ENGLAND.   201

sovereign, whenever public wisdom, public care, public justice and piety shall advise the measure. This point obtained, the American church will soon go

BY ISAAC BACKUS

out of its infant state, be able to stand upon its own legs and without foreign help support and spread itself. Then the business of this society will have been brought to the happy issue intended."*

The society, to whom this was preached, had expended vast sums, for sixty-six years, to propagate what they called the gospel in America; and they now discovered what they were after; which was to have Episcopacy supported by force in our country. By the abstract at the end of this sermon, it appears that their society had then only seven ministers in the whole of North Carolina, when they had twenty-three in the Massachusetts and Connecticut. Yet their profession was, to send ministers to gospelize the heathen, or to teach others who had not a sufficient support for ministers among them. And Dr. Chandler, of New-Jersey, now wrote upon the same argument, which I before referred to; and the danger of their succeeding appeared to be so great, that Dr. Chauncy wrote a large answer to him, wherein he said,

"We are in principle against all civil establishments in religion; and as we do not desire any establishment in support of our own religious sentiments or practice, we cannot reasonably be blamed, if we are not disposed to encourage one in favour of the Episcopal colonists.—It does not appear to us, that God has entrusted the state with a right to make religious establishments. If the state in England has this delegated authority, must it not be owned, that the state in China, in Turkey, in Spain, has this authority also? What should make the difference in the eye of true reason?

* Sermon in London, February 20, 1767, by the Bishop of Landaff, p. 24, 25.

202　　　　　　　　A CHURCH HISTORY　　　　　　　[CH. XI.

Hath the state in England been distinguished by Heaven by any particular grant beyond the state in other countries? If it has, let the grant be produced. If it has not, all states have in common the same authority. And as they must severally be supposed to exert their authority in establishments conformable to their own sentiments in religion; what can the consequence be, but infinite damage to the cause of God and true religion? And such in fact has been the consequence of these establishments in all ages, and in all places."*

The general association of ministers in Connecticut published a letter of thanks to Dr. Chauncy, for writing this book, in a Boston paper, in 1768. But Chandler wrote again, and Chauncy replied, and said, "The religion of Jesus has suffered more from the exercise of this pretended right, than from all other causes put together; and it is, with me, past all doubt, that it will never be restored to its primitive purity, simplicity and glory, until religious establishments are so brought down as to be no more."† And yet he had published more, for thirty years, to uphold the Congregational establishments in New-England, than any other man. And if any should plead that he held these not to be real establishments, that plea cannot be truth, because they hold fast three principles here, that are the foundation of all worldly establishments that ever were made under the name of Christianity. The first is, infant baptism, which lays bands upon children before they can choose for themselves; and education, honour, gain and self-righteousness, hold them in that way all their days, in the general custom of the world. The second is, the supporting of religious teachers by force, by the power of the magistrate. The third is, the al-

* Answer to Chandler, p. 152, 153.
† Reply, 1770, p. 144, 145.

1770.]   OF NEW-ENGLAND.   203

lowing religious ministers a power of office which the people cannot give nor take away. The church of Rome, and the church of England, were built and are now upheld entirely by these three principles: and the Congregational churches that are established by law in the Massachusetts and Connecticut, hold each of them fast. As long as rulers force the people to support religious teachers, it bribes them to use all their influence in favour of such rulers, and this bribes rulers to continue in that way. And God says, "A gift doth blind the eyes of the wise, and pervert the words of the righteous." Deut. xvi. 19. And so many wise and righteous men have gone in that way, that it is very difficult for their children to get out of it. But the word of God points out a clear light, which is to direct our feet in the way of peace. And he gives a most solemn warning to all, against adding to, or taking from his words. Rev. xxii. 18, 19. And no men can force others to support any religious teachers, without adding to the holy Scriptures, our only safe rule of conduct. What vast expenses would be saved to worldly governments, if that evil was entirely renounced! For the costs of Legislatures to make laws about worship, parishes and ministers, is a main part of the expenses of all governments who go in that way. Religious pretences have caused the most of the wars that have been in the world, under the name of Christianity; and the expenses which are occasioned by wars, are as much as half of the support of government in Europe and America.

BY ISAAC BACKUS

Yet the holding of ministers above the churches is still a darling point in our country, against all the light which God has given us. For the minister of Bolton, in Worcester county, drank to excess on a sacrament day, so as to shock his whole congregation. His church called him to account for it, but he did not give them satisfaction. Three councils,

204 A CHURCH HISTORY [CH. XI.

one after another, were called about it, but they were all for continuing him in office there; but as he had assumed the power to negative the acts of the church, and to dissolve their meeting, they called another, and chose a moderator and clerk, and made some proposals to their minister, and adjourned. But as he gave them no satisfaction, they met on August 8, 1771, and dismissed him from them, and the town concurred in it.

Upon this, ministers were much alarmed, and things were published against the church, as daring usurpers of an unwarrantable power; upon which two editions of Mr. Wise's works were printed at Boston, to shew what power the church once had. But the general convention of ministers at Boston, in May, 1773, published a pamphlet, to try to prove that no church had a right to dismiss their minister, without the direction of a council therein. And in August following, a council of seven churches met at Boston, and tried hard to have that minister restored again to his office there; and because they could not obtain it, they printed their result at Boston as their testimony against any such power in their churches. Dr. Chauncy was moderator of that council.

In 1772, a man from England, by the way of New-York, came to Boston, and artfully held up that Christ had paid the debt to justice for all mankind, so that none of them would suffer in hell after the day of judgment. This gave so great a shock to the ministers who held so general redemption, that they published nothing against him in ten years; but in 1782, an anonymous pamphlet came out in Boston against him. And Dr. Chauncy published a book in 1784, wherein he held forth, that the *fire of hell* would purge away the sins of all the race of Adam, so that they would be all saved, after ages

1773.] OF NEW-ENGLAND. 205

of ages.* This the pamphlet, in 1782, had called PURGATORY.†

Now an inspired apostle says, "If the blood of bulls, and of goats, and the ashes of an heifer sprinkling the unclean, sanctifieth to the purifying of the flesh; how much more shall the blood of Christ, who through the eternal

Spirit offered himself without spot to God, *purge your conscience* from dead works to serve the living God!" Heb. ix. 13, 14. This must be done in the present life, or else they who die in their sins will lift up their eyes *in torment*, and find a great gulf fixed between them and the righteous, which none pan pass over. Luke xvi. 22—26. And what madness is it to hold that the fire of hell can purge away any sins, instead of the blood of Christ! Dr. Jonathan Edwards published a full answer to Chauncy, in 1790.

But let us return to more agreeable things. A Baptist church was formed at Newton in New-Hampshire, in 1755, and one at Haverhill, in 1765, which were the first that were formed any where northward of Boston. A great revival of religion then prevailed in New-Hampshire, and the Baptist principle spread therein, until a Baptist church was constituted in Stratham, and a minister was ordained there in 1771, and their increase has been great that way ever since. And a powerful work came on in Swansea and Rehoboth, which increased the Baptist churches there, and raised a new one in Dighton, which is since very large. Old churches gained great light now, about doctrines and gospel order, and more than twenty new churches were formed in New-England, in three years. And in the close of 1774, such a work came on in Providence, that Dr. Manning baptized an hundred and ten persons in nine months; and many joined to

* Salvation for all men, p. 324.

† Said pamphlet, p. 21.

206   A CHURCH HISTORY   [CH. XI.

other churches in that town, and the work was extensive in other places.

Mr. Whitefield was taken to his rest before this, after his extraordinary labours, for thirty-four years, in England, Scotland, Ireland and America. He came over seven voyages to our country, in the last of which he landed in South-Carolina, in November, 1769, and went to Georgia. From thence he travelled through all the country, as far as the district of Maine; and in fifty-eight days he preached fifty-one sermons, before he died at Newburyport, September 30, 1770; as appears in funeral sermons for him, and in his life published since. And how wonderful were these things!

The first Baptist church in Vermont was formed in Shaftsbury in 1768, and the second was in Pownal in 1773. In the three following years, Baptist churches were constituted at Suffield, Ashford, Hampton and Killingly in Connecticut, and Medfield, Harvard and Chelmsford, in the Massachusetts; when the terrible calamities of the war could not stop this

156

work. Neither could the ill-treatment which the Baptists had met with, turn them against their country, who had oppressed them; for though they had received relief from the British court, several times, yet they saw that this was done for political ends, by men who now aimed to bring all America into bondage. And we shall here take a concise view of the partiality that was often discovered, even when our rulers pretended to relieve us.

The certificate acts which were made from time to time, to exempt us from ministerial taxes, were often violated by our oppressors, especially where new churches were formed. The Baptist church that was formed at Sturbridge in 1749, gave in certificates according to law, and yet they were all taxed to the parish minister; and in two years five men were imprisoned for it at Worcester, and

1773.]   OF NEW-ENGLAND.   207

three oxen and eight cows were taken away, beside a great deal of other property. Several men sued for recompence, and at length judgment was given for them in one case; but then other cases were non-suited, under the pretence that the actions were not commenced against the right persons. The Baptists judged that their damages in these cases were not less than four hundred dollars. And a representative from Sturbridge prevailed with our Legislature to make a new law, in 1752, to exclude all Baptist churches from power to give legal certificates, until they had obtained certificates from three other Baptist churches, that they esteemed said church to be conscientiously Anabaptists; that is, *rebaptizers*, which they never did believe. Yet, rather than to suffer continually, most of the Baptists conformed in some measure to their laws, until they were convinced that true help could not be had in that way, and therefore they concluded in 1773 to give no more certificates, and published their reasons for so doing.

The town of Ashfield was planted in 1751, and a Baptist church was constituted and organized there in 1761, with a large majority of the inhabitants in their favour. They had upheld worship there through all the perils of a long war; yet after it was over, others came in, and ordained a Congregational minister, and taxed the Baptist minister and his people for his support. One condition in the grant of the town was, that they should settle an orthodox minister, and build a meeting-house; and as the Baptists were taxed for doing that for a Congregational minister they paid it. But after they had done it, a law was made in 1768, which took the power out of the hands of the inhabitants, and put it into the hands of the proprietors, many of whom did

CHURCH HISTORY OF NEW ENGLAND

not live in the town, to tax all the inhabitants of the town for the *support* of said minister, and to lay the tax

208 A CHURCH HISTORY [CH. XI.

wholly upon the lands, be they in whose hands they might, and to sell the lands if the owners refused to pay it. The word *support* was not in the original grant of the town from the government. Yet in 1770, three hundred and ninety eight acres of land, owned by the Baptists, was sold, because they refused to pay a tax laid contrary to the original grant of said lands. They sought to the Legislature for relief, without any success, for near three years, and then sent to the King in council, and got that law disannulled. But no sooner was the news of it published here, than a malicious prosecution was commenced against the character of a chief father of that Baptist church; and though he was fully acquitted upon trial, yet he got no recompence for his costs and trouble. This plainly discovers what wickedness is the consequence of supporting religious ministers by force.

More of this appeared in other places. After the Baptist church was formed in Haverhill, in 1765, they gave in certificates to the other denomination according to law, and yet they were all taxed to them; and in 1766, a large quantity of goods were taken from one of their society, and they sued for recompence in several courts, until judgment was given in their favour in 1767, by our superior court. Their opponents had promised that this should be a final trial, yet they violated that promise, and procured another trial in June, 1769, when the case was turned against the Baptists, which cost them two hundred and fifty dollars. And they suffered much other ways for several years, but they have been well treated since. At Montague they made distress upon the Baptist committee, who signed their certificates, and not upon others; and when they sued for recompence, the case was turned against them, both in their inferior and superior courts, upon a pretence that they could not witness for themselves,

1774.] OF NEW-ENGLAND. 209

though there were three of them, and if their names had not been in the lists, they could not have been exempted. And both there and in Haverhill case, Baptists were not admitted as witnesses of plain facts, because they were parties concerned; though judges and jurors were as much so as they. The Baptists in Berwick and Goreham suffered much in these ways, as many others also did. And as their exempting law expired in 1774, another was

BY ISAAC BACKUS

made, which required that their certificates should be recorded in each parish where the Baptists lived, who must give four-pence for a copy of it, in order to clear themselves, which is three-pence sterling, the same as was laid on a pound of tea, which brought on the war in America.

The Baptist churches began an annual association at Warren, September 8, 1767, who have done much to defend their privileges, as well as to unite and quicken each other in religion. And when they met at Medfield, September 13, 1774, they chose an agent to go to Philadelphia, when the first Congress was sitting there, to join with the Philadelphia association, to endeavour to secure our religious rights, while we united with our country in the defence of all our privileges. And when he came there, said association elected a large committee to help in the affair; and they obtained a meeting of the four delegates from the Massachusetts, before other members of Congress, in the evening of October 14; to whom a memorial of our grievances about religious matters was read. This, two of those delegates endeavoured to answer, and denied that we had any reason to complain on those accounts. But when leave was given for a reply, plain facts silenced that plea. They then shifted their plea, and would have all the blame of our sufferings laid upon executive officers, and they asserted that our Legislature was entirely free from

210   A CHURCH HISTORY   [CH. XI.

blame. Three of them joined in this plea, and one of them denied that it could be a case of conscience to refuse to give them certificates, and said it was a matter of conscience with them to support ministers by law, and that we denied them liberty of conscience, in denying their right to do it. But when our agent was allowed to speak, he brought up the case of Ashfield, where near four hundred acres of land were sold for a condition that was not in the original grant of the town, for which the blame lay directly on the Legislature; and if the King in council had not disannulled that law, the Baptists might have been robbed of all their lands, as far as any thing has since appeared. He also told them that he could not in conscience give the certificates which they required, which would implicitly allow a power to man, which in his view belongs only to God. And said he, "Only allow us the liberty in the country, that they have long enjoyed in Boston, and we ask no more." This was so plain, that said delegates promised to use their influence towards having that liberty granted to all our government.

But as one of them returned before said agent got home, a report was spread in the country, that he had been to Philadelphia to try to break the union

CHURCH HISTORY OF NEW ENGLAND

of these colonies in the defence of all their privileges. He therefore soon met our Baptist committee at Boston, who sent in a remonstrance upon this subject to our provincial Congress at Cambridge, and they passed a resolve, which acquitted us of all blame in that affair; and we are now to look into their following proceedings.

A Congress, elected by the people in twelve colonies, met at Philadelphia, September 5, 1774, and sent a petition to the king for the restoration and continuance of our former privileges, and also made the best preparations that they could to defend them; but their petition was treated with con-

1776.]   OF NEW-ENGLAND.   211

tempt, and an army was sent to compel us to yield to be taxed where we were not represented. A part of the army was sent from Boston in the night, and on the morning of April 19, 1775, they killed eight men at Lexington, and some more at Concord. But the people arose against them, and they fled back the same night, and were confined in Boston eleven months, and then their army fled from thence by sea. And such things then took place in America, as never were seen upon earth before. A minister who came from England, and then lived at Roxbury, said upon a view of our country at that time,

"Now some hundred thousand people are in a state of nature, and yet as still and peaceable, at present, as ever they were when government was in full vigour. We have neither legislators, nor magistrates, nor executive officers. We have no officers, but military ones; of these we have a multitude, chosen by the people, and exercising them with more authority and spirit, than ever any did who had commissions from a Governor. The inhabitants are determined never to submit to the act destroying their charter, and are every where devoting themselves to arms."* And a man who was born in this country, and carefully observed the events in it, inserted a note in his private diary, in January, 1776, which said, "Great and marvellous have been our dangers and our escapes. In the midst of the worst kind of wars, we have both peace and plenty. I scarce ever knew the country to be better off for provision. This is a state of trial, and the great changes which are passing over us, serve greatly to shew what is in man. As every one saw himself to be interested in the war, men were forward enough to enlist into the army, and others to supply them; so that perhaps no army

* Gordon's History, vol. i. p. 427, 428.

BY ISAAC BACKUS

212   A CHURCH HISTORY   [CH. XI.

was ever supplied more plentifully with provision than ours has been."

Yet a party spirit about religion still remained, and it was remarkably discovered in one place. A young Baptist minister was invited to preach in Pepperell, forty miles northwesterly from Boston, and it had so much effect, that a number of people met with a change; another minister was sent for, and six persons declared their experiences before them, who were judged to be fit subjects for baptism. And on June 26, 1776, they met in a field, by the side of a river, for worship and the administration of that ordinance. But in the midst of their worship, the chief men of the town came at the head of a mob and broke it up. The ministers tried to reason with them about their conduct, but in vain; and a dog was carried into the river, and dipped, in contempt of their opinion. A gentleman of the town then invited the Baptists to his house, near another river, and they held their worship there; but the chief men of the town followed them, and two dogs were plunged in that river; and one young man dipped another there with scorn and derision of the Baptists; and an officer of the town went into the house, and advised these ministers to depart immediately out of town for their own safety. They asked if their lives would be in danger if they did not go, but received no answer. But they secretly agreed with their friends to disperse, and to meet at another place of water; and they did so, and those six persons were baptized, after which the mob offered them some further abuse. These things were laid before the Warren Association in September, by whose direction an account of them was published in Boston, which the town of Pepperell answered, and the Baptists replied thereto, and made the town ashamed of what they had done.

1778.]   OF NEW-ENGLAND.   213

At the same time an event took place which weakened the society of Quakers, more than any thing had done before, since they first came into existence. With much art and labour, their church had become numerous, in England and America, which they held to be but one church, and that all their children were born in it, and they did not allow them to hear any teachers but their own. And they had five houses for public worship in the town of Dartmouth, which then included what is now three towns. But after our war began, one of their most noted ministers published a pamphlet, to persuade them to pay what they were taxed for the war, to defend America against Britain. Upon which they dealt with him as a transgressor of the rules of their church, and they expelled him from it in 1778. But this caused a division

CHURCH HISTORY OF NEW ENGLAND

among them, and it reached to Philadelphia, and it opened a door for their children to go to hear other teachers; and two Baptist churches have been formed since, where there were none before.

The Baptists were so generally united with their country in the defence of their privileges, that when the General Court at Boston passed an act, in October, 1778, to debar all men from returning into their government, whom they judged to be their enemies, and named three hundred and eleven men as such, there was not one Baptist among them. Yet there was scarce a Baptist member in the Legislature who passed this act.

In the same year a new plan of government was formed for the Massachusetts, which took in their old taxing laws of ministers, who were exceeding earnest for its adoption; but they then failed of their design. But they, by deceitful arts, at length obtained what they were after. And in the mean time. Dr. Chauncy published a sermon in September, 1778, wherein he held up to the world, that the neglect of our Legislature, to make an act to

214   A CHURCH HISTORY   [CH. XI.

compel the people to make up to ministers what their salaries had lacked from the depreciation of our public currency, was an *accursed thing*, which caused the defeat of our army on Rhode Island.

CHAP. XII.

A new constitution formed.—Unjust accusations against the Baptists.—A plea of conscience against them.—Ministers discover their mistakes.—The kingdom of Christ described.—Connecticut schemes against it.—Yet God now revived his work greatly.—Methodism described.—Bishops come over from England.—Episcopacy abolished in Virginia.—A new constitution of government established in America.—President Washington favours the Baptists.—A great revival on our eastern coasts.—Also to the westward.

A CONVENTION met at Boston, September 1, 1779, to form a new constitution of government for us, and they chose a committee to make a draught for it, and adjourned. A general fast was appointed, to pray for direction in the affair, on November 4; and on the tenth, the article was brought in, to give rulers power to support ministers by force; and in order to get a vote for it, Mr. John Adams accused the Baptists of sending an agent to Philadelphia, when the first Congress was setting there, to try to break the union of these colonies in the defence of all our privileges. And Mr. Paine accused the Baptists of reading a long memorial there, in which were some things against our government, which he believed never existed. Many in the Convention were greatly inflamed thereby, and a vote was obtained to adopt said article. And did not these men, "fast for strife and

1779.]   OF NEW-ENGLAND.   215

debate, and to smite with the fist of wickedness?" Isaiah lviii. 4.

As the Baptist agent was soon informed of these things, he wrote a narrative of the affair, naming his accusers, and challenging them to a fair hearing upon it, before any proper judges, and published it in the Chronicle at Boston, December 2, 1779; and he has never heard of any answer since. Though when the first General Court upon the Constitution, met at Boston, October 25, 1780, a chief minister of the town said in a sermon before them, "I know there is diversity of sentiments respecting the extent of civil power in religious matters. Instead of entering into the dispute, may I be allowed from the warmth of my heart to recommend, where conscience is pleaded on both sides, mutual candour and love."*

But do any men plead conscience for violating their own promises? Or are any conscientious in denying all the country the liberty which they have long enjoyed in Boston? Yea, what do they do with their consciences in Boston, where the laws are made, since they are not enforced there? And if men call interest conscience, where is their religion? A just answer to these questions may be very serviceable. The views of another minister, who had a hand in forming our Constitution, discover how far they were from right ideas about the kingdom of Christ; for he said to our General Court,

"The law of self-preservation will always justify opposing a cruel and tyrannical imposition, except where opposition is attended with greater evils than submission; which is frequently the case where a few are oppressed by a large and powerful majority. This shews the reason why the primitive Christians did not oppose the cruel persecutions that were inflicted upon them by the heathen magistrates;

* Cooper's Sermon. p, 37, 38.

216   A CHURCH HISTORY   [CH. XII.

they were few compared with the heathen world, and for them to have attempted to resist their enemies by force, would have been like a small parcel of sheep endeavouring to oppose a large number of ravening wolves and

CHURCH HISTORY OF NEW ENGLAND

savage beasts of prey; it would without a miracle have brought upon them inevitable ruin and destruction. Hence the wise and prudent advice of our Saviour to them was, "When they persecute you in this city, flee ye to another."*

But this is so opposite to truth, that our Lord said to his heathen judge, "My kingdom is not of this world: if my kingdom were of this world, then would my servants fight, that I should not be delivered to the Jews; but now is my kingdom not from thence." John xviii. 36. And Paul says, "The weapons of our warfare are not carnal, but mighty through God to the pulling down of strong holds, casting down imaginations, and every high thing that exalteth itself against the knowledge of God, and bringing into captivity every thought to the obedience of Christ." 2 Cor. x. 4, 5. Therefore all the use of carnal weapons, to support religious ministers, that ever has been in the world, has been a violation of the laws of Christ; for he is the only head of his church, and each church that supports her ministers in the name of any earthly head, is a harlot. And the power of spiritual weapons was such, that God again revived his work in 1779, and it prevailed so far for three years, as greatly to increase the old Baptist churches, and to form above thirty new ones in New-England, beside many more in the southern parts of America. And as pure religion is directly against all offensive wars, and fills the people of God with an earnest desire and pursuit of justice and equity, this revival had a great influence in procuring the peace of 1783.

* West's Election Sermon, May 29, 1776, p. 19.

1784.]   OF NEW-ENGLAND.   217

But as it came on, many discovered more of their own blindness; for a minister of great note in Connecticut said to their Legislature, "The pastors are orderly and regularly set apart to the ministry, by the laying on of the hands of the presbytery, or of those who have regularly derived office power, in a lineal succession, from the apostles and Jesus Christ." And though he knew that the first ministers in our country were ordained by their churches, and did not hold to such a succession, yet he said, "These were all ordained before by the bishops in England."* And they had theirs from Rome, the mother of harlots, the great city which reigneth over the kings of the earth. Rev. xvii. 5, 18. Great Britain has lost all her power here, and our rulers have sworn to renounce all foreign power over America, and yet they compel the people to support ministers who claim a power of office from England. How shocking is this!

They also accuse us of renouncing the true God, because we have renounced a successive baptism which came from Rome. For so many had been baptized in Connecticut, that their general association set one of their number to write against the Baptists; and he said to them, "When you rebaptize those in adult years, which we have baptized in their infancy, you and they jointly renounce that Father, Son and Holy Ghost, whom we adore and worship, as the only living and true God, and on whom we depend for all our salvation."† Whereas we have only renounced an invention of men, which came from Rome, and is never named in the word of God. Yet we are

* Election sermon at Hartford, May 8, 1783, by Ezra Stiles, D. D. President of Yale College, p. 58, 61.

† An address to his Anabaptist brethren, by Joseph Huntington, D. D. 1783, p. 23.

218   A CHURCH HISTORY   [CH. XII.

constantly complained of, because we cannot receive it as his ordinance.

In the year 1784, the year in which Dr. Chauncy held up the doctrine of PURGATORY in Boston, laws were made in Connecticut to force people to support such ministers, and the like was soon done in the Massachusetts. The chief rulers of New-Hampshire, for many years, were not of the Congregational denomination, and therefore the people did not suffer so much from them, as they did in the Massachusetts and Connecticut, and so I have passed them over. And there is such a mixture in Vermont, that I have no account of great sufferings there. But the behaviour of various parties in England at this time, may deserve some notice.

Mr. John Wesley was with Mr. Whitefield in Oxford College, where they obtained the name of Methodists, because of their strict method of acting about religion; and they appeared to be united in one cause, until Wesley came out against particular election and final perseverance, about 1739; after which Mr. Wesley travelled and laboured earnestly, in England, Scotland and Ireland, to promote a particular sect, until America became independent of Britain; and then he took the thirty-nine articles of the church of England, and reduced them to twenty-four, with new forms of prayer and discipline, and printed them in London, in 1784, and called them, "The Sunday service in North America;" thus presuming to be a lawgiver for this great country. Many of his followers met in Maryland, December 27, 1784, and drew up a pamphlet, called, "A form of discipline for the Methodist Episcopal church in America." They hold to three orders of office, one above another, called

CHURCH HISTORY OF NEW ENGLAND

Bishops, Elders and Deacons, beside preachers who are not ordained. They plainly give up the opinion of a lineal succession from the apostles, because it cannot be proved. They hold to perfection in

1784.]   OF NEW-ENGLAND.   219

this life, and yet that saints may fall away and perish forever. They hold that Christ died equally for all mankind, and that no man is elected until he is converted. And if any one who was sprinkled in infancy, is not satisfied with it, and will join with them, they will go into the water and baptize him. And they have preached these sentiments through these United States, and into Canada and Nova-Scotia. Many have doubtless been reformed by their means, and some converted; but they readily receive awakened persons to communion, without a profession of regeneration. Hereby church and world are as really bound together, as they were in old worldly establishments; whereas the Son of God says to his children, "If ye were of the world, the world would love his own; but because ye are not of the world, but I have chosen you out of the world, therefore the world hateth you." John xv. 19. He chose, or *elected* them out of the world, and so they are elect according to the foreknowledge of God the Father, through sanctification of the Spirit unto obedience, and sprinkling of the blood of Jesus Christ. 1 Peter, i. 2. God the Father hath chosen us in Christ, before the foundation of the world, that we should be holy, and without blame before him in love. Eph. i. 3, 4. He chose them that they *should be holy*, and not as they become holy in conversion. If our conversion and holiness were the cause of God's electing us, our salvation would be of works, and not of grace; and this would also exclude all men from hope, who see that they are wholly under sin, and have naturally no good thing in them.

There were many others in England, that held to a lineal succession of office, who wanted to have power in America; but as no bishop could be ordained in England, without swearing to the king's supremacy, Dr. Samuel Seabury went into Scotland, and obtained the name of bishop of Connecticut,

220   A CHURCH HISTORY   [CH. XII.

from men who claimed a succession from bishops in England, who refused to swear allegiance to king William, after he came to the throne in 1689. But as this was not liked in England, letters were written to America about it, and one minister went over from New-York, and another from Philadelphia, and a special act of Parliament then exempted them from said oath, and they were ordained bishops of the states where they belorged, to which they returned in 1786. So that America has men now, whom England allows to be regular bishops, and who can make others so; but as Britain cannot compel us to receive or support them, they have increased their denomination but very little any where, and they have but one minister in all the old colony of Plymouth; and their establishment is abolished in Virginia.

That colony was first planted in 1607, the first of all our colonies, and the church of England had all the government there until 1775, when Britain commenced a war against us, in which dissenters from them prevailed, and took away the support of those ministers by law. And though they tried hard to regain their power afterwards, yet in the beginning of 1786, a law was made, which said,

"Well aware that Almighty God hath created the mind free; that all attempts to influence it by temporal punishments or burthens, or by civil incapocitations, [sic.] tend only to beget habits of hypocrisy and meanness, and are a departure from the plan of the holy Author of our religion, who, being Lord both of body and mind, yet chose not to propagate it by coercions on either, as was in his almighty power to do; that the impious presumption of Legislatures and rulers, civil or ecclesiastical, who being themselves but fallible and uninspired men, have assumed dominion over the faith of others, setting up their own opinions and modes of thinking as the only true and infallible, and as such endeavour-

1786.]   OF NEW-ENGLAND.   221

ing to impose them on others, have established and maintained false religions over the greatest part of the world, and through all time; that to compel a man to furnish contributions of money for the propagation of opinions which he disbelieves is sinful and tyrannical; that even the forcing him to support this or that teacher of his own religious persuasion, is depriving him of the comfortable liberty of giving his contributions to the particular pastor whose morals he would make his pattern, and whose powers he feels most persuasive to righteousness, and is withdrawing from the ministry those temporal rewards, which proceeding from an approbation of their personal conduct, are an additional incitement to earnest and unremitting labours for the instruction of mankind; that our civil rights have no dependence on our religious opinions, more than on our opinions in physics or geometry; that therefore the proscribing any citizen as unworthy the public confidence, by laying upon him an incapacity of being called to offices of trust and emolument, unless he profess or renounce this or that religious opinion, is depriving him injuriously of those privileges and advantages to which in common with his fellow-citizens he has a natural right; that it tends also to corrupt the principles of that very religion it is meant to encourage by bribing with a monopoly of worldly honours and emoluments, those who will externally profess and conform to it; that though indeed those are criminal who do not withstand such temptations, yet neither are those innocent who lay the bait in their way; that to suffer the civil magistrate to intrude his powers into the field of opinion, and to restrain the profession or propagation of principles on supposition of their ill tendency, is a dangerous fallacy, which at once destroys all religious liberty, because he being of course judge of that tendency, will make his opinions the rule

222   A CHURCH HISTORY   [CH. XII.

of judgment, and approve or condemn the sentiments of others, only as they shall square with or differ from his own; that it is time enough for the rightful purposes of civil government for its officers to interfere when principles break out into overt acts against peace and good order; and finally, that truth is great and will prevail if left to itself, that she is the proper and sufficient antagonist to error, and has nothing to fear from the conflict, unless by human interposition disarmed of her natural weapons, free argument and debate; errors ceasing to be dangerous when it is permitted freely to contradict them.

"*Be it therefore enacted by the General Assembly,* That no man shall be compelled to frequent or support any religious worship, place or ministry whatsoever, nor shall be enforced, retrained, molested, or burthened in his body or goods, nor shall otherwise suffer on account of his religious opinions or belief; but that all men shall be free to profess, and by argument to maintain, their opinions in matters of religion, and that the same shall in no wise diminish, enlarge, or affect their civil capacities.

"And though we well know that this Assembly, elected by the people for the ordinary purposes of legislation only, have no power to restrain the acts of succeeding Assemblies, constituted with powers equal to our own, and therefore to declare this act irrevocable, would be of no effect in law, yet we are free to declare, and do declare, that the rights hereby asserted are of the natural rights of mankind, and that if any act shall be hereafter passed to repeal the present, or to narrow its operation, such act will be an infringement of natural right."*

Though many have imagined that such liberty favours infidelity, yet Christianity is in full favour of it; and the power of the gospel, against all the

* Jefferson's Notes on Virginia, p. 242–244.

1788.]   OF NEW-ENGLAND.   225

powers of Rome, prevailed as far and farther than the Roman empire extended, for two hundred years. And Christianity has never appeared in the world, in its primitive purity and glory, since infant baptism was brought in, and after it the sword of the magistrate to support religious teachers. Yea, the foregoing declaration of Dr. Chauncy plainly says as much; and the inconsistencies and contradictions, that he and others have been guilty of, serve to confirm the above observations.

The credit of the paper money, which supported our war for several years, gradually declined, until it entirely failed in 1781; so that if a kind Providence had not opened other ways for us, the independence of America could not have been established. And when that was granted, private and public debts, and the fierce methods that were taken to recover them, brought on an insurrection in the Massachusetts, where the war began. It was then found to be necessary for a new plan to be formed for the government of all these states; and this was done in 1787. A large convention met at Boston, in January, 1788, to consider of this new constitution, where men discovered what was in their hearts in various ways. I before observed that a constitution for the Massachusetts was formed in 1778, which was not accepted. But I would observe now, that when it was in suspence, a noted minister said to our rulers, "Let the restraints of religion once be broken down, as they infallibly would be by leaving the subject of public worship to the humours of the multitude, and we might well defy all human wisdom and power to support and preserve order and government in the state."* Yet this same man was in the Convention of 1788, wherein much was said against adopting a constitution of government, which had no religious tests

* Payson's Election Sermon, May 27, 1778, p. 20.

224   A CHURCH HISTORY   [CH. XII.

in it; and he was then in favour of the constitution, and to promote the adoption of it, he said, "The great object of religion being God supreme, and the seat of religion in man being the heart or conscience, that is, the reason God has given us, employed on our moral actions, in their most important consequences, as related to the tribunal of God, hence I infer, that God alone is the God of the conscience, and consequently, attempts to erect human

CHURCH HISTORY OF NEW ENGLAND

tribunals for the consciences of men, are impious encroachments upon the prerogatives of God."*

Can these two paragraphs, from one man, possibly be reconciled together? Yea, or can any men support ministers by the sword of the magistrate, without acting contrary to a good conscience? The support of the ministers of Christ is as plainly a matter of conscience towards God, as any ordinance of his worship is. This I shall more clearly prove hereafter. In the mean time, the sentiments and example of the greatest men in America, deserve our serious notice.

After General Washington was established as President of these United States, a general committee of the Baptist churches in Virginia presented an address to him, in August, 1789, wherein they expressed an high regard for him; but a fear that our religious rights were not well secured in our new constitution of government. In answer to which, he assured them of his readiness to use his influence to make them more secure, and then said, "While I recollect with satisfaction, that the religious society of which you are members, have been throughout America, uniformly and almost unanimously the firm friends of civil liberty, and the persevering promoters of our glorious revolution, I cannot hesitate to believe, that they will be the faithful supporters of a free, yet efficient general

* Debates in Convention, p. 148.

1789.]   OF NEW-ENGLAND.   225

government."* And an amendment to the constitution was made the next month, which says,

"Congress shall make no law, establishing articles of faith, or a mode of worship, or prohibiting the free exercise of religion, or abridging the freedom of speech, or of the press, or the right of the people peaceably to aftemble, and to petition to the government for a redress of grievances."

This was dated September 23, 1789; and it has been adopted by so many of the States, that it is part of the constitution of our general government, and yet the Massachusetts and Connecticut act contrary to it to this day. And so all the evils that worldly establishments have ever produced, ought to be considered as a warning to them; for our Lord assured the Jews, that all the blood which had been shed by former persecutors, whom they imitated, should be required of them. Mat. xxiii. 29—35. And the blood that was shed at Boston, an hundred and forty years ago, brought the greatest reproach upon New-England, of anything that was ever done in it. A mistaken idea of good, in maintaining the government of the church over the world, was the cause of that evil; but the worst of men in our land have equal votes with the best, in our present government. A view of this caused many fathers in Boston to procure an act to abolish the use of force there for the support of religious ministers; and all that is done of that nature in the country, is contrary to that example, as well as to our national government.

A work of the Spirit of God at this time discovered the glory of a free gospel; for many new plantations on our eastern coasts had scarce any ministers at all to preach to them, as a view to worldly gain could not draw them there; but a

* Leland's Virginia Chronicle, p. 47, 48,

man, who was born in 1734, and settled near Kennebec river, was converted in October, 1781, and then said, "Now I began to see the base views I formerly had of the Lord Jesus Christ, and of the plan of salvation; for when I had a discovery of actual sins, and of the danger I was exposed to thereby, I would repent and reform, and think what a glorious Saviour Christ was, and that some time or other he would save me from hell, and take me to glory, with a desire to be happy, but no desire to be holy. But, glory to God! he now gave me another view of salvation. Now I saw his law to be holy, and loved it, though I and all my conduct was condemned by it. Now I saw that God's justice did not strike against me as his creature, but as a sinner; and that Christ died not only to save from punishment, but from sin itself. I saw that Christ's office was not only to make men happy, but also to make them holy; and the plan now looked beautiful to me, and I had no desire to have the least tittle of it altered, but all my cry was to be conformed to this glorious plan."

It appeared to him to be his duty to leave the care of his farm to his wife and children, and to go from house to house, for many miles round, to converse with all he could meet with, about the concerns of their souls and eternal salvation. And though many were stupid at first, yet in the beginning of 1782, powerful effects appeared, so that they set up religious meetings, and one after another came out into spiritual liberty, and he and others were led into the Baptist principles, even before they had seen a Baptist minister. But hearing of these things at a distance, some preachers went among them, and the work was promoted thereby, and it went on through the year 1783. In May, 1784, a Baptist church was formed in Bowdoinham, and another in

Thomaston, and pastors were settled in each of them. A church was also formed in Harps-

1790.]   OF NEW-ENGLAND.   227

well, January 20, 1785, and a pastor was ordained there the fall after. These three churches began an association in 1787, which increased to six churches in 1790, and 317 members.

These new churches had many secret and open enemies to encounter in a wilderness; yet God was pleased to revive his work again in 1791, so that five churches were formed in that year, and four in 1792. And by August, 1802, they had increased to forty-one churches, and twenty-five ordained ministers, in the counties of Cumberland, Lincoln and Kennebec, and 1754 members, beside many preachers who were not ordained. So many in eighteen years. In the mean time there was such a revival granted in and near Swansea, in 1789, and on our western borders in that and the year, before, that above five hundred persons were baptized in those places. To open still more clearly the nature of what these people call religion, I shall give a distinct account of one new church on our western borders.

In the adjoining borders of Bethlehem, Sandisfield and Tyringham, in the county of Berkshire, a number of people, who lived remote from parish meetings, set up a meeting among themselves, in 1784, to pray, sing, and to read sermons; and they concluded not to admit any man who was not a Pædobaptist to carry on among them. And they went on in that way, until a man who was a Baptist came to their meeting in the fall of 1787; and as he spake in public at times, they allowed him to do so once among them. This he did to their satisfaction, so that they desired him to proceed in that way, and such a blessing was granted on his labours, that a Baptist minister was sent for in March, 1788, when nineteen persons were baptized and formed into a church, called the Second Baptist church in Sandisfield. And they increased to forty members, when Mr. Benjamin Baldwin was

228   A CHURCH HISTORY   [CH. XII.

ordained their pastor, June 9, 1790. They afterwards met with cruel oppression from the Congregational party, from which they in vain sought for relief in courts; though their oppressors at length gave up such proceedings. Yet declension and coldness came on among the Baptists, until the work of God was again revived among them in June, 1798, and prevailed through the winter after. And they say, "conferences and lectures were attended in

Sandisfield, Bethlehem and Tyringham, and in the two last places almost every night in the week. Neither storms of snow, nor piercing cold could obstruct their attending divine worship. The most delicate characters did not observe the severity of the weather, in following Jesus down the banks of Jordan into the liquid grave. This work appeared to go on with great solemnity, and scarce an instance appeared of any overheated zeal, or flight of passion. Both sinners under conviction, and those who were newly brought into the liberty of the gospel, conversed in their meetings with the greatest freedom; they spake one at a time, in the most solemn and impressive manner. Their enemies were bound, and there was not a dog to move his tongue. It appeared also in the first church, and in neighbouring towns. In one year there were added to this church about sixty, and about as many to the first church, and some to other churches. In the following years, about twenty were added to our church each year. Our present number is 175, November 12, 1801."

1793.]   OF NEW-ENGLAND.   229

CHAP. XIII.

Manning's character and death. Others raised to supply his place.—The increase of the Baptists makes others expose themselves.—Cruelty shown to the Baptists.—Their first church in Connecticut better treated.—They increase there.—Religion greatly revived through the country.—Even to Virginia, Georgia and Kentucky.—A book from England reprinted against them.—Remarks upon it.

Dr. Manning was a faithful preacher of the gospel, and President of our College, for twenty five years, until he was called out of our world, July 29, 1791, in his fifty-third year. He was a good instructer [sic.] in human learning, but at every commencement he gave a solemn charge to his scholars, never to presume to enter into the work of the ministry, until they were taught of God, and had reason to conclude that they had experienced a saving change of heart. And a tutor in the college, who appeared to have met with such a change in October, 1789, was instrumental of a revival of religion, both in the college and in the town, and he was called into the ministry, and then was a President of the College eleven years. And then another tutor was hopefully converted, and called into the ministry, and has been President ever since. And I hope succeeding ages will follow these examples.

But as the Baptists increased much, in many parts of our land, a minister in the west part of the Massachusetts endeavoured to make an improvement upon the plan which Dr. Stiles had published in Connecticut; and his book was so pleasing to many, that it passed six editions in about two years, the last of which was at Boston, in 1793. His text is Mat. vii. 15, 16; and he tried all his art to

230   CHURCH HISTORY   [CH. XIII.

represent all teachers in our land to be wolves in sheep's clothing, who were not ordained by ministers who hold a succession from England, and who do not regard parish lines. And he says, "A good shepherd attends to his own proper charge; the wolf is a rapacious, prowling animal, not satisfied with taking out of one flock, he roams from flock to flock, and can never have enough." And of an uninterrupted succession from the apostles, he says, "It is by no means necessary, that by historical deduction, we should prove an uninterrupted succession; we have a right to presume it, until evidence appears to the contrary."* But God says, "Who hath *required* this at your, hands to tread my courts? Your hands are full of *blood*." Isaiah i. 12, 15. And the *bloody hands* of teachers in Rome and England, could never convey just authority to any other ministers.

This was so evident to the fathers of this country, that they allowed none to be pastors of their churches, but such as each church elected and ordained, as I before proved. And Mr. Cotton said, "The power of the ministerial calling is not derived from ordination, whether Episcopal, or Presbyterial, or Congregational. The power of the ministerial calling is derived chiefly from Christ, furnishing his servants with gifts fit for the calling; and nextly from the church (or congregation) who observing such whom the Lord hath gifted, do elect and call them forth to come and help them."†

From hence came the name Congregational, the meaning of which many have departed from, though they still usurp the name. But it is well known in America, that it is the election of the people, that gives our civil officers their power, and not the oaths which they take from other offi-

          * Lathrop's Discourses, p. 26, 56.
          † Answer to Williams, part second, p. 82.

1793.]   OF NEW-ENGLAND.   231

cers. And ordination of ministers is no more than swearing them to be faithful in that office. Their being furnished with grace and gifts for it, is the most essential thing in the affair; for an inspired apostle says, "As every man hath received the gift, even so minister the same one to another, as good stewards of the manifold grace of God. If any man speak, let him speak as the oracles of God; if any man minister, let him do it as of the ability which God giveth; that God in all things may be glorified through Christ Jesus. The Elders which are among you I exhort, who am also an Elder, and a witness of the sufferings of Christ, and also a partaker of the glory that shall be revealed; feed the flock of God which is among you, taking the oversight thereof, not by constraint, but willingly; not for filthy lucre, but of a ready mind; neither as being lords over God's heritage, but being ensamples to the flock. And when the chief Shepherd shall appear, ye shall receive a crown of glory that fadeth not away. Likewise ye younger, submit yourselves unto the elder; yea, all of you be subject one to another, and be clothed with humility; for God resisteth the proud, and giveth grace to the humble." 1 Peter iv. 10, 11. v. 1—5.

Here we may plainly see, that the gifts and graces which God bestows on men for the ministry, gives them their internal call to go into that work; and the union of the church in calling and receiving them, and the acting as a united body, is the essence of the government which Christ has established in each of his churches. All men who claim a power of office above the churches, desire to be lords over God's heritage. And we must not forget, that teachers are to be known by their fruits, and not by ordination. Thorns and thistles wound the flesh, or tear away the property of others; which is done by imprisoning their persons, or taking away their goods unjustly. If we regard

232   A CHURCH HISTORY   [CH. XIII.

this rule, which Christ has given to know false teachers by, how plainly do they appear in our land? A great many instances of imprisonment, and spoiling of goods, to support ministers whom the people did not choose, have been given already, and more are before us.

The Baptist church in Barnstable was formed, June 20, 1771, and they were not free of sufferings, though they were not great, until God revived his work there in 1781, and it increased their church and society, and they ordained a pastor therein, in 1788, who had preached to them five years. Yet in that time, and in two years after, more than an hundred and fifty dollars were forced from them for ministers whom they did not hear. But the committee of the Warren Association met at Boston, in January, 1791, and wrote to the officers of the parishes who oppressed them, in such a manner as caused them to refrain from proceeding in that way, though they did not restore the money which they had taken away unjustly. Much greater evils were soon after done in another place; for a Baptist church was formed and organized in the south part of Harwich in 1757, and they built them a meeting-house, and carried on their worship for about forty years, when there was no Congregational minister in that parish. But when the Baptists were without a pastor, in the fall of 1792, a Congregational minister was ordained there, and the Baptists treated him in a friendly manner, while they still maintained their own worship, and soon got them another minister. Yet after they had done it, a few of the Congregational party, in the beginning of 1794, taxed all the Baptist church and society to their minister; and near the close of 1795, they imprisoned six men for it, and forced away much property from others. This was so glaringly unjust, and even contrary to the law of the government, that the Baptists sued for

1796.] OF NEW-ENGLAND. 233

recompense, in 1796, and obtained judgment in their favour, in their county court. But their oppressors appealed to their superior court, and obtained judgment against the Baptists, who in the whole lost above five hundred dollars. False witnesses had an evident hand in this. And as the Congregational party found that their courts favoured them, they thought they might do as they pleased.

An aged and pious Baptist deacon, who never was of the Congregational party, wrote to Boston November 12, 1799, and said, "On the 26th of last July, the Collector of Harwich came and seized about four or five bushels of my rye, and carried it off, and sold it for one dollar, and made above two dollars charge on it; and on the 13th of August, the same Collector, Edward Hall, came and seized about three tons of my hay, and carried it off, and sold it for forty nine shillings, and returned me five shillings and six pence. For all this I was taxed to their minister but seven shillings and a penny. I have given you as exact account as possible. These from yours in gospel bonds,

ABNER CHASE."

Therye was taken out of the field before it was threshed, so that the exact quantity was not known. Now the only reason that is given in our constitution of government, for empowering rulers to support teachers by force, is because "the happiness of a people, and the good order of civil government essentially depend upon piety, religion and morality." But how opposite hereto is the above conduct! Our Lord says, "All things whatsoever ye would that men should do to you, do ye even so to them; for this is the law and the prophets." Mat. vii. 12. And is there one man among us, who would be willing to be compelled to support any teacher that he never chose? Yet this is the natural consequence of allowing any men to sup-

234 A CHURCH HISTORY [CH. XIII.

port teachers by the sword of the magistrate. And this practice has caused the effusion of blood, among all nations, more than any other means in the world. And the combination of rulers and teachers herein, I believe, is the beast and false prophet, which will finally be cast into the burning lake. Rev. xix. 20. When this shall be done, the glory of the later day will come on, as it is described in the next chapter; though this great event is freely left with Him to whom it belongs. But as God never allowed Israel to use any force for the support of his priests, how can any be willing to use compulsion for the support of religious ministers? No man can be satisfied that others have a right to take away his property for nothing, yea, and worse than nothing.

Any Congregational minister may avoid oppressing the people if he will. This appeared plain in the case of the first Baptist church in Connecticut. It was formed about 1705, in the town of Groton, under the ministry of Mr. Volentine Wightman. They suffered some at first, but when Mr. John Owen became the minister of the town, he was not for forcing any money from the Baptists; and when the great revival of religion came on, he and Wightman were agreed in it, until the latter died in 1747. His son, Timothy Wightman, was ordained in his place, May 20, 1756, and he was a faithful and successful minister, until he died joyfully, November 14, 1796, aged near 78, when he left 215 members in his church. After which his son, John Gano Wightman, succeeded him in that office. A daughter of their first pastor married a Mr. Rathbun, two of whose sons, and two of his grandsons, are ordained Baptist ministers, and so have been some others of the Wightman family.

Their first minister assisted in forming a Baptist church in Stonington, in 1743, and a second was formed there in 1765. But a number there and

1799.] OF NEW-ENGLAND. 235

more in Groton were then for continuing the communion of the two denominations together, and many churches were formed upon that plan; and they began a yearly meeting in 1785, called, The Groton Conference. But they have given up mixed communion in later years, and are come into connexion with the rest of our associations.

Much declension and coldness about religion came on in 1797, which was lamented by the faithful of different denominations; but a great work came on in the spring of 1798, in many parts of America. It began at Mansfield in Connecticut, in a remarkable manner. A letter from Windham in October mentions it, and says, "The Spirit of the Lord seemed to sweep all before it, like an overflowing flood, though with very little noise or crying out. It was wonderful to see the surprising alteration in that place in so short a time. I conclude there are not less than an hundred souls converted in that town since the work began. It soon after began in Hampton, but did not spread with that degree of rapidity as it did in Mansfield. The same happy work has lately taken place in Ashford." Soon after this, Hartford, their capital city, experienced the like work among the Congregational and Baptist societies. A Presbyterian minister, who went from the Massachusetts to a town above them, said on February 6, 1799, "I stopped at Hartford, and preached five sermons. The spirit of hearing at Hartford is greater than any representations which have been made. Young people of both sexes flock by hundreds, and the prospect is flattering in the extreme. Conference meetings are held every night in different private houses. In Mr. Strong's society sixty are thought to be under conviction, and twenty have been hopefully brought into gospel liberty. In *Mr. Nel-

* Nelson's church are Baptists.

236   A CHURCH HISTORY   [CH. XIII.

son's thirty, and some in Mr. Flint's. This sacred flame has spread into many neighbouring towns, and the pious are flocking into Hartford to be eye witnesses of this glorious work. I have felt myself so much engaged in preaching, visiting and conversing with old and young, that my attention has been literally taken off from wife, children, flock, and bodily infirmities." It was said that this work spread, more or less, into an hundred towns in Connecticut.

In April, 1798, Mr. Blood, pastor of a Baptist church at Shaftsbury in Vermont, had his soul greatly affected with the low state of religion among them, with earnest cries that God would pour out his spirit upon the souls of men, and save them from sin and ruin. In July following, a person who had been converted before, came forward in baptism; and her declaration and example awakened many others, and four were baptized in August, and seventeen in September. And the work went on in such a manner, that on February 21, 1799, he said, "The whole number added to this church, since last May, is 175; 25 by letter and other ways, and 150 by baptism. Our whole number is 346. Many of this number are removed into different parts, of the country; there are, however, nearly 300 that live in the vicinity, the remotest of them not more than six miles from our meeting-house. There are also about 70 added to the west church in this town since the work began; and 13 to the east church. In years past there has not been the most cordial fellowship between the three churches in this town; but the Lord has now effected a happy union between us. On the last Lord's-day in January, we all met at one communion table. That happy day my soul had desired for years. Nothing but experience could have made me believe it possible, that I could have felt so much solid delight, anticipated so much trouble, and rejoiced

1799.]   OF NEW-ENGLAND.   237

with so much trembling, at one and the same time. That day I trust will never be forgotten by me. In about two months after the work began, the whole town seemed to be affected. Conference meetings were attended two or three times in a week in almost every neighbourhood; and it was surprising to me, that scarcely a single instance appeared of any overheated zeal, or flight of passion. Both sinners under conviction, and those newly brought into the liberty of the gospel, conversed in their meetings with the greatest freedom; they spake one at a time a few words, in the most solemn manner I ever heard people in my life. And in general they spake so low, that their assemblies must be perfectly still, or they could not hear them; yet a remarkable power attended their conversation. Sinners would tremble as though they felt themselves in the immediate presence of the great Jehovah. Some of all ranks and characters among us have been taken; from the most respectable members of society, to the vilest in the place. Some of our most noted Deists have bowed the knee to King Jesus; and a number of Universalists have forsaken their delusions, and embraced the truth." And when the Shaftsbury Association met in June, 1799, they had accounts that 259 had been added in the year, to the three churches in Shaftsbury, and not one member had died in that time. Also that the addition to their whole association that year was 732.

This work was also great on our eastern coasts. Mr. Peter Powers, a Congregational minister on Deer-Island in Penobscot Bay, wrote from thence, March 20, 1799, and said, "In the beginning of June last, I was called to Mount-Desert to administer sacraments to a church who have not a stated pastor, and tarried with them about nine days; when, in preaching my second sermon, the glory of the Lord came down in a wonderful manner. One

A CHURCH HISTORY [Ch. XIII.

convicted, and hopefully converted under the sermon, was added to the church about two days after, and three others who had before obtained a hope. Three months after this I went again to administer the Lord's Supper, at which time I admitted twenty-eight who had hopefully been brought home in the interval. The work of conviction was then going on powerfully in the town, and spreading into those adjoining on the same island. Our association had licensed dear Mr. Ebenezer Eaton to preach, who improved his talent, labouring night and day among them, whom the Lord remarkably owned. How many have been brought out since I was there, I am not informed; but according to the best accounts, there are many. The Lord multiply the number, and add to the church of such as shall be saved.

"I now come a little nearer home. In the beginning of winter, this glorious work began in Sedgwick, under the pastoral care of the Rev. Daniel Merrill. Perhaps there hath not been a work so powerful, and so much like the work fifty-eight years ago. In a time of such extraordinaries, it could not reasonably be expected but some things would be a little wild and incoherent, considering the various tempers, infirmities and dispositions of mankind: but I believe my young dear brother Merrill, together with experienced Christians, were very careful to distinguish the precious from the vile; to correct errors, *to set them in the way of his steps*, so that there appears to be no prevalence of enthusiasm among them, according to the best information. How great the number is of those who have been brought to hope, I am not able to give any tolerable account. Some say there are about an hundred, others about double that number; I believe they are all very uncertain. Blessed be God, the work is yet going on there, though not with equal rapidity.

1799.] OF NEW-ENGLAND. 239

"And now, dear Sir, let your imagination paint to your view the striking scene of an hundred souls, men, women, and children, at the same time under the work of the law. The tears, sobs, groans and cries issuing from scores at a time! All the terrors of the law crowding and pressing in upon them; their sins, in infinite number and aggravations, staring them in the face; all their old vain hopes gone, and cut off, and every refuge failing! Hear them freely confessing their old abominations, their former enmity to the great doctrines of original sin, election, the sovereignty of divine free grace, the power of God displayed in effectual vocation; above all, the justice of God in their damnation! How often are souls brought out into peace and comfort of the love of God, and the sweet consolations of the Holy Spirit! The dead hear the voice of the Son of God, and live. Children are brought to cry, "Hosanna to the Son of David." Indeed this glorious work has been wonderful among children; and God has made instruments of them to perfect praise in carrying on his work.

"This blessed work of God has begun in Blue-Hill; but as yet has not gained the ascendency. I shall therefore come to my own dear people of Deer-Isle. And here, perhaps, the work is as remarkable as at Sedgwick, but not so rapid. Not more than eight months ago it appeared to me that religion was near expiring among us, except in a very handful of professors. Deism had taken an unaccountable stride, and spread itself over a great number of the inhabitants. And now, no Bible, no Christ; but the Christian religion, and Christians, were the song of the drunkard; and every drunkard, and every vice, was deemed harmless, and inoffensive to God. I had no reason to think but by the next annual meeting of the town, they would vote the gospel out from them. When the aforementioned work at Penobscot and

240   A CHURCH HISTORY   [CH. XIII.

Mount-Desert was going on, it seemed to have no influence on our people. This, you may be sure, was very grievous to me. However, I think I was enabled to bear witness to the truth with great freedom. In October, I perceived a more close attention to the word, but nothing special as yet. After I was confined to my house, the work began to appear; and though I could not go abroad to preach at the meeting-house, there was seldom a day but more or less visited me under their trouble, and I preached in my own house when I was not able to stand on my feet. At length we had the assistance of Mr. E. Eaton, whom God remarkably owns. I believe there are about forty, men, women, and children, who have obtained a hope; and great numbers are under pressing conviction. The work is now on the increase. May the Lord continue and still increase it, till they are all brought in. The mouth of deism is at present stopped, and against the children of Israel not so much as a dog is suffered to move his tongue."

A Baptist minister of Lyme in Connecticut, on June 30, 1799, wrote to Boston, and said, "Though the severity of last winter was tedious, yet I have not heard any one complain, or shrink at the cross, on account of the coldness of the weather. This work has been gloriously carried on in the spirit of love. In the first part of it, there was great crying out, but it gradually subsided into free deliberate conversation on the dreadful situation they were in by nature, and their full determination to continue seeking till they should

CHURCH HISTORY OF NEW ENGLAND

find him of whom Moses and the prophets did write. I never saw less opposition to any work of God I ever was acquainted with.—More than a hundred we hope have received the grace of God, and more than eighty have joined with our church.—The present number of members, is three hundred and thirty-six."

1800.] OF NEW-ENGLAND. 241

Extracts from these and other letters were printed in a pamphlet at Boston, and afterwards at Philadelphia. At the same time they had a great work among the Baptists near Kennebec river. Elder James Potter, the instrument of beginning the revival there, had ninety-seven members added to his church in Bowdoin, in 1798 and '99; and five hundred and seventy-five were then added to the whole of their association. And Boston, Bridgwater, Middleborough, and many other places had a share of these blessings; and so had some places to the southward.

I received a letter from elder Benjamin Watkins of Virginia, dated June 30, 1801, in which he says, "I have lived to see several revivals in our parts, but the last has been the greatest, which originated about two years ago, in several churches belonging to the middle district association. Before the revival began, wickedness had gotten to a great height. Deism and irreligion abounded on every hand. Professors had become very carnal, many had apostatized, so that there were but a few names in Sardis who had not defiled their garments; so that I had some awful fears about our condition, and was dreading that some great judgment would befall our wretched land. But contrary to my fears, the Lord visited us in a way of mercy, by stirring up his church often to assemble together, and to carry on worship by prayer and fasting, called *prayer meetings*. And he came amongst us, and the sacred flame has spread in various parts of Virginia; so that we may truly say, The lines are fallen unto us in pleasant places, and we have a goodly heritage.

"Our church, called Spring Creek, has an addition by baptism, since the revival began, of upwards of 200 members; brother Clay's about the same number, or more; Brother Smith's about an

242 A CHURCH HISTORY [CH. XIII.

hundred; Tomahawk Church about fifty; Skinquarter near an hundred; elder Webber's church two hundred or more; and several other churches have had some smart additions. The work has chiefly been among the young people; there has not been nigh so much noise amongst us, as there was in 1785 and

'86. Many would come and give a declaration of the work of God upon their souls, that made no noise at all; and, what was remarkable, a number of children, from ten to fifteen years of age, would come and tell of the goodness of God, while the old people, who had lived to see several revivals, are still left out, exposed to the wrath and displeasure of God."

All the churches mentioned above, are in the three counties of Powhatan, Chesterfield and Goochland, in the middle part of Virginia, a little above the city of Richmond, their capital. I had much delight in preaching in all of them, when I was there in the spring of 1789, when they had about two hundred Baptist churches in the whole of Virginia. And the work has been great since in many places farther southward. A minister in the upper part of Georgia wrote to his friend in Savannah, Nov. 17, 1801, and said, "several churches here, within three or four months past, have received and baptized from twenty to fifty persons; and one in Elbert county has had an addition by baptism of about an hundred and forty. And according to the best accounts from Kentucky, there have been added to the Baptist churches, since last March, near six thousand, while multitudes were joining to the Methodists and Presbyterians."

This was put into our public papers, and sent into all the country. Those who held to infant baptism were very uneasy under such things, which they discovered in a remarkable manner; for early in 1802, a book from England was reprinted at Exeter, in New-Hampshire, written by a minister who

1802.]   OF NEW-ENGLAND.   243

had been a Baptist, who held up to the world, that the greatest writers in England against infant baptism were guilty of sophistry and deceit in their arguments, as he had clearly found by experience. And it was said that this testimony had been published seven years in England, and no answer had been made to it. This was so wonderful, that it passed four or five editions in about a year, in the different States of New-England. But when this glorying was at the highest, an answer came out of the press at Boston, in December, 1802, which was first published in London the same year that the first book came out there. The facts here follow.

Mr. Peter Edwards was first a zealous advocate for infant baptism in London, and then turned suddenly from it; became a Baptist preacher, and was ordained in a Baptist church near Portsmouth in England; but in about ten years he changed again, and published this book, to give the reasons for his renouncing the principles of the Baptists, in the beginning of 1795; and

Dr. Joseph Jenkins of London answered him in the same year. Edwards holds up, with much confidence, that faith and repentance were required of all adult persons, in order for circumcision as well as baptism; and therefore that all which is said in the gospel about the baptizing of believers, is no argument against believers having their infants baptized. He accuseth the Baptists in general of denying the use of inferences and consequences, in arguments for infant baptism, but of using them against that practice, which he calls sophistry and deceit. Having disarmed the Baptists, as he imagined, he lays down his foundation in these words: "1. God has instituted in his church the membership of infants, and admitted them to it by a religious rite. 2. The church membership of infants was never set aside by God or man; but continues in force, under the sanction of God, to the present day." p. 90.

244   A CHURCH HISTORY
[CH. XIII.

But as the Baptists never denied the true use of inferences and consequences in any argument, the charge of deceit and sophistry must be turned back upon him who advanced it; and whether his foundation can stand, may be judged of by the following things.

1. Circumcision was not known in the world, for above two thousand years after it was created; and who will say that God had no church in the world for all that time? Yea, when circumcision was instituted, Lot, and other righteous men had no concern in it; neither had any females among the posterity of Abraham, though women are baptized under the gospel as well as men. 2. God said to Israel, "The life of the flesh is in the *blood*, and I have given it to you upon the altar, to make an atonement for your souls." Levit. xvii. 11. And no worship was ever accepted of God from the beginning without *blood* in sacrifices. Abraham shed his own *blood* in circumcision, as the father of all believers in all nations. Rom. iv. 18. And thus he was a type of Christ who shed his *blood* to atone for the sins of all true believers, even to the end of the world. 3. Abraham had no right to circumcise any male but such as were born in his house, or bought with his money; and he circumcised all the *men* of his house, the same day that he circumcised himself, of whom he had before three hundred and eighteen soldiers. Gen. xiv. 14. xvii. 13, 27. And how far is this from a warrant for *infant* baptism! 4. No females were to be circumcised, to shew that it was a *man* and not a woman who was to die for us. 5. The bloody sign of circumcision weakened men so much, that two men destroyed a whole city, three days after the men in it were circumcised. Gen. xxxiv. 25. But no infant that ever was sprinkled, could know that it was done,

if they were not told of it by others. So far are they from answering a good conscience

1802.]   OF NEW-ENGLAND.   245

in baptism. 1 Peter iii. 21. None but believers can do it. 6. Abraham was not to circumcise any stranger, until he had bought him as a servant with his money, which was a type of our being bought with the blood of Christ; and after he had done it, he said, "Circumcision is nothing, and uncircumcision is nothing, but the keeping the com-mandments of God. Ye are bought with a price; be not ye the servants of men." 1 Cor. vii. 19, 23. Which is a plain repeal of the covenant of circumcision. It was a type of the death of Christ to come, and baptism is to be done by faith in him who is already come. This is a reason why men might be circumcised before they believed, and why baptism is only for professing believers. 7. Since he is come, he says, "Ye are all the children, of God by faith in Christ Jesus. For as many of you as have been baptized into Christ, have put on Christ. There is neither Jew nor Greek, there is neither bond nor free, there is neither male nor female; for ye are all one in Christ Jesus. And if ye be Christ's, then are ye Abraham's seed, and heirs according to the promise. Gal. iii. 26—29. Three things are here excluded from baptism, which were essential in circumcision. 8. The children of Israel had no right to admit strangers by households, to circumcision and the passover, until the day in which they came out of Egypt. Exod. xii. 43— 51. But when they were going into Babylon, it was said, "Behold the days come, saith the Lord, that I will make a *new* covenant with the house of Israel, and with the house of Judah, not according to the covenant that I made with their fathers in the day that I took them by the hand, to bring them out of the land of Egypt (which my covenant they break, although I was an husband unto them, saith the Lord ;) but this shall be the covenant that I will make with the house of Israel, After those days, saith the Lord, I will put my law

246   A CHURCH HISTORY   [CH. XIII.

in their inward parts, and write it in their hearts, and I will be their God, and they shall be my people. And they shall teach no more every man his neighbour, and every man his brother, saying, Know the Lord; for they shall all know me, from the least of them unto the greatest of them, saith the Lord; for I will forgive their iniquity, and I will remember their sin no more." Jer. xxxi. 31—34. This is the pure covenant of grace, since the death of Christ hath taken away the *old* covenant. Heb. viii. 7—13. Language cannot distinguish two covenants more clearly, than God hath here done it. And until old and new, first and second, can be made to mean but one covenant, men can never prove infant baptism by said covenant. 9. God promised that kings should come out of Abraham. Gen. xvii. 6. And this was fulfilled in David and his race, and in the King Messiah; and this shews that no man now can stand in such a relation to his children as Abraham did to his. Aaron was also a type of Christ, and his lawful posterity were the only priests in Israel until Christ came, when the priesthood was *changed*; and Christ is both our king and priest. Heb. vii. 12. And God says to those who are *born again*, among all nations. "Ye are a chosen generation, a royal priesthood, an holy nation, a peculiar people; that ye should shew forth the praises of him who hath called you out of darkness into his marvellous light." 1 Peter i. 23. ii. 9. And such are the only priests, and holy nation, that are ever named in the church of Christ. By his death he abolished all those ancient types, and formed his church of all souls who are born again among all nations; and officers in his church are never called priests therein, in distinction from other children of God. Worldly churches have been built upon infant baptism, which is not named in the Holy Scriptures.

1802.]   OF NEW-ENGLAND.   247

CHAP. XIV.

A view of the Baptist churches in South-Carolina.—In Pennsylvania and New-Jersey.—In Virginia.—Presbyterians there.—A difference among the Baptists healed. The cause of equal liberty among them.—A view of them in North-Carolina.—In Georgia.—Of Negro Baptists.—Of the Baptists in the State of New-York.—In Kentucky.—Of Associations.—Of the number of Baptists in all America.—Of late revivals.—Of their likeness to the first fathers of our country.—How infant baptism originated.—A happy change in our government.—Light from the case of Israel.—Of the latter day glory.

TRUTH and love, and persecution for the same, caused the first planting of New-England; and it also caused the planting of Baptist churches in the southern parts of America. Some men from here, and some from England, Wales and Ireland, all had a hand in it. When elder William Scraven was cruelly persecuted in the province of Maine, in 1682, he went to Charleston in South-Carolina, and became pastor of a Baptist church there. How long it had been formed I know not. But when the Baptist church in Boston wanted a pastor, and sent for him, who had been one of them, he wrote to them, June

2, 1707, and said, "Our minister who came from England is dead, and I can by no means be spared. I must say it is a great loss, and to me a great disappointment; but the will of the Lord is done." And he wrote again, August 6, 1708, and said, "I have been brought very low by sickness, but I bless God, I was helped to preach, and administer the communion last Lord's-day; but am still weak. Our society are for the most part in health, and I hope thriving in grace. We are about ninety in all." And his posterity have

248   A CHURCH HISTORY   [CH. XIV.

been honourable, and useful in those parts ever since. Mr. Isaac Chanler was a Baptist minister among them for many years, and a book of his upon the doctrines of the gospel was printed at Boston in 1744. Mr. Oliver Hart, from Pennsylvania, got to Charleston in 1749, just after Mr. Chanler died, and was pastor of that church thirty years. But as he was heartily engaged for liberty in America, he left Charleston, before the British forces took it, in 1780, and settled as pastor of the Baptist church at Hopewell in New-Jersey the same year, where he was very useful, till he died in 1795. But the Baptist cause has prevailed much in that State to this day.

       Thomas Dungen of Newport was one of the signers of the request to Mr. Clarke, to go as their agent to England in 1651, the original of which I now have. And about 1684, two years after Pennsylvania began, Bungen went there, and preached the Baptist principles among the people, with considerable success; and his posterity are numerous among them ever since. And about 1686, Elias Keach, son to elder Benjamin Keach of London, came over to Philadelphia, a wild young man, but was soon after converted, and laboured earnestly to collect the Baptists together; and they formed a church at Pennepeck, eleven miles from Philadelphia, in 1688. Mr. Keach also was helpful in forming a Baptist church at Middletown, and another at Piscataway in 1689; and one at Cohansey in 1690, all three in New-Jersey. And these four, with that at Charleston, were all the Baptist churches that were formed south of New-England, before the year 1700. Many of those who constituted the church at Cohansey, came from Ireland; though one of them was Obadiah Holmes, Esq. a son of the sufferer at Boston in 1651; and others of his posterity have since been members of the church in Middletown. Piscataway, on Raritan

1802.]   OF NEW-ENGLAND.   249

CHURCH HISTORY OF NEW ENGLAND

river in the Jersey, sprang partly from people who came from Piscataqua river, which has Kittery upon the north side of it, where the Baptist church was formed in 1682, who were scattered by persecution. Other members of those churches went from Rhode Island colony, as appears by the publications of Mr. Morgan Edwards, in 1770, and 1792. He was born in Wales, from whence also came many ministers and members of those churches; and I took many of the above things from him.

And he informs us of many people who came over from Wales in 1701, and resided near their brethren at Pennepeck, until they removed in 1703, and planted a church in a place they called Welshtract, then under the government of Pennsylvania, but now under Delaware State. In 1770, they had increased to ten churches in Pennsylvania, and 668 members, besides a few who kept the seventh-day sabbath. He gives an account also of the Tunkers, the first of whom came from Germany in 1719, and had increased to fifteen societies, and a large number of communicants, who were not in fellowship with the English churches. They dip persons with their faces forward, three times over. They hold to general redemption, and are much like the old Quakers in their general conduct, though more strict than they are now. The Mennonists also came from Germany, and are of like behaviour, but they are not truly Baptists now. Their fathers were so in Luther's day, until confinement in prison brought them to pour water on the head of the subjects, instead of immersion; and what was then done out of necessity, is now done out of choice, as other corruptions are. When Edwards published his book in 1792, the first-day Baptists in the Jersey had 24 churches, and 2994 members; and those who kept the seventh day,

250   A CHURCH HISTORY   [CH. XIV.

3 churches and 249 members. And in 1802, the Philadelphia Association had 2695 members.

North-Carolina had but little appearance of religion in any part of it, until late years. Some Baptist ministers from New-Jersey and Pennsylvania travelled and laboured there with some success, and some who went from New-England settled there. Shubael Stearns was born in Boston, January 28, 1706; but he went to Connecticut, where he was baptized, and was ordained at Tolland, March 20, 1751, and continued there three years. But then his soul was fired with zeal to carry light into those dark parts; and in August, 1754, he and others set off for that purpose, and some of them got into North-Carolina before him; and he wrote to Connecticut from the south part of Virginia, that they informed him from Carolina, "That the work of God was

188

great, in preaching to an ignorant people, who had little or no preaching for an hundred miles, and no established meeting. But now the people were so eager to hear, that they would come forty miles each way, when they could have opportunity to hear a sermon." This was dated June 13, 1755; and Stearns went and settled upon Sandy Creek, which runs into Cape Fear river, where he formed a church, November 22, 1755, which increased to 606 members, in a few years, and several other churches were soon formed round him.

Daniel Marshall was born at Windsor in Connecticut, and after he was called to preach, he went and laboured some time among the Indians, in the upper part of New-Jersey, and then followed Stearns into North-Carolina, where he was very successful. And in and after 1758, many were converted and baptized near the south borders of Virginia, and they began an association in 1760, of five churches in Carolina, and one in Virginia, and they increased fast. On October 16, 1765, Stearns wrote to

1802.]   OF NEW-ENGLAND.   251

Connecticut, and said, "The Lord carries on his work gloriously, in sundry places in this province, and in Virginia, and in South-Carolina. There has been no addition of churches, since I wrote last year, but many members have been added in many places. Not long since, I attended a meeting on Hoy river, about thirty miles from hence. About seven hundred souls attended the meeting, which held six days. We received twenty-four persons by a satisfactory declaration of grace, and eighteen of them were baptized. The power of God was wonderful."

But we must now come to Virginia, of which it may be said, The first is last, and the last first. It was planted in 1607, the first of all our English colonies; and though it was done entirely from worldly motives, yet the worship of the church of England was established by law, and no other worship was allowed of there for an hundred years. In 1643, three Congregational ministers went there, at the request of a number of the inhabitants, but they were forced to depart the colony, after preaching a few sermons. And directly upon it, the savages were let loose upon the English, and destroyed about five hundred of them. This one of them declared in England afterwards, where he again suffered from Episcopalians.* In 1644, Daniel Gookin left Virginia, and became a very useful man in the Massachusetts for many years.†

The first Baptist church in Virginia was formed in Prince George county, in 1714, by Robert Norden, who then came from England, and was

CHURCH HISTORY OF NEW ENGLAND

their pastor till he died, in 1725. In 1727, Mr. Richard Jones was ordained their pastor; and in 1742, they had about 40 members, as one of them then wrote to Newport, which letter I have. About

* Calamy's Account, vol. ii. p. 607.
† Historical Society, vol. i. p. 228.

252 A CHURCH HISTORY [CH. XIV.

the same time, a man went from thence and formed a church on the sea coasts of North-Carolina. But these all held to general redemption, and their churches are since dissolved.

In the mean time, religion was revived in Virginia by other means; for Samuel Morris, of Hanover county, was converted in 1740, by reading some old books; and Upon his reading them to his neighbours, they set up a meeting at his house, instead of going to church. And in 1743, he obtained a book of sermons, taken down in short hand, as Mr. Whitefield delivered them in Glasgow, and printed there. The reading of these had such an effect upon the people, that more came to hear them than his house could hold, and they built a meeting-house for the purpose. He was also called to read them in several other places, and many were affected thereby. But they were called to account for not going to church, and they pleaded the act of toleration for dissenters, though they knew not what to call themselves. At length they called themselves Lutherans, because they had received much benefit from the writings of that reformer. And hearing of a wonderful preacher, near an hundred miles off, they sent for him, in July, 1743, and he preached to them four days, with exceeding great effect; and he advised them to pray and sing in their meetings, which they had not done before; so great is the influence of tradition. Mr. William Robinson was the man whose labours had then been so much blessed among them; and when he was going away, they asked him what he called himself; he said, "A Presbyterian." "Then we are Presbyterians too," said they, "for your religion is just like ours."

They then sent for other ministers of that denomination, from Pennsylvania and New-Jersey, and obtained help from them, from time to time, until Mr. Samuel Davies settled there in 1748.

1802.] OF NEW-ENGLAND. 253

And in 1751, he published an account of this work, and of other Presbyterians in those parts. Mr. Davies became the President of New-Jersey college afterwards, and died there; and his sermons are now much esteemed in Europe, as well as America. Those ministers met at Philadelphia in 1789, and formed a society which they called, "The General Assembly of the Presbyterian Church, in the United States of America." In 1793, it was said that they had about two hundred churches in all the States south of New-England.* But they have very few of them in the old part of Virginia, where the Baptists have increased greatly.

Mr. Samuel Harris was born in Hanover county, January 12, 1724, and he was so much esteemed, that he became a Colonel of their militia, a member of their Legislature, and a judge of their courts, before he was converted in 1758; when he not only became a Baptist preacher, but also much of a father among their churches for above thirty years. And some ministers from Pennsylvania went and formed some Baptist churches in the north part of Virginia, about 1760, who were not fully agreed with those southern Baptists, for the following reasons: The Philadelphia association had adopted the confession of faith which was composed by the Baptists in London in 1689, with the addition of an article which required the laying on of hands upon every member of the church, which the others did not hold. Some eminent ministers in England had also carried the doctrine of particular election so far, as to deny that any minister had a right to address the calls of the gospel to all sinners without distinction, and the Philadelphians had adopted this opinion; and they called themselves Regular Baptists, while those who went from Connecticut were called Separates.

* Rippon's Register, vol. ii. p. 131.

And there were unhappy contentions between them for many years; for the New-England Baptists in general do not hold to the laying on of hands upon every member, nor to the above restriction of the calls of the gospel.

We generally believe the doctrine of particular election, and the final perseverance of every true believer, while we proclaim a free salvation to all the children of men, and even to the chief of sinners; and we hold that God has appointed the means as well as the end, and the means in order to the end of every event. When the Jews were obstinate against receiving Jesus as the true Messiah, he said, "I thank thee, O Father, Lord of heaven and earth, because thou hast hid these things from the wise and prudent, and hast revealed them unto babes. Even so, Father, for so it seemed good in thy sight. All things are delivered unto me of my Father; and no man knoweth the Son, but the Father; neither knoweth any man the Father, save the Son, and he to whomsoever the Son will reveal him. Come unto me, all ye that labour, and are heavy laden, and I will give you rest. Take my yoke upon you, and learn of me, for I am meek and lowly in heart, and ye shall find rest unto your souls: for my yoke is easy, and my burden is light." Mat. xi. 25—30. The only reason why any one is chosen, called and saved, rather than another, is because so it seemed good in the sight of God. But many men imagine that the choice and doings of men are the cause of it, and so would take the glory of it to themselves, instead of giving it to God alone. God never fails of doing justice to all, while he says, "I will be gracious to whom I will be gracious, and will shew mercy on whom I will shew mercy." And his glory essentially requires this. Exod. xxxiii. 18, 19. Therefore he says, "Is it not lawful for me to do what I will with mine

1802.]   OF NEW-ENGLAND.   255

own?" Mat. xx. 15. The meanest person upon earth has a right to give his own property to whom he will; and how mad are those who deny this right to the eternal God! Many ruin their souls by fighting against God, but it is impossible for him to be deceived or disappointed in any of his designs of mercy, as well as of justice. And free salvation by the Son of God is held forth to all men in the gospel, as openly as the brazen serpent was to the camp of Israel; and the condemnation of all who do not receive him, is because they *hate the light*. John iii. 14—20. Therefore the most moving methods ought to be taken with sinners in general, to enlighten and turn them from sin to God.— Light concerning these things gained gradually among the Baptists in Virginia, so as to unite them as one people in 1787, and they have increased much since.

Mr. John Leland, from whom I had many of these things, was born at Grafton in the Massachusetts, May 14, 1754; and after he was baptized and called to preach, he set off with his young wife, in the fall of 1776, and went into Virginia, and settled in the county of Orange. He travelled and laboured much in those parts, and had a considerable hand in procuring the law for equal liberty, before inserted. Though the behaviour of Episcopal ministers themselves did more towards it; for many of them would play cards, swear profanely, and get drunk, while they imprisoned about thirty Baptist ministers for preaching the gospel to precious souls, without licence from them. This moved their rulers to abolish such tyranny. Mr. Leland baptized about an hundred persons in and near York-town, the year before the British army was captivated there; and in the whole he baptized above six hundred in those parts. He published a Virginia Chronicle, before referred to, and some other things; and in 1791, he returned to New-

256 A CHURCH HISTORY [CH. XIV.

England, and settled in Cheshire in the Massachusetts.

But Mr. Stearns spent his life in those parts, and died in peace, November 20, 1771. And the Baptists have been increasing in North-Carolina ever since, and have been so highly esteemed by their fellow-citizens, that many members of their churches have been representatives and senators in their legislature, judges in their courts, and in other offices of their government.

Mr. Daniel Marshall, after much service there, went on to Georgia, where he formed a church in 1772, and was the pastor of it until he died, it being the first Baptist church in that State; and his son Abraham Marshall has been pastor of it ever since. The Baptists have been the most numerous of any religious denomination in Georgia, for many years past. They have lately increased much in Savannah, their capital. The late honourable Joseph Clay, who had been one of the federal judges of the District Court, was ordained a Baptist minister there, in January, 1804. There are many associations in those parts, in one of which were fifty-six churches, and three thousand, seven hundred and ninety-six members, in 1792; and they have greatly increased since. One minister baptized about an hundred persons there, in the year 1803; and when the first association of South-Carolina met that fall, they received the report of Mr. John Rooker, one of their ministers, who had been sent to preach among the Catawba Indians, that his preaching among them was received with much attention, and they were very thankful for his being sent among them; and they not only desired him to come again, but also that a school-master might be sent to teach the Indian youth in human learning, and also in Christian principles. The association agreed to send him among them again, and also a school-master, according to their request,

1804.] OF NEW-ENGLAND. 257

and to bear their expenses. Some of the English near them appeared to have a gracious work begun among them, and it was hoped that the Indians would share in the same blessing.

A great many Negroes in those parts have been converted and baptized, and some of them have been called to preach the gospel. George Liele was so a little before our American War; and in the time of it he fell into

CHURCH HISTORY OF NEW ENGLAND

British hands, and went down and baptized a number in Savannah, and then was carried to Jamaica, where he began to preach to the blacks in 1784; and he behaved so well as to be favoured by the government there, and his success was so great that he had 350 members in his church in 1791.* And we have heard of much increase among them since. There is one such minister and church in Virginia, beside a great number of blacks who have joined to the English churches there. And Andrew Bryan has a large negro church in Savannah in Georgia; and Mr. Abraham Marshall assisted in his ordination. The Charleston association, in 1803, received an account from the Bethel association, that more than fourteen hundred persons had joined to all their churches in a year. Such has been the work in those parts.

The first Baptist church in the State of New-York was formed at Oyster bay on Long-Island. Elder Robert Feke wrote from thence to Newport, November 29, 1741, and said, "God has begun a glorious work among us, and I hope he will carry it on to his own glory, and the salvation of many souls. There have been seventeen added to our little band in about three months." I suppose their church had not been formed long.

* Rippon's Register, vol. i. p. 334.

258   A CHURCH HISTORY   [CH. XIV.

The first Baptist church in the city of New-York was formed in 1762, under the ministry of Mr. John Gano, who is since in Kentucky. There were a few Baptist churches before, northward of the city, near Connecticut line. And soon after the British army was captivated at Saratoga, in 1777, many such churches were formed in those parts, and they have been increasing ever since. And a large number of people have removed from New-England, and planted the lands near the heads of the Mohawk, Susquehanna, and Genesee rivers; and a Baptist church was formed in 1789 near the Otsego lake, which is the first church in the Otsego association, which was formed in 1795, and it increased in three years to 28 churches, and 1292 members. They have been increasing to this day, and have formed another association further westward. These associations have sent ministers to preach to the Six Nations of Indians, and also among the English in Upper Canada, where they have been well received, and an association is formed there. Several Baptist ministers in those parts were preachers before in Congregational churches. If we look again to the southward, we may still see greater wonders of grace, as well as of Divine Providence.

The lands upon the river Ohio were so much esteemed, both by the French and English nations, that they commenced a war about them in 1755, which ended in yielding those lands, as well as all Canada, to Great-Britain. Our people began to plant Kentucky about 1777, and inhabitants have increased so much in that state, as now to have six representatives in Congress, which is one more than New-Hampshire has. Many of the inhabitants went from Virginia, and the Baptists have increased to six associations, and to 14076 communicants in their churches, as we had a printed account in 1802. And there are a large number of such

churches on both sides of the Ohio, besides those in Kentucky; and they are scattered into each of these United States.

As associations have been often mentioned, I will now describe the nature of them. Associations had been very cruel and oppressive in Connecticut, as they were there established by law; and many Baptists could not believe, for a long time, that they could be so conducted as to be serviceable any way; and it has ever been difficult to keep a clear distinction in our minds, between the real nature of things, and the abuse of them which is very common. When difficulties arise in churches, few have the patience and wisdom which is necessary, for the carrying the laws of Christ into effect against offenders, without looking to any earthly power for help in such cases.

The Warren Association was formed, September 8, 1767, upon the following principles. They refuse to hear and judge of any personal controversy in any of their churches, or to intermeddle with the affairs of any church which hath not freely joined with them. When any church desires to join with them, they send messengers and a letter to the association, shewing when their church was formed, the faith and order of it, and their number of members. If satisfaction is gained, they are received by a vote of the Association, and the moderator gives the messengers the right hand of fellowship. Each church is to send messengers and a letter, or a letter at least, to the annual meeting of the association, to give an account of the date of their church, and how many have been added, dismissed, excluded, or that have died in the year. If this is neglected for a number of years, or if the church departs from her former faith and order, she is left out of the Association. In 1771, they began to print the minutes of their annual proceedings, which any may have if they

CHURCH HISTORY OF NEW ENGLAND

will. By these means, mutual acquaintance and communion hath been begotten and promoted; errors in doctrine or conduct have been exposed and guarded against; false teachers have been detected, and warnings published against them; destitute flocks have been occasionally supplied; the weak and oppressed have been relieved, and many have been animated and encouraged in preaching the gospel through the land, and in new plantations in the wilderness.

A collection is made at our annual meetings for the widows and children of poor ministers. A society has also been incorporated, to collect money to assist pious youths in obtaining learning, with a view to the ministry. And a Missionary Society is formed to collect money for the support of travelling ministers, and to instruct and direct them therein, according to their best discretion. And several of them have visited many destitute flocks, and some have gone into Upper Canada, with great acceptance.

The Warren Association has extended over all the old colony of Plymouth, and over the Massachusetts as high as Connecticut river, and into the borders of three other States; and its benefits soon became visible to others. The Stonington Association began in 1772, and it extends over the east part of Connecticut, and the west of Rhode Island State. The New-Hampshire Association began in 1776, and it extends over the east part of that State, and over the county of York in the District of Maine. The Shaftsbury Association began in 1781, and it is in the southwest part of Vermont, the west of the Massachusetts, and east of New-York State. The Woodstock Association began in 1783, and is in the easterly part of Vermont, and westerly of New-Hampshire. The Groton Conference began in 1785, and it extends from Connecticut river near the sea, across the State of

1804.]   OF NEW-ENGLAND.   261

Rhode Island, into the county of Bristol in the Massachusetts. The Bowdoinham Association began in 1787, and it extends over three counties in the District of Maine. The Vermont Association began the same year, and it is in the northwest part of that State. The Meredith Association began in 1789, and is in the northerly part of New-Hampshire, and the adjoining part of Vermont. The Danbury Association began in 1790, and it extends from the south borders of the Massachusetts, across Connecticut to the sea, west of their great river. The Leyden Association began in 1793, on the north borders of the Massachusetts, and it extends into the corners of New-Hampshire and Vermont, on both sides of Connecticut river. The Richmond Conference began in 1795, and is in the northeast part of Vermont. The Sturbridge Association began in 1801, and it is in the southerly part of the middle of Massachusetts, and northerly of Connecticut.

Thus we have thirteen associations in New-England, in which are 312 churches, and 23638 members, where there were but nine Baptist churches in 1700, and but five more in all America. We have also many other churches in New-England beside what are in these Associations; and I conclude that in the whole of these United States, there are now about twelve hundred Baptist churches, and an hundred thousand members. And the main of them have been formed within forty years past. The work of God in late years has given much light to our old Baptist churches. The darkness that was in the first Baptist church in Boston, caused the forming of the second in 1742; but light gradually gained among them, until they settled a pastor there in 1765, who was clear in gospel doctrines; and religion was soon after revived there, and the two churches were united, and they have been increasing to this

262   A CHURCH HISTORY   [CH. XIV.

day. They have gained such credit in our government, that Dr. Stillman, pastor of their first church, was called to preach the election sermon at Boston in 1779, and Dr. Baldwin, pastor of the second, in 1802. In the spring of 1803, religion was again revived in Boston, which still continues, and their two churches have increased to 640 members. This work is now powerful in Charlestown, Malden, Woburn, Reading, Danvers, Salem and Beverly; the first of which churches was formed in 1793, and the rest since, all within about twenty miles of Boston. Our churches in general hold to the doctrines of grace, Christian experience, and the importance of a holy life, much as the chief fathers of New-England did. They differ very little from the fathers of Plymouth colony, only about infant baptism. And though the fathers of the Massachusetts made laws to establish the government of the church over the world, yet when that power was lost, Boston renounced the government of the world over the church, as we have proved. And this practice cannot now be vindicated by Scripture, reason, nor by the example of any of the fathers of New-England, for seventy years after it was planted. And it is also contrary to the general government of these United States.

Infant baptism was not named in the holy Scriptures, nor in any history, for two hundred years after the birth of Christ. And when it was first named, ministers called it *regeneration*. Because Christ says, "Except a man be born of water, and of the Spirit, he cannot enter into the kingdom of God," they held that baptism washed away original sin, and that infants could not be saved if they were not baptized. And because Christ says, "Except ye eat the flesh of the Son of man, and drink his blood, ye have no life in you," they held that no person could be saved without eating the Lord's Supper; and they brought infants to it, as well as

1804.]   OF NEW-ENGLAND.   263

to baptism. For the truth of these facts, we appeal to the most noted writings of the third and fourth centuries. A noted minister of the third century said, "It is for that reason, because by the sacrament of baptism the pollution of our birth is taken away, that infants are baptized."*

This, and more of like nature, was quoted by an eminent advocate for infant baptism in our day, to defend the practice, though not the opinion of its being regeneration. But the church of Rome, and the church of England, have long held that ministers could regenerate persons by baptizing them. And they who renounced that practice have been called Anabaptists to this day. Natural affection for children, and for the sick and dying, has caused an amazing attachment to ministers who they thought could save persons from hell by baptizing them; and from thence came the notion of the necessity of an external succession of ministerial ordinations, even through the corruptions of antichrist.

But as fire and wind, as well as water, are of a cleansing influence, they are all made use of to explain the nature of regeneration, which is effected only by the power of the Holy Ghost. Mat. iii. 11. John iii. 5, 8. The work of sanctification in believers is carried on by the ordinances of baptism and the holy supper, but they are not spoken of in Scripture as the means of begetting faith in any person; for faith cometh by hearing the word of God. Rom. x. 17. But in all nations where ministers have been supported by force, only one party of teachers and rulers have shared in the gains of it, to the constant injury of all the rest of the community. And this way has been upheld by perverse disputers, who have supposed that gain was godliness. 1 Tim. vi. 5. But if the vengeance of

* Clark's defence of infant baptism, 1752, p. 111.

264   A CHURCH HISTORY   [CH. XIV.

God came upon men who were *partial* in his law, what will he do to those who make *partial* laws of their own? Mal. ii. 9.

And since a door is now opened in our land for a clear deliverance from these evils, can any man be free of guilt if he tries to shut it? This consideration is enforced by late experience; for the man, who was the Chief Magistrate of these United States for four years, was very fond of such *partiality*. But a man was elected into that office in 1801, who is for equal liberty to all the nation. And if the Holy Scriptures are well regarded, we shall be the happiest people upon earth; for they shew that every man, who is fit for a ruler, is like good trees and vines, which yield sweet fruits to all around them, without injuring anyone; and that tyrants are like the bramble, which would set the whole community on *fire*, and burn up the best characters in it, if they stood in the way of their gratifying their own lusts of pride and covetousness. Judges ix. 7—15. Therefore our Lord says, "By their fruits ye shall know them." Mat. vii. 20. And this should ever guide all electors of officers, as well as all men in office.

A review of the dealings of God with his ancient people, may afford much help to us all. For the highest rulers in Israel had no right to make any laws at all, but were to govern the people by the laws of God, which he had given them by Moses and the prophets. The tribe of Levi, in which was the family of Aaron, were to have the whole government of their worship, and to offer sacrifices upon the altar of God. Those offerings, with the tenth part of the produce of the good land which he had given them, were freely to be brought in annually to the place which God chose, and the Priests and Levites were to have their living in that way, and they were to have the care of the poor. Each man in Israel was to bring in those tithes and offerings

1804.] OF NEW-ENGLAND. 265

to the place which God chose, in such a manner as to be able to say before him, "I have brought away the hallowed things out of mine house, and also have given them unto the Levite, and unto the stranger, to the fatherless and the widow according to all thy commandments which thou hast commanded me; I have not transgressed thy commandments, neither have I forgotten them. I have not eaten thereof in my mourning, neither have I taken ought thereof, for any unclean use, nor given ought thereof for the dead; but I have hearkened to the voice of the Lord my God, and have done all that thou hast commanded me. Look down from thy holy habitation, from heaven, and bless thy people Israel, and the land which thou hast given us, as thou swearest unto our fathers, a land that floweth with milk and honey. This day the Lord thy God hath commanded thee to do these statutes and judgments; thou shalt therefore keep and do them with all thine heart, and with all thy soul. Thou

CHURCH HISTORY OF NEW ENGLAND

hast avouched the Lord this day to be thy God, and to walk in his ways, and to keep his statutes, and his commandments, and his judgments, and to hearken to his voice. And the Lord hath avouched thee this day to be his peculiar people, as he hath promised thee, and that thou shouldst keep all his commandments; and to make thee high above all nations which he hath made, in praise, and in name, and in honour, and that thou mayest be an holy people unto the Lord thy God, as he hath spoken." Deut. xxvi. 13—19.

Thus we may see that the support of religious ministers in Israel, as well as the poor, was to be done voluntarily, as each man would desire the blessing of God upon his labours, as well as the salvation of his soul; and also that they could not be a holy people in any other way, but by obeying the

266   A CHURCH HISTORY   [CH. XIV.

voice of God with all their hearts, and with all their souls. And for any community to call themselves a holy people, only because they have an established worship by the laws of men, enforced by the sword, is directly contrary to the national worship of Israel which was owned of God. Christ was tempted in all points like as we are, and the devil tempted him to presume upon being supported by the promise of God, without going in the ways of his precepts. Mat. iv. 6, 7. Psalm xci. 11, 12. And how full is the world of this iniquity!

The nation of Israel was advanced above all other nations, when they obeyed the revealed will of God, in the days of David and Solomon, according to this promise. But in after generations they declined from that way, until God said, "As troops of robbers wait for a man, so the company of priests murder in the way by consent." Hosea vi. 9. "The heads thereof judge for reward, the priests thereof teach for hire, and the prophets thereof divine for money; yet will they lean upon the Lord, and say, Is not the Lord among us? None evil can come upon us. Therefore shall Zion for your sake be ploughed as a field, and Jerusalem shall become heaps, and the mountain of the house as the high places of the forest." Micah iii. 11, 12. This prophecy was partly accomplished by the Babylonians, and fully by the Romans. And the Jews are now monuments of warning to all nations. Isaiah xxx. 17. Thus present events prove the truth of revelation.

Before the destruction of the second temple, God gave the Jews a new warning, and said, "Will a man rob God? Yet ye have robbed me; but ye say, Wherein have we robbed thee? In tithes and offerings. Ye are cursed with a curse; for ye have robbed me, even this whole nation. Bring ye all the tithes into the store-house, that there may be meat in mine house, and prove me now herewith,

1804.]   OF NEW-ENGLAND.   267

saith the Lord of hosts, if I will not open you the windows of heaven, and pour you out a blessing, that there shall not be room enough to receive it." Mal. iii. 8—10.

Here we may see that a voluntary obedience to God about his worship and ministers, or the contrary, brought his blessings or curses upon his people and he now says to people under the gospel, "Do ye not know that they which minister about holy things, live of the things of the temple, and they which wait at the altar are partakers with the altar? Even so hath the Lord ordained, that they which preach the gospel should live of the gospel." 1 Cor. ix. 13, 14. But as some ministers of the devil had prejudiced many in the church of Corinth against this apostle, he refused to take any support of them, though he said "Forgive me this wrong." 2 Cor. xi. 13—15. xii. 13. Thus it appears, that there is a stronger guard set against deceitful teachers, by the laws of Christ, than there was by the law of Moses. Yet such is the depravity of human nature, that the supporting of ministers of the devil by force hath filled the world with war and blood, under the name of Christianity, much more than the nation of Israel ever did. And this is now the greatest handle that infidels have to use against revealed religion. The command is, "Let God be true, but every man a liar;" while many bring the lies of men against the truth of God, and so discover that he hath said the truth concerning them.

Upon the case before us, he says, "Let him that is taught in the word, communicate unto him that teacheth in all good things. Be not deceived, God is not mocked; for whatsoever a man soweth, that shall he also reap. For he that soweth to the flesh, shall of the flesh reap corruption; but he that soweth to the Spirit, shall of the Spirit reap life everlasting." Gal. vi. 6—8. So that everlasting life, or

268   A CHURCH HISTORY   [CH. XIV.

endless misery, are connected with faithfulness or unfaithfulness in this affair. Yea, and these things are personal between God and individuals, as much as faith and unbelief are; and therefore they are entirely out of the jurisdiction of the magistrate. And we have a glorious promise of God, which says, "In the last days it shall come to pass, that the mountain of the house of the Lord shall be established in the top of the mountains, and it shall be exalted above the hills, and people shall flow unto it. And many nations shall come and say, "Come and let us go up to the mountain of the Lord, and to the habitation of the God of Jacob, and he will teach us of his ways, and we will walk in his paths; for the law shall go forth of Zion, and the word of the Lord from Jerusalem. And he shall judge among the people, and rebuke strong nations afar off, and they shall beat their swords into ploughshares, and their spears into pruning hooks; nation shall not lift up sword against nation, neither shall they learn war anymore. But they shall sit every man under his vine, and under his fig-tree, and none shall make them afraid; for the mouth of the Lord of hosts hath spoken it. For all people will walk every one in the name of his god, and we will walk in the name of the Lord our God, forever and ever." Micah iv. 1—5.

Now it is most certain that this prophecy hath never yet been fulfilled; but it will as surely come to pass hereafter, as ever the promise did of Christ's being born of a virgin. The mountains and hills here mean the kingdoms and states of this world, and the mountain of the house of the Lord, is the kingdom of Christ, who will subdue all other kingdoms, and reign forever. And he says, "The kingdom, and dominion, and the greatness of the kingdom under the whole heaven shall be given to the people of the saints of the Most High; whose kingdom is an everlasting kingdom, and all dominions shall serve and obey him." Daniel ii. 35, 44.

1804.]   OF NEW-ENGLAND.   269

vii. 27. People shall go up to the house of God, and personally obey his revealed will, as freely as the water *flows* in its channels. And what can be freer than water? Every idea of force is excluded from the support of his worship; and all the force for the support of religious teachers, that ever was used under the name of Christianity, was done by adding to his word. And Christ says, "I testify unto every man that heareth the words of the prophecy of this book, If any man shall add unto these things, God shall add unto him the plagues that are written in this book; and if any man shall take away from the words of the book of this prophecy, God shall take away his part out of the book of life, and out of the holy city, and from the things which are written in this book." Rev. xxii. 18, 19.

O how solemn are these things! Mystery Babylon was built by adding to the word of God, and by taking away what is plainly written in it; and all religious establishments by the laws of men, that ever were made in our world, were made in that way, and so are parts of that great city. She is the mother of harlots, and she hath many daughters. And as Christ is the only head of his church, every community that supports her ministers in the name of any earthly head, is a harlot. And in Babylon was found the blood of prophets, and of saints, and of all that were slain upon the earth. Rev. xviii. 24. The blood of Abel was shed by Cain, because his own works were evil, and his brother's righteous. 1 John, iii. 12. And the guilt of blood will come upon all men who imitate old persecutors. Mat. xxiii. 35, 36. And God says, "In the last days perilous times shall come; for men shall be lovers of their ownselves, covetous, boasters, proud, blasphemers, disobedient to parents, unthankful, unholy, without natural affection, truce breakers, false accusers, incontinent,

270 A CHURCH HISTORY [CH. XIV.

fierce, despisers of those that are good, traitors, heady, high minded, lovers of pleasures more than lovers of God; having a form of godliness, but denying the power thereof: from such turn away." 2 Tim. iii. x—5.

Language cannot describe our times more exactly, than it was thus done by God, near eighteen hundred years ago. And how blind must men be, if they imagine that godliness can be supported by such characters! and yet such have equal votes in government with the best men in it. The best churches that ever supported their ministers by force, had no more than *a form* of godliness; and all men have denied the *power* of it, who have denied that the laws and Spirit of Christ were entirely sufficient to support his ministers, without any arm of flesh in the case. And God says, "Hold fast *the form* of sound words, which thou hast heard of me, in faith and love which is in Christ Jesus." And *the form* says, "All scripture is given by inspiration of God, and is profitable for doctrine, for reproof, for correction, for instruction in righteousness; that the man of God may be perfect, thoroughly furnished unto all good works." 2 Tim. i. 13. iii. 16, 17.

The men of the world are allowed to make laws, and to enforce them with the sword, to punish immoralities, and to keep the civil peace; and real Christians are best subjects of civil government in the world, while they obey God rather than man *in the form of godliness*. And though the worst of wars have lately been carried on by sea, yet it will hereafter be said, "Look upon Zion, the city of our solemnities; thine eyes shall see Jerusalem a quiet habitation, a tabernacle that shall not be taken down; not one of the stakes thereof shall ever be removed, neither shall any of the cords thereof be broken. But there the glorious Lord will be unto us a place of broad rivers and streams; wherein shall go no

1804.] OF NEW-ENGLAND. 271

CHURCH HISTORY OF NEW ENGLAND

galley with oars, neither shall gallant ships pass thereby. For the Lord is our judge, the Lord is our lawgiver, the Lord is our king, he will save us. Thy tacklings are loosed; they could not well strengthen their mast; they could not spread the sail: then is the prey of a great spoil divided; the lame take the prey." Isaiah xxxiii. 20—23. And though the merchants of Babylon, and her mariners, will make great lamentations for the loss of their *bloody* gains, yet the Holy Spirit says, "Rejoice over her, thou heaven, and ye holy apostles and prophets, for God hath avenged you on her." Rev. xviii. 20. The apostles explained the prophets, and finished writing the book of God; and heaven and earth will rejoice to see his truth and justice glorified.

FINIS.

IN our third volume are many accounts of particular churches, and of other things which are not in this volume, and it may be had by itself where this is sold.

ERRATA.

Page 10, line 34, r. apostle.

15, l. 3, r. had, instead of has.

73, l. 1, r. the, instead of that.

212, l. 11, r. 1778, instead of 1776.

Bibliography

A full bibliography of religion in North America during Backus's lifetime is beyond the scope of this work. This is an abbreviated bibliography on Backus and related topics.

Backus, Isaac. *A History of New England, With Particular Reference to the Denomination of Christians Called Baptists. Second Edition, with Notes. By David Weston*. Newton, MA: Backus Historical Society, 1871.

———. *A History of New-England, with Particular Reference to the Denomination of Christians Called Baptists*. Boston, MA: Printed by Edward Draper, at his printing-office in Newbury-Street, 1777.

———. *A Seasonable Plea for Liberty of Conscience Against Some Late Oppressive Proceedings Particularly in the Town of Berwick*. Boston, MA: 1770.

———. *An Abridgment of the Church History of New-England, From 1602 to 1804*. Boston, MA: Manning & Loring, 1804.

Balmer, Randall Herbert. *Blessed Assurance: A History of Evangelicalism in America*. Boston: Beacon Press, 1999.

———. *Encyclopedia of Evangelicalism*. Rev. and Expanded ed. Waco, TX: Baylor University Press, 2004.

———. *Evangelicalism in America*. Waco: Baylor University Press, 2016.

Bebbington, David W. *Evangelicalism in Modern Britain: A History from the 1730s to the 1980s* London and New York: Routledge/Taylor & Francis Group, 1989. ProQuest Ebook Central, http://ebookcentral.proquest.com/lib/vand/detail.action?docID=179445.

Bozeman, Theodore Dwight. *To Live Ancient Lives: The Primitivist Dimension in Puritanism*. Chapel Hill: Published for the Institute of Early American History and Culture, Williamsburg, Virginia, by the University of North Carolina Press, 1988.

Brackney, William H. and Janet Thorngate, eds. *Baptists in Early North America: Newport, Rhode Island, Seventh Day Baptists*. Baptists in Early North America Series, vol. III. Macon, GA: Mercer University Press, 2016.

Brackney, William H., and Charles K. Hartman, eds. *Baptists in Early North America: Swansea, Massachusetts*. First edition. Baptists in Early North America Series, vol. I. Macon, Georgia: Mercer University Press, 2013.

CHURCH HISTORY OF NEW ENGLAND

Butler, Jon. "Enthusiasm Described and Decried: The Great Awakening as Interpretive Fiction." *Journal of American History* 69, September (1982): 305–325.

Byrd, James P. *Sacred Scripture, Sacred War: The Bible and the American Revolution*. New York: Oxford University Press, 2013.

Carroll, Bret E. *The Routledge Historical Atlas of Religion in America*. Routledge Atlases of American History Series. New York: Routledge, 2000.

Chauncy, Charles. *Seasonable Thoughts on the State of Religion in New England, A Treatise in five Parts*. Boston, MA: Rogers and Fowle, 1743.

_____. *The Appeal to the public answered, in behalf of the non-Episcopal churches in America*. Boston, MA: Kneeland and Adams, 1768.

Coffey, John, and Paul Chang-Ha Lim, eds. *The Cambridge Companion to Puritanism*. Cambridge Companions to Religion. New York: Cambridge University Press, 2008.

Constitution of the United States, The Avalon Project, Yale Law School, https://avalon.law.yale.edu/18th_century/rights1.asp#1.

Cotton, John. *The Bloudy Tenent, Washed, and Made White in the Bloud of the Lambe: Being Discussed and Discharged of Bloud-Guiltinesse by Just Defence*. London: Crowne in Popes-Head-Alley, 1647.

Declaration of Independence, Avalon Project, Yale Law Library, https://avalon.law.yale.edu/18th_century/declare.asp.

Dunn, E. *Backus, Isaac (1724-1806), Baptist clergyman. American National Biography*. Retrieved 12 Jul. 2021, https://www-anb-org.proxy.library.vanderbilt.edu/view/10.1093/anb/9780198606697.001.0001/anb-9780198606697-e-0100041.

Edwards, Jonathan. "Faithful Narrative" in *The Great Awakening*, ed. C. C. Goen. New Haven, CT: Yale University Press/WJE Online Vol. 4.

_____. "Sinners in the Hands of an Angry God" in *Works of Jonathan Edwards, Volume 22, Sermons and Discourses, 1739–1742*, ed. Harry S. Stout, Nathan O. Hatch, and Kyle P. Farley. New Haven, CT: Yale University Press, 2003.

_____. *An Humble Inquiry into the Rules of the Word of God, in Works of Jonathan Edwards, Volume 12, Ecclesiastical Writings*, ed. David D. Hall. New Haven, CT: Yale University Press, 1994.

_____. *Some Thoughts Concerning the Revival, in Works of Jonathan Edwards, Volume 4, Great Awakening*, ed. C. C. Goen. New Haven, CT: Yale University Press, 1970.

208

BIBLIOGRAPHY

Goen, C. C. *Revivalism and Separatism in New England, 1740–1800: Strict Congregationalist and Separate Baptists in the Great Awakening*. New Haven, CT: Yale University Press, 1962.

Gordon-Reed, Annette. *The Hemingses of Monticello: An American Family*, 1st ed. New York: W.W. Norton & Co, 2008.

_____. *Thomas Jefferson and Sally Hemings: An American Controversy*. Charlottesville, VA: University Press of Virginia, 1997.

Grenz, Stanley J. *Isaac Backus—Puritan and Baptist: His Place in History, His Thought, and Their Implications for Modern Baptist Theology*. NABPR Dissertation Series, no. 4. Macon, GA: Mercer University Press, 1983.

Holifield, E. Brooks. *Theology in America: Christian Thought from the Age of the Puritans to the Civil War*. New Haven, CT: Yale University Press, 2003.

Hovey, Alvah. *A Memoir of the Life and Times of the Rev. Isaac Backus. The Era of the American Revolution*. New York: Da Capo Press, 1972.

Howe, Daniel Walker. *What Hath God Wrought: The Transformation of America, 1815–1848*. The Oxford History of the United States. New York: Oxford University Press, 2007.

Kidd, Thomas S. *God of Liberty: A Religious History of the American Revolution*. Philadelphia, PA: Basic Books, 2010), Kindle edition.

_____. *The Great Awakening: The Roots of Evangelical Christianity in Colonial America*. New Haven, CT: Yale University Press.

Knight, Janice. *Orthodoxies in Massachusetts: Rereading American Puritanism*. Cambridge, Mass: Harvard University Press, 1994.

Larsen, Timothy, and Daniel J. Treier, eds. *The Cambridge Companion to Evangelical Theology*. Cambridge Companions to Religion. Cambridge New York: Cambridge University Press, 2007.

Leland, John and L. F. Greene, *The Writings of the Late Elder John Leland: Including Some Events in His Life*. New York: Printed by G.W. Wood, 1845.

"The Life of Sally Hemings," https://www.monticello.org/sallyhemings/.

Marsden, George M. *Jonathan Edwards: A Life*. New Haven, CT: Yale University Press, 2003.

Maston, T. B. *Isaac Backus: Pioneer of Religious Liberty*. Rochester, NY: American Baptist Historical Society, 1962.

McDermott, Gerald R., ed. *The Oxford Handbook of Evangelical Theology*. New York: Oxford University Press, 2010.

McLoughlin, William G. and Isaac Backus. *Isaac Backus on Church, State, and Calvinism: Pamphlets, 1754–1789*. Cambridge, MA: Belknap Press of Harvard University Press, 1968.

_____. *The Diary of Isaac Backus*. Providence, RI: Brown University Press, 1979.

McLoughlin, William G. *Isaac Backus and the American Pietistic Tradition*, The Library of American Biography. Boston, MA: Little, Brown, and Co., 1967.

_____. *New England Dissent, 1630–1833; The Baptists and the Separation of Church and State*. Cambridge, MA: Harvard University Press, 1971.

_____. *Soul Liberty: The Baptists' Struggle in New England, 1630-1833*. Hanover, MA: University Press of New England and Brown University Press, 1991.

Miller, Perry. *Orthodoxy in Massachusetts, 1630–1650: A Genetic Study*. Cambridge: Harvard University Press, 1933.

_____. *The New England Mind, from Colony to Province*. Cambridge, Mass: Belknap Press of Harvard University Press, 1953; repr., 1983.

_____. *The New England Mind: The Seventeenth Century*. New York: The Macmillan Company, 1939.

Morgan, Edmund S. *Visible Saints: The History of a Puritan Idea*. Ithaca, NY: Cornell University Press, 1963.

New England Dissent, 1630–1833; The Baptists and the Separation of Church and State. Cambridge, MA, Harvard University Press, 1971.

Noll, Mark A. *America's God: From Jonathan Edwards to Abraham Lincoln*. New York: Oxford University Press, 2002.

Paine, Thomas. *Common Sense*, Liberty Fund, Online Library of Liberty, https://oll.libertyfund.org/pages/1776-paine-common-sense-pamphlet.

Perl-Rosenthal, N. "The 'Divine Right of Republics': Hebraic Republicanism and the Debate Over Kingless Government in Revolutionary America." *The William and Mary Quarterly* 66, no. 3 (July 2009): 535–564;

Pope, Robert G. *The Half-Way Covenant: Church Membership in Puritan New England*. Princeton, NJ: Princeton University Press, 1969.

Proceedings of the Massachusetts Historical Society, 1862–1863. Boston, MA: John Wilson and Son, 1863.

Shalev, Eran. "'A Perfect Republic': The Mosaic Constitution in Revolutionary New England, 1775–1788." *The New England Quarterly* 82, no. 2 (2009): 235–263.

_____. *American Zion: The Old Testament as a Political Text from the Revolution to the Civil War*. New Haven, CT: Yale University Press, 2013.

Stout, Harry S. *The New England Soul: Preaching and Religious Culture in Colonial New England*. 25th anniversary ed. New York: Oxford University Press, 2012.

BIBLIOGRAPHY

Washington, George. The Papers of George Washington Digital Edition. Charlottesville, VA: University of Virginia Press, Rotunda, 2008. Canonic URL: https://rotunda-upress-virginia-edu.proxy.library.vanderbilt.edu/founders/GEWN-05-02-02-0309.

Wigger, John. "Francis Asbury and American Methodism," in *The Oxford Handbook of Methodist Studie*s. Edited by James E. Kirby and William J. Abraham. New York and London: Oxford University Press, 2011.

Williams, Roger. *The Bloudy Tenent of Persecution for Cause of Conscience.* London, 1644; repr., Macon, GA: Mercer University Press, 2001.

_____. *A Key into the Language of America*, ed. James Hammond Trumball, vol. 1 of *The Complete Writings of Roger Williams*. Providence, RI: Narragansett Club Publications, 1866; repr., New York: Russell & Russell, 1963.

_____. *Christenings Make Not Christians* (London: Iane Coe, 1645); repr. in *Rhode Island Historical Tracts*, no. 14, ed. Henry Martyn Dexter. Providence, RI: Sidney S. Rider, 1881.

_____. *George Fox digg'd out of his burrowes*. Boston, MA: John Foster, 1676.

_____. *The Bloody Tenent yet More Bloody: By Mr Cottons Endevour to Wash It White in the Blood of the Lambe*. London: Giles Calvert, 1652.

Winiarski, Douglas L. *Darkness Falls on the Land of Light: Experiencing Religious Awakenings in Eighteenth-Century New England*. Chapel Hill: Published for the Omohundro Institute of Early American History and Culture, Williamsburg, Virginia, by the University of North Carolina Press, 2017.

Winship, Michael P. *Godly Republicanism: Puritans, Pilgrims, and a City on a Hill*. Cambridge, Mass: Harvard University Press, 2012.

Wood, Gordon S. *Empire of Liberty: A History of the Early Republic, 1789–1815*. The Oxford History of the United States series. Oxford; New York: Oxford University Press, 2009.

Index

Aaron, 38, 186, 199
Abraham, 74, 112, 123, 152, 184, 185, 186
Adams, John (founder), xxxii, xxxiii, 162
Adams, John (minister), 121
Adams, Samuel, xxxii
Ahab, 44
Alden, John, 18, 20
Allerton, Isaac, 18, 20
American Revolution, xi, xii, xiii, xvii, xix, xxx, xxxi, xxxii, xxxiii, xxxv, xxxvii, 54, 209, 210,
Anabaptists, 29, 39, 62, 64, 66, 78, 80, 98, 198,
Andros, Sir Edmond, 101, 102,
Angels, 15, 89, 118,
Antichrist, xxi, 12, 28, 33, 42, 44, 45, 47, 66, 89, 97, 101, 198
Arminian, xxxvi, 4, 13, 40,
Ayris, Alex, viii,
Babcock, Stephen, 136,
Backus, Elizabeth Tracy, xxiii, 90, 143,
Backus, Isaac
On American Revolution, xi, xii, xiii, xvii, xix, xxx, xxxi, xxxii, xxxiii, xxxv, xxxvii, 54, 209, 210,
On Baptism, xi, xxiv, xxviii, xxix, xxxvii, 6, 21, 23, 38, 39, 40, 51, 72, 74, 80, 81, 87, 88, 100, 111, 112, 118, 119, 123, 124, 138, 145, 152, 154, 161, 165, 178, 179, 182, 183, 184, 185, 186, 197, 198,
On Baptists, ix, xi, xiii, xiv, xvi, xvii, xx, xxi, xxiv, xxvi, xxix, xxx, xxxiii, xxxviii, xxxix, 1,

36, 51, 57, 66, 77, 78, 79, 91, 103, 112, 113, 120, 128, 136, 139, 140, 145, 147, 152, 158, 159, 177, 182, 183, 184, 186, 187, 188, 192,
On Religious liberty, x, xi, xii, xiv, xv, xvii, xviii, xix, xx, xxi, xxix, xxx, xxxi, xxxii, xxxiii, xxxiv, xxxv, xl, 1, 13, 14, 23, 24, 28, 35, 36, 37, 39, 41, 44, 51, 52-55, 58, 65, 73, 75, 77, 80, 81, 89, 98, 99, 101-102, 114, 121-122, 134, 138-139, 143, 145, 159, 163, 167-168, 170, 171, 173, 178-179, 186, 187, 192, 199,
Early life of, ix-x,
On Revival, ix, x, xi, xii, xxi, xxii, xxiii, xxiv, xxv, xxvi, xxvii, xxviii, xxx, xxxiii, xxxvi, xxxvii, 113, 116, 119, 120, 123, 145, 150, 156, 162, 164, 172, 173, 177, 182, 183, 186,
Slavery in family, ix
Slavery views, ix-x, xi, xv, xxxix, 80, 101
Backus, Samuel, ix
Baldwin, Benjamin, 172, 197,
Baldwin, Benjamin, 172, 197,
Baptism (infant), xxiv, xxxii, 10, 39, 40, 41, 52, 55, 66, 74, 75, 97, 112, 154, 169, 183, 184, 186, 197,
Baptism, (believers') xi, xxix, 58,
Baptism, xi, xxiv, xxviii, xxix, xxxvii, 6, 21, 23, 38, 39, 40, 51, 72, 74, 80, 81, 87, 88, 100, 111, 112, 118, 119, 123, 124, 138,

145, 152, 154, 161, 165, 178, 179, 182, 183, 184, 185, 186, 197, 198,

Baptists, ix, xi, xiii, xiv, xvi, xvii, xx, xxi, xxiv, xxvi, xxix, xxx, xxxiii, xxxviii, xxxix, 1, 36, 51, 57, 66, 77, 78, 79, 91, 103, 112, 113, 120, 128, 136, 139, 140, 145, 147, 152, 158, 159, 177, 182, 183, 184, 186, 187, 188, 192, Denominational competition, xxxvi, xxxvii, Growth, x, xii, 173, 191, 193, 195, Persecution of, 79, 93, 94, 96, 98, 99, 101, 106, 116, 119, 122, 146, 157, 162, 165, 176, Revivalism of, xi, visible sainthood of, xi, Worship of, 118, 127, 161, 172,

Bay Colony, Massachusetts, xi, xiii, xv, xvi, xvii, xviii, xix, 19,

Bebbington, David, xxi, xxii,

Bellamy, Joseph, 127, 152,

Bible, (Scripture), vi, vii, xv, xvii, xx, xxi, xxx, xl, 66, 95, 181, 208,

Blunt, John, 136,

Bourn, Richard, 95,

Bowdoinham Association, 171, 196,

Brackney, William H., vi, vii, viii,

Bradford, William, 18, 20, 25, 57, 71

Brainard, David, 128, 148,

Brewster, William, 18, 20, 21,

Bryan, Andrew, xxxviii, 194,

Byrd, James P., vi-vii,

Callender, Elisha, 120, 121,

Callender, Ellis, 112, 113,

Callender, James, xxxix,

Callender, John, 119, 120,

Calvin, Calvinists, xxxvi, xxxvi, 13, 15, 97,

Carpenter, Joseph, 75,

Carpenter, William, 37, 136,

Carver, John, 18-19,

Cathcart, William, vi,

Chandler, Thomas Bradbury, 153-154,

Chanler, Isaac, 187,

Charles, King I, 22, 32, 74,

Charles, King II, 73, 74,

Chauncy, Charles, xxvi, xxvii, xxxi, xxxii, 8, 9, 38, 128, 129, 130, 150, 153, 155, 156, 162, 165, 169, 208,

Circumcision, 74, 123, 184, 185,

Clap, Nathanael, 121,

Clark, Peter, 146

Clarke, John, xviii, xix, xxi, xxxi, 7, 36, 39, 54, 57, 58, 59, 62, 64, 66, 67, 68, 74, 77, 84, 85, 87, 88, 89, 90, 93, 100, 187,

Clay, Joseph, 193;

Coddington, William, 36, 52, 56, 68, 84, 85,

Coke, Edward, 24,

Cole, Ezekiel, 136,

Cole, Robert, 37,

Collins, William, 99, 100,

Comer, John, 7, 86, 114, 117, 118, 119, 120, 121, 122,

Conant, Roger, 22,

Conant, Sylvanus, 137, 138,

Congress, xxxii, xxxv, 159, 160, 162, 170, 195,

Constitution (United States), x, xxxiii, xxxiv, xxxv, 9, 162, 163, 169, 170, 176, 208,

Cotton, John, xvii, xviii, xix, xx, 23, 26, 27, 33, 36, 40, 41, 46-52, 55, 59, 63-66, 97,

Cotton, Josiah, 122,

Coxe, Nehemiah, 99, 100,

Craghead, Thomas, 114,

Cushman, Isaac, 104,

Danbury Association, 196,

Danforth, Samuel, 116, 122,

Davenport, James, xxiii, 32,

Davenport, John, 32,

David, 181, 186, 200,

Davies, Samuel, 190-191,

Davis, Sarah, 90,

Declaration of Independence, xxx,

INDEX

Deism, Deists, xii, 179, 181, 182,
Dennison, Thomas, 136,
Devil, 41, 42, 47, 66, 200, 201,
Dexter, Gregory, xviii, 54,
Dickinson, Jonathan, 146,
Draper, Nathanael, 136,
Drown, Samuel, 136,
Dudley, Thomas, 33, 56, 62, 95,
Dunham, Jonathan, 104,
Dunstar, Henry, 66, 75,
Dyke, Daniel, 99, 100,
Dyre, Mary, 73,
Dyre, William, 36, 56, 68,
Eaton, Ebenezer, 180, 181,
Eaton, Theophilus, 32,
Edward, King VI, 55,
Edwards, Jonathan, vi, xxii, xxiv, xxv, xxvii, xxviii, xxix, 8, 123, 124, 126, 128, 132, 133, 138, 139, 156, 208, 209, 210,
Edwards, Morgan, 188,
Edwards, Peter, 183,
Edwards, Timothy, 110,
Eelles, Edward, 148
Egypt, xv, 28, 116, 128,
Elizabeth, Queen I, 12, 56,
Episcopalians, 9, 106, 115, 116, 145, 189
Ewer, Nathanael, 136,
Exodus, 111,
Feke, Robert, 194,
Finley, Samuel, 8, 131,
First Amendment, xxxiv, xxxv, 170,
Fletcher, Jane, 90
Franklin, Benjamin, xxvi, 96,
French Revolution, xii, xiii,
Frothingham, Ebenezer, 136-137
Fuller, John, 136,
Fuller, Samuel, 19, 104,
Gano, John, 177, 194,
Gaustad, Edwin S., vi,
Gill, John, 146,
Goen, Clarence C., vi,
Gookin, Daniel, 95, 189,

Gorton, Samuel, 5, 16, 28, 36, 41, 42, 43, 44, 45, 67, 83,
Gould, Thomas, 75, 76, 77, 78, 82, 122,
Great Awakening, ix, xii, xxv,
Green, Nathanael, xviii, 54,
Groton Conference, 196,
Hall, Edward, 176,
Hall, Theophilus, 148,
Harges, Elizabeth, 90,
Harris, John, 99,
Harris, Samuel, 191,
Harris, Thomas, 37,
Harris, William, 37,
Hart, Oliver, 187,
Hart, William, 148,
Harvard, xxix, 5, 111, 112, 113, 126, 139, 156,
Hastings, Joseph, 136,
Hathorne, John, 67,
Haynes, John, 23, 35,
Hazel, John, 61, 122,
Hemings, Sally, xxxix,
Henry, King VII, 55,
Henry, King VIII, 55,
Hide, Jedidiah, 136,
Hide, Jonathan, 136,
Hide, Samuel, 136,
Higginson, Francis, 22
Higginson, John, 105,
Hobart, Noah, 148,
Hollis, Thomas, 103, 113,
Holmes, Obidaiah, xix, 52, 57, 59, 61-62, 63, 64, 100, 122, 187,
Hooker, Thomas, 5, 6, 23, 35, 55, 103, 109,
Hovey, Alva, vi
Hovey, John, 136,
Hovey, Samuel, 136,
Howland, John, 20,
Hubbard, Samuel, 54, 56, 71, 77, 78, 81, 94,
Hubbard, William, 96, 105,
Huntington, Hezekiah, 131, 137,
Huntington, Joseph, 165,

215

CHURCH HISTORY OF NEW ENGLAND

Hutchinson, Ann, 34,
Hypocrisy, hypocrites, xi, xii, xix,
    xx, xxxi, xxxix, 12, 17, 62, 64,
    65, 125, 126, 167,
Jefferson, Thomas, xxx, xxxix, xl,
    169, 199,
Jenkins, Joseph, 184,
Jenks, Joseph (Governor), 64, 84,
    119, 121,
Jennings, Samuel, 113,
Jesus, xvi, xx, xxxvi, 21, 26, 36, 44,
    48, 49, 52, 58, 59, 60, 73, 76, 77,
    85, 86, 98, 112, 119, 121, 141,
    142, 143, 144, 147, 153, 164,
    166, 171, 173, 175, 179, 185,
    191, 203,
Jews, Judaism, xx, 85, 106, 112,
    119, 150, 164, 170, 185, 191,
    200,
Johnson, Edward, 29, 32, 33, 45, 66,
    67, 70,
Johnson, Obadiah, 137,
Jolley, Marc, viii,
Josiah, 64
Judson, David, 149,
Keach, Elias, 187,
Kidd, Thomas S., xxii,
Kiffen, William, 62, 99, 100,
King Philip (Metacom), 70, 92, 94,
Knollys, Hanserd, 5, 36, 39, 99, 100,
Laud, William, 32, 33,
Leddra, William, 73,
Leland, John, xxxiv, xxxv, xxxvi,
    xxxix, 171, 192, 209,
Levi, tribe of, 78, 184, 199;
Leyden Association, 196,
Liele, George, xxxviii, 193-194,
Lord, Benjamin, xxii, xxiii,
Lord's Supper (holy supper), xxviii,
    21, 38, 72, 75, 87, 106, 111, 112,
    123, 138, 146, 180, 198,
Luther, Lutherans, 15, 188, 190,
Mack, Ebenezer, 136,
Madison, James, xxxiv,
Magna Charta, 101,

Manning, James, 151, 152, 156, 173,
Marsh, Benjamin, 120,
Marsh, Elihu, 136,
Marsh, Thomas, 136,
Marshall, Abraham, 194,
Marshall, Daniel, xxxvii, 189, 193,
Mary, Queen I, 12, 55, 56, 74,
Massassoit, 19, 92,
Mather, Cotton, 39, 56, 66, 77, 81,
    112, 113, 115, 116, 117, 130,
Mather, Increase, 97, 98, 99, 104,
    105, 111, 112, 114, 115, 117,
    132,
Mather, Moses, 152,
Mather, Richard, 24,
Matson, Thomas B., vi,
Mayhew, Jonathan, 150,
Mayhew, Thomas, 95, 96,
McLoughlin, William G., vi, xxxvi,
    xxxiv,
Meredith Association, 196,
Merrill, Daniel, 180,
Methodists, vii, xxvi, xxxvi, xxxvii,
    165-166, 183, 211,
Miantenimo, 5, 31, 82,
Miles, John, 75, 92, 98, 100, 122,
Millennium, xxxvii,
Mitchel, Jonathan, 66, 77, 78, 105
Mohegan peoples, 31, 43, 94, 96,
Moody, Samuel, 110,
Morris, Samuel, 190,
Morse, Joshua, 136,
Moses, 35, 36, 77, 118, 182, 199,
    201,
Moulton, Ebenezer, 120, 146,
Narragansetts, xv, xvi, 19, 28, 30, 31,
    37, 43, 45, 82, 83, 91, 92, 94, 96,
    120,
Native American, ix, xvi, 70, 83,
New Testament, xviii, xxxvi, 36, 80,
    141,
Newman, Samuel, 57,
Nickerson, Joshua, 136,
Ninagret, 96,
Noll, Mark A., x, xxix, xxxi, xxxii,

216

INDEX

Norden, Robert, 189,
Noyes, Joseph, 148,
Occum, Samsom, 96,
Old Testament (Hebrew Bible), xvii, xviii, 49, 141, 210,
Oldham, John, 29-30,
Olney, Thomas, 37, 38, 54, 100,
Osburne, Thomas, 76-77
Owen, John, 36, 50, 81, 105, 131, 177,
Oxford, xxvi, 25, 124, 165,
Paine, Elisha, 133, 134, 136, 137, 143-144,
Paine, John, 136,
Paine, Solomon, 147,
Paine, Thomas, xiii, xvii, xxx, 214, 210,
Palmer, John, 136, 137,
Park, Paul, 136,
Pequots, xv, xvi, 5, 22, 29, 30, 31, 45, 82, 83,
Philadelphia Association, 159, 188, 191,
Pilgrims, xiii,
Pope, xvi, xvii, 48, 55, 81,
Potter, James, 182,
Potter, Robert, 42,
Powers, Peter, 179;
Prince, Thomas, 12, 13, 15, 20, 21, 23, 25, 125, 132,
Providence (doctrine), xxxiii, 14, 17, 18, 25, 30, 48, 169, 194,
Providence (Rhode Island), xv, xvii, xviii, 5, 6, 28, 29, 32, 36, 37, 38, 42, 44, 45, 46, 52, 53, 54, 56, 61, 66, 67, 69, 74, 82, 84, 85, 90, 91, 93,100, 114, 119, 121, 122, 125, 133, 136, 150, 156,
Providence College, 145, 151,
Pumham, 42-44, 70, 94,
Purgatory, 155, 165,
Puritans, xi, xiii, xiv, xv, xvi, xvii, xix, xx, xxvii, 209, 211,
Racism, xvi,

Religious liberty, x, xi, xii, xiv, xv, xvii, xviii, xix, xx, xxi, xxix, xxx, xxxi, xxxii, xxxiii, xxxiv, xxxv, xl, 1, 13, 14, 23, 24, 28, 35, 36, 37, 39, 41, 44, 51, 52-55, 58, 65, 73, 75, 77, 80, 81, 89, 98, 99, 101-102, 114, 121-122, 134, 138-139, 143, 145, 159, 163, 167-168, 170, 171, 173, 178-179, 186, 187, 192, 199,
Revelation, Book of, xvi, xxxviii, 202,
Revival, ix, x, xi, xii, xxi, xxii, xxiii, xxiv, xxv, xxvi, xxvii, xxviii, xxx, xxxiii, xxxvi, xxxvii, 113, 116, 119, 120, 123, 145, 150, 156, 162, 164, 172, 173, 177, 182, 183, 186,
Richmond Conference, 196-197,
Robbins, Philemon, 8, 127, 133, 140, 141, 142, 147, 148,
Robinson, John, 4, 5, 11, 12, 13, 14, 15, 18, 20, 21, 32, 36, 52,
Robinson, William, 73, 190,
Rogers, Daniel, 126,
Rome, Church of (Roman Catholicism), xiii, xvi, xvii, xxxii, xxxv, 48, 85, 144, 154, 164, 165, 169, 174, 198,
Rooker, John, 193;
Russell, John, 98-100, 122,
Saltonstall, Gurdon, 107, 115,
Saltonstall, Richard, 62,
Sandy Creek, 189,
Sassacus, 29, 31,
Satan, 16, 40, 71, 98
Saybrook platform, 133, 140-142, 147, 149,
Scraven, William, 100, 186,
Seabury, Samuel, 166;
Separates (Congregationalists), xxiv, 8, 12, 41, 57, 77, 87, 137, 146, 191, 209,
Shaftsbury Association, 179, 196,
Shepard, Nathanael, 136,

Skelton, Samuel, 22, 25,
Slavery, ix-x, xi, xv, xxxix, 80, 101
Smith, Hezekiah, 152,
Smith, Ralph, 21,
Snow, Joseph, 136,
Socononco, 42, 44,
Spilsbury, John, 62,
Sprague, Jonathan, 121, 122,
Sprague, William B, vi,
Spur, John, 61,
Standish, Miles, 18, 20,
Stearns, Shubael, xxxvii, 136, 188-189, 193,
Stevens, Thomas, 136,137,
Stevenson, Marmaduke, 73,
Stevenson, Thomas, 147,
Stiles, Abel, 134,
Stiles, Ezra, 165, 174,
Stiles, Isaac, 148
Stoddard, Solomon, xxviii, 78, 103, 106, 107, 110, 111, 112, 123, 130, 138, 139,
Stone, Samuel, 23,
Sturbridge Association, 197,
Tabor, Philip, 114,
Talcot, Governor, 127,
Tennant, Gilbert, 125, 128,
Thatcher, Peter, 137,
Todd, Jonathan, 148,
Torry, Samuel, 105,
Turner, William, 76, 78, 82, 93, 94,
Uncas, 31, 43-44,
Universalism, xii, 145,
Vane, Henry, 33, 34, 45, 46, 68,

Vermont Association, 196,
Wadsworth, Ebenezer, 136,
Wadsworth, Samuel, 136,
Warren Association, xxxviii, 161, 175, 195, 196,
Washington, George, xxxiv, xxxv, xxxviii, 162, 170, 211,
Werden, Peter, 136,
Wesley, Charles, xxvi,
Wesley, John, xxvi, xxxvi, xxxvii, 165,
Wheelwright, John, 34, 35,
White, Ebenezer, 149,
White, John, 22, 110,
Whitefield, George, xxvi, xxix, 8, 124, 125, 126, 128, 129, 130, 133, 139, 145, 156, 165, 190,
Whiting, Samuel, 117,
Whittlesey, Chauncy, 148,
Whittlesey, Samuel, 148,
Wightman, Daniel, 119, 120,
William King III, 166,
Williams, Roger, vi, vii, xi, xiv-xxi, xxxi, xl, 22, 22, 24-27, 29, 30-32, 34-39, 42, 45-50, 52-55, 65-69, 74, 83-86, 89, 100, 101, 152,
Wilson, John, 23,
Winslow, Edward, 16, 18, 20, 28, 33, 68,
Wise, John, 101, 103, 106, 107, 110, 111, 115, 155,
Woodstock Association, 196,
Woodward, John, 109

Index of Biblical Citations

Genesis 14:14; 17:13, 27, 184; 17:6, 186; 18:20-21, 63; 24:25, 184; 39-43, xv,
Exodus 12, 111; 12:43-51, 185; 23:2-3, 49; 33:18-19, 192;
Leviticus 17:11, 184;
Deuteronomy 13:1-3, 134; 13:5, 49; 13:9-10, 50; 16:19, 154; 17:8-12, 78; 17:12, 106; 26:13-19, 200;
Judges 9:7-15, xxxix, 199;
2 Samuel 20:19, 63;
Ezra 62:1, 38;
Psalms 33:11, 89; 91:11-12, 200;
Proverbs 19:21, 89;
Isaiah 1:12, 15, 174; 23:20-23, 204; 30:17, 200; 46, xxviii, 132;
Jeremiah 23, xxviii, 132; 31:31-34, 185;
Ezekiel, 34, xxviii, 132;
Daniel 2:35, 44, 202; 7:27, 202;
Hosea 6:9, 200;
Micah 3:11-12, 200; 4:1-5, 202;
Zechariah 10, xxviii, 132,
Malachi, 2:9, 198; 3:8-10, 201;
Matthew 3:11, 198; 4:6-7, 200; 6:15, 49; 7:1-3, 17; 7:12, 176; 7:20, 199; 11:25-30, 191-192; 13:30, 38, 47; 18:7, 16; 18:20, 38; 20:15, 192; 23:29-35, 170; 23:35-36, 203; 28:19-20, 38;
Luke 12:32, 89; 16:22-26, 156;
John 1:12, 42; 3:3, 103; 3:5, 8, 198; 3:14-20, 192; 18:36, 52, 164;
Acts 2:23, 89; 4:28, 89; 5:5-14, 65; 20:29, 49;
Romans 2:29, 139; 3:22, 152; 4:18, 184; 6:1-4, 139; 8:29-30, 89; 9:13-14, 89; 9:18, 89; 9:23, 89; 10:17, 198; 11:33, 89; 13:30, 89; 14, 81; 14:23, 62, 64; 15:20, 129; 16:17, 12; 16:17-18, 147;
1 Corinthians 5:1, 12; 6:9, 47; 6:20, 52; 7:19, 23, 185; 9:15, 16; 10:4, 49; 10:9, 49; 14:3 and 31, 21; 11:13-15, 201; 12:13, 201;
2 Corinthians 10:4-5, 164;
Galatians 3:26-29, 185; 6:6-8, 201;
Ephesians 1:3-4, 166; 1:6, 89; 1:11, 89; 1:4-5, 89;
Philippians 3:3, 139;
Colossians 2:11-12, 139;
1 Thessalonians, 1:4, 89; 5:9, 89; 5:14, 12;
2 Thessalonians, 2:13, 89; 3:6, 12; 3:6-11, 129;
1 Timothy, 6:5, 12, 198;
2 Timothy, 1:13, 203; 2:16-18, 49; 3, 203; 3:16-17, 203;
Titus, 3:10-11, 48;

CHURCH HISTORY OF NEW ENGLAND

Hebrews 6:17, 89; 7:12, 186; 8:7-13, 185; 9:13-14, 156;
James 1:17, 89;
1 Peter 1:2, 166; 1:23, 11:9, 38; 1:23, 186; 2:9, 186; 3:21, 185; 4:10,11, 21, 175;
    5:1-5, 175;
2 Peter 1:10, 89;
1 John 1:5, 89; 2:18, 22, 42; 3:12, 203; 4:5, 124; 15:19, 166;
Revelation 2:14-16, 20; 17:16, xvi, 47, ; 17:6, xvi; 17:5, 18, 164; 18:20-23, 204;
    18:24, 203; 19:20, 177; 22:18-19, 154, 202;